CLOTILDE'S

—

EDIBLE

—

ADVENTURES

—

IN PARIS

Clotilde Dusoulier

BROADWAY BOOKS · NEW YO

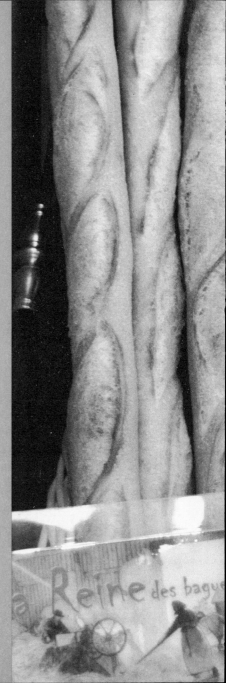

BROADWAY

PUBLISHED BY BROADWAY BOOKS

Copyright © 2008 by Clotilde Dusoulier

Published in the United States by Broadway Books,
an imprint of The Doubleday Broadway Publishing
Group, a division of Random House, Inc., New York.
www.broadwaybooks.com

BROADWAY BOOKS and its logo, a letter B bisected on
the diagonal, are trademarks of Random House, Inc.

Photography by Clotilde Dusoulier
Map by Andrew Barthelmes
Book design by Elizabeth Rendfleisch

Library of Congress Cataloging-in-Publication Data
Dusoulier, Clotilde, 1979–
            Clotilde's edible adventures in Paris /
Clotilde Dusoulier. —1st ed.
                                    p.   cm.
1. Restaurants—France—Paris—Guidebooks. 2. Grocery
trade—France—Paris—Guidebooks. I. Title. II. Title:
Edible adventures in Paris.

    TX907.5.F72D976 2008
    647.9544'361—dc22

2007032079

ISBN 978-0-7679-2613-3

PRINTED IN THE UNITED STATES OF AMERICA

10 9 8 7 6 5 4 3 2 1

First Edition

Un après-midi à Paris
Que je garde près de moi
Comme un jour où chaque seconde
Dure toute une vie.

—Philippe Katerine

CONTENTS

I am an enthusiastic list-maker: I keep lists of books I want to read, places I want to travel to, stories I want to write, and projects I want to take on. And ever since I got passionately interested in food in my early twenties, I have been keeping endless lists of dishes I want to cook, restaurants I want to try, and shops I want to visit.

My Paris lists are especially copious, as I eagerly collect recommendations, tips, and news from multiple sources, then trek around the city to see, smell, and taste for myself. And when I find a gem—a shop that sells honey on tap or artisanal beer, a restaurant that serves superb oysters or handles game exceptionally well—I love nothing more than spreading the word about it, allowing my friends and readers to enjoy it, too. In dining as in cooking, I don't believe in hoarding secrets.

This book is a window onto my Paris, this delicious stomping ground for the food enthusiast. It is the companion I wish I had for every city I visit, pointing me to the edible highlights and giving me the lowdown on the dining scene, the best food shopping haunts, and the locals' favorites.

I hope it finds its place on your nightstand, as you plan your future (or perhaps imaginary) trip to Paris, and in your pocket, as you walk around the City of Light and Good Food and munch on its endless wonders.

This volume is divided into two main sections. The first one, **EATS,** takes you around restaurant favorites: they are ordered alphabetically by *arrondissements* (Paris's twenty districts). (Note: when the name of a restaurant begins with Le, La, Les, Chez, or Aux, the leading article is ignored.) In the second section, **SHOPS,** recommendations are organized by specialty—bread, pastries, wine—and, within each specialty, by arrondissement.

Telephone numbers are given in the format as they should be dialed when you're in France. To call from the States, replace the leading zero with 011 33. (For example, if the phone number is **01** 23 45 67 89, dial **011 33** 1 23 45 67 89.)

If **multiple locations** are listed for the same business, the first one is either the historical location or the one that most warrants a visit. The nearest métro stations are listed after the M° sign, as well as the closest cross street.

Terrace space is a rare commodity in this city, but some restaurants do offer a handful of sidewalk tables that Parisians dart to at the first sign of balmy weather. Outdoor seating is noted for these establishments.

Restaurant menus change often, to reflect the season and the inspiration of the chef, so the **dish examples** are simply included for illustration purposes, to give you an idea of the style of cuisine.

The **hours** listed for restaurants are service hours, i.e., the time periods during which diners can come in and be seated; the dining room remains open for a couple of hours after that. For stores, the hours listed are actual hours of operation.

Business slows down drastically in July and August: most shops and restaurants close for three to four weeks for their *congés annuels,* and those that remain open often switch to a more limited summer schedule, with fewer opening days—Mondays and Sundays are the first to get nixed.

All practical details in the book were double-checked for accuracy, but they are, of course, subject to change. Prices in particular tend to creep up by a euro or two when no one's looking, and days and hours of service are sometimes loosely interpreted: it is not infrequent to drop by a store within the hours of operation and find a hastily written sign on the door that reads *"Je reviens"* (back later), or even a good old *"Fermeture exceptionnelle"* (sorry, we're closed). If you're planning a ride all the way across the city to visit a specific place, consider calling ahead to make sure that it is, indeed, open.

Log on to Chocolate & Zucchini (http://chocolateandzucchini.com) to check for updates and corrections, and if you have changes of your own to report, they will be very welcome.

Let me first raise my glass to my favorite dining companions, without whom table-hopping and bread-breaking wouldn't be half as fun: Maxence, Alisa, Caroline, Céline, Estérelle, Laurence, Marie-Laure, Meredith, Pascale, Patricia and Stephan, Shelli and Gene, and my parents.

I would like to thank the chefs who have shared recipes for this book—Sébastien Gaudard of Délicabar, Stéphane Molé of Les Ormes, Rémi Van Peteghem of Le Sensing, Dominique Saugnac of Boulangépicier, Christophe Vasseur of Du Pain et des Idées, Antoine Westermann of Drouant—and Mary Sue Hayward, my recipe tester extraordinaire, who has helped adapt these recipes for cooks like you and me.

Thank you, also, to the Broadway Books team—Jennifer Josephy and Tammy Blake in particular—for supporting my work, and to Claudia Cross, for being the best agent I could dream of.

Finally, thank you Paris, for letting me traipse around your streets, and providing inspiration at every turn. I feel lucky to know you.

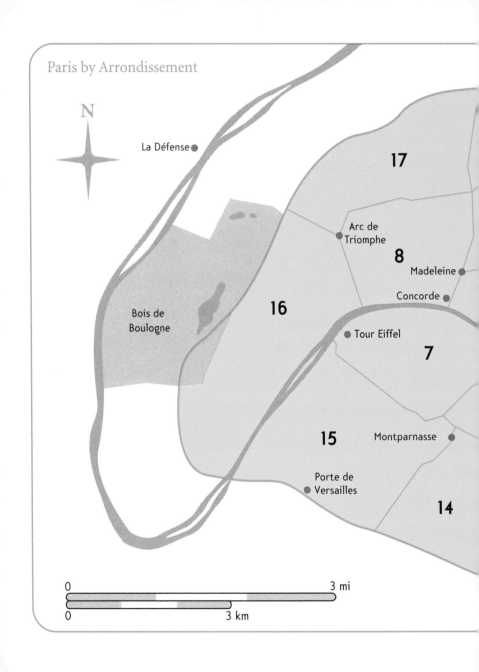

Paris by Arrondissement

N

La Défense

17

Arc de
Triomphe

8

Madeleine

Concorde

16

Tour Eiffel

7

Bois de
Boulogne

15

Montparnasse

Porte de
Versailles

14

0   3 mi

0   3 km

eats

When it comes to eating out in Paris, the difficulty lies not so much in finding a good restaurant—there is no dearth of those—as in deciding what you feel like, in your heart of hearts. A glass of wine and a few nibbles? A wholesome bistro meal? A creative take on French classics? A colorful salad? A four-hour gastronomic extravaganza? A crisp, golden crêpe? A cup of tea and a pastry?

Whatever the itch, this book should include a restaurant to scratch it. I have strived to put together a selection that covers a wide variety of occasions, moods, appetites, and budgets within eight categories:

LUNCH. For a quick, light meal—soups, salads, sandwiches, savory tarts, and simple *plats du jour*. These restaurants are usually open during the daytime only, and in most cases, no table service is provided: you order and pay at the counter, then take your purchases to go (*à emporter*) or sit down at a table to eat them (*sur place*). No reservation necessary. Dress code: come as you are.

CASUAL. For traditional French cuisine in a laid-back and often bustling atmosphere. Expect little room between tables and hectic service. Dress code: casual.

NEO BISTRO. For bistro food taken to a new level. The ambiance is casual, but there is serious action in the kitchen as the chef revisits the classics with creative riffs. See page 46 for more on the neo bistro trend. Dress code: casual-chic.

CHIC. For special-occasion meals in a more upscale environment. Expect smooth tablecloths, polished silverware, attentive service, and sophisticated food. Dress code: chic.

GASTRONOMIC. For a memorable dining experience at a high-flying establishment. Reputations can be deceiving, as a number of visits to renowned restaurants have disappointingly revealed. The ones I have highlighted here, however, truly provide an excellent level of cuisine, service, and décor. I have limited the selection to those that offer affordable weekday lunch menus, giving you the most sparkling and the most delicious run for your money. Dress code: chic, but not to the point of evening wear. Men should wear a shirt and a jacket—in addition to the pants and shoes, I mean.

SALON DE THÉ. For tea and pastries in the afternoon. Most tea salons also serve a light fare at lunchtime, and brunch on weekends. Dress code: casual.

BAR À VIN. For great wines, and food to match. The fare may be reduced to platters of tapas-like nibbles (charcuterie, cheese, etc.) or there may be cooking involved, from simple to elaborate. See page 20 for more on wine bars. Dress code: casual.

INTERNATIONAL. Much as I regret it, the average French palate is not particularly adventurous. Consequently, our ethnic restaurants tend to edit—some would say "dumb down"—the cuisines they represent so as not to disorient sensitive taste buds. The ones I have selected provide as authentic a dining experience as you will find in Paris: most are fuss-free joints that the immigrant communities frequent, and you will enjoy them if you're interested in observing how these cuisines respond to the influence of local ingredients, tastes, and habits. Dress code: casual, unless otherwise specified.

CARTE, MENU, FORMULE ET MENU-CARTE

The list of dishes that a restaurant offers is referred to as **la carte** or **le menu.** Ordering **à la carte** means you choose individual dishes from the list: each has its own price, and your total bill will simply be the sum of these prices. (The à la carte prices in this book indicate the average cost of a typical meal—two or three courses depending on the style of the restaurant—without drinks.)

A **fixed-price menu** is a subset of these dishes, from which you pick two or three courses and pay a set price, regardless of the specific dishes you choose. A **formule** is similar to a fixed-price menu, except it is cheaper and the choices are more limited, if you have a choice at all. Formules are usually lunchtime deals, in which case they may be called *menu déjeuner;* some include a glass of wine and/or a cup of coffee.

More and more restaurants simplify the equation by serving a fixed-price menu only; it is then referred to as a **menu-carte.** You may be charged a few more euros for some dishes on the menu-carte. This is called a **supplément,** and the amount will be indicated next to the dish ("+2€," "+5€").

DINING TIPS

Parisian waiters have a terrible reputation and some deserve every last crumb, but good service is at your fingertips if you play by the rules of this strange little world called the French restaurant.

These rules all derive from a significant cultural difference: in France, a restaurant is not perceived as a public place so much as the extension of the chef's or owner's home, a fact that is well illustrated by the traditional name of many restaurants—Chez Michel, Chez Jean, Chez Ramulaud . . .

Diners are seen as paying guests rather than just customers, and the restaurant staff as their hosts rather than just the people who cook and serve the food. Waiters often feel proprietorial about the restaurant they work in, and they want to be sure its value is recognized and appreciated: the relationship they establish with the diners is thus based on grounds more personal and more emotionally charged than what you may be used to.

But if you keep this in mind and follow the tips outlined below, you will find it easy to make them want to make you happy. Humor goes a long way, too: many waiters are the teasing kind, and playing along is the surest way to win them over.

Date and time

With the exception of brasseries, which offer nonstop service, Parisian restaurants typically start serving at noon for lunch and 8pm for dinner, with a break between the two shifts, during which the restaurant is closed. Most Parisians arrive a bit later than the beginning of the service hours—around 1pm for lunch, and 9pm for dinner.

Restaurants are busiest on Thursdays and Fridays, with a peak on Saturday nights. Many restaurants are closed on Sundays and Mondays, and restaurants that cater chiefly to an office crowd may be closed on weekends. Restaurants that serve both lunch and dinner often skip the lunch service on Mondays and Saturdays.

The vast majority of Paris restaurants close for three to four weeks in July or August, when the entire country is on vacation, and for a week or two in late December, for Christmas and New Year's Eve. These are, consequently, tough times for dining out, as the choice of restaurants is very limited.

Reservations

It is always a good idea to make a reservation: not only does this guarantee you a table, but it is also a matter of courtesy to your hosts, who will welcome you more warmly if you have called ahead to announce your visit. In some exceptional cases, you need to book a table weeks or even months in advance, but most of the time, calling a few days ahead or even on the same day will suffice.

A reservation is essential on the busiest days of the week, especially Fridays and Saturdays, and if there are more than two of you. If you don't have a reservation, your best bet is to arrive at the beginning of the service (around 12:30pm for lunch, or 8pm for dinner) and ask if they can accommodate you. Don't be upset if you see that the restaurant is empty but you're told they can't seat you: it's not that you have grime on your face, it's that they're holding the tables for diners who have made a reservation and will show up a bit later.

Reservations are taken on the phone—fax and e-mail are not reliable means of communication—during the service hours of the restaurant. Outside of these hours, you may be able to leave a message on an answering machine, but you will need to leave a phone number at which the staff can call and confirm your reservation.

When you call, you will be asked for the date and time you would like to come, how many people will be in your party (they may be referred to as *couverts,* or place settings), your name (if your name is difficult to understand or spell, just pick an easier one, or give your first name), and sometimes a phone number—the reason they ask is so they can call you if there is a problem, or if you are late for your reservation.

A typical conversation would go:

"Bonjour, je voudrais réserver une table pour quatre pour vendredi soir. C'est possible?" (Hello, I'd like to make a reservation for four on Friday night. Is it possible?)

"Pas de problème, vous voulez venir à quelle heure?" (No problem, what time would you like to come?)

"Vers vingt heures trente." (Around 8:30pm.)

"C'est à quel nom?" (Under what name?)

"Au nom de Bernard." (Bernard.)
"Parfait—quatre couverts pour vendredi, vingt heures trente. À vendredi!" (Okay—table for four on Friday at 8:30pm. See you then!)
"Merci, à vendredi!" (Thanks, see you on Friday!)

If you don't speak French, start the phone call by saying *"Bonjour, je voudrais faire une réservation, s'il vous plaît. Vous parlez anglais?"* The person you're talking to often will, or will at least understand enough to take a reservation if you give the information slowly and clearly. And if you're staying at a hotel, ask the concierge or receptionist to place the call for you.

If you have a reservation, you will rarely be made to wait. In the event that the table is not ready, ask how long it will be, and go out for a stroll or have an apéritif at the bar (it will be added to your bill).

Most restaurants hold the table for fifteen minutes or so after the appointed time. If you think you will be later than that, or that there will be fewer or more people in your party, call the restaurant to let them know and ask if it's okay.

And of course, if your plans change and you can't come at all, be sure to call and cancel as soon as you know: Paris restaurants don't overbook and they may turn people away to hold your table, so if you fail to show up, you're effectively hurting their business.

First contact

When you enter the restaurant, say *"Bonjour!"* during the day, and *"Bonsoir!"* in the evening—the magical switch from *bonjour* to *bonsoir* happens around 6pm. Mention whether or not you have a reservation, and if so, under what name—*"Nous avons une réservation pour quatre, au nom de Bernard"*—then wait for the staff to point you or show you to your table. Don't seat yourself at a table without asking first: it would be seen as brash, and that table may be reserved. (This seating etiquette is also valid in cafés, even if they seem more casual.)

Generally speaking, smile—without excess—and use as much French as you can, even if it's just the basics: *bonjour, bonsoir, excusez-moi, s'il vous plaît, merci, au revoir.* It shows that you are making an effort, and this is always appreciated. Try to establish a rapport with the wait staff by joking, asking for advice, and demonstrating your interest in the restaurant and the food that it serves.

Be attentive to the level of noise in the room, and adjust your voice accordingly: Paris restaurants are typically small and the tables close to one another, so keeping one's voice down is common courtesy.

No one calls the waiter "*Garçon!*" outside of black-and-white movies. If you need to catch the staff's attention, raise your arm slightly (but do not—I repeat, do not—snap your fingers) and say "*Excusez-moi?*" or "*S'il vous plaît?*"

Ordering

You should be brought the **menu** minutes after being seated. It can be a printed menu that is handed to each diner, or a chalkboard menu that is passed around from table to table (see page 67). The waiter may have **plats du jour** (specials) to announce—ask him to repeat if you haven't had time to register them all—and these dishes may be listed on a chalkboard somewhere in the room.

As you are handed the menu, you will be asked if you would like an **apéritif** drink (see page 112). Order one if you like, but you will not look cheap if you decline. When the waiter comes to take the **food order,** each diner announces in turn the first and main course he's chosen. (See page 14 for more on courses.)

If you're unsure what to order, or if you have a hard time deciding between two dishes, don't hesitate to ask the waiter for his recommendation or personal preference. And if you order a dish of seared meat or red tuna, you will be asked how you want it cooked (see page 109).

The **dessert** order is usually placed after the main courses have been cleared, unless it's a dessert that takes time to prepare, in which case it will be indicated as such on the menu ("*à commander en début de repas*") or the waiter will tell you.

A basket of **bread** is placed on your table once you've ordered, or as the first course is served. It is free, but does not come with butter, except at gastronomic restaurants.

Drinks

Once you've ordered the food, you will be asked about drinks; at fancier places, the sommelier will come to take your order. The French don't typically drink sodas with their meals, but rather water and wine, or beer in some cases—in Alsatian and Asian restaurants in particular.

Ordering **wine** by the bottle gives you the widest choice, but a smaller selection is often offered by the half-bottle, by the *pichet* (pitcher), or by the glass (see page 90). Don't hesitate to ask for advice, specifying how much you can spend and the sort of wine you enjoy.

Water isn't necessarily brought to the table; you may have to request it ("*On peut avoir de l'eau, s'il vous plaît?*"). Waiters often try to sell you bottled water by asking if you want still or sparkling ("*Plate ou pétillante?*"). For tap water, which is free and fine to drink, ask for *une carafe d'eau*. The water will be cold, but it won't be served with ice.

Table manners

No one will think twice if you just follow the rules you grew up with, but should you wish to adopt the French dining etiquette while in Paris, here are a few basics:

- Keep your hands on, not under, the table, but don't put your elbows on the table as you eat.
- Place your piece of bread on the table next to your plate (or on the bread plate if one is provided), not on the rim of your plate.

- If there is more than one set of silverware around your plate, start with the outermost set and work your way in from course to course.
- The French way of using silverware is to hold the fork, tines down, in your left hand and the knife in your right hand—no switching between the two.
- To signify that you are done with your dish, place your fork and knife together at four o'clock on your plate. Note, however, that the waiter won't clear your plate until everyone at the table has finished eating; this is so the slowest eater won't feel rushed.
- In most restaurants you will get fresh silverware for each dish, but at casual places you may be asked to keep your fork and knife throughout the meal. If that is the case, put the fork tines down on the table to your right, and balance the blade of the knife over the fork so as not to soil the table.
- There is no such thing as a doggie bag in France, and restaurants don't have takeout boxes handy, so you can't take the remains of your meal home—sorry.

Coffee

The French typically end their meals with a cup of espresso, caffeinated (*un café* or *un express*) or decaffeinated (*un déca*). This is ordered instead of, or after dessert, not alongside dessert. You can also opt for one of the variations: *un café serré* (an espresso with less water poured in), *un café noisette* (a regular espresso with a drop of milk), or *un café allongé* (a regular espresso with double the amount of water). You can also order a cup of tea or tisane, but *café au lait,* which is really referred to as *café crème* in cafés, is considered a morning beverage only.

Tab and tipping

At the end of your meal, you have to ask for the check explicitly: it is considered bad form to bring it unprompted, as that would give the impression that they are rushing you out. Ask for *"L'addition, s'il vous plaît!"* or just make eye contact with your waiter and mime a scribbling gesture in the air. Always check the tab to make sure that there is no mistake; if there is, tell your waiter politely and in a low voice so he can correct it.

The price indicated on the menu and on your check includes a 15 percent gratuity. You are not required to leave anything beyond that, but if you are happy with the service, you are welcome to tip. Regardless of your means of payment, credit card or cash, the tip is paid in change and left on the table as you leave. (The credit card system works differently in France than in the States, and you can't add the tip on your credit card receipt.)

How much you tip depends on how happy you are, how much the meal cost overall, and how much change you have, but 5 percent is a good baseline. The easiest thing to do is to round off the amount, especially if you've paid in cash: for instance, if the meal cost 94 euros and you've paid 100 in cash, you could leave the extra six euros as a tip.

BUDGET DINING

Let me start with the bitter truth: Paris is not a cheap city, and its food is no exception. Some restaurants offer a better price-to-quality ratio than others but quality has a price, true bargains are few and far between, and it usually isn't long before success drives the prices upward. But there are a few guidelines to follow if you wish to limit your expenses:

FAVOR THE LUNCH SERVICE. Most restaurants serve gently priced formules at lunchtime (see page 5). The choice may be limited, but this still provides the best bang for your buck. The difference is most notable when it comes to gastronomic restaurants, which often offer a weekday lunch menu that's three to four times cheaper than the same meal served in the evening.

DON'T EAT OUT AT EVERY MEAL. So many ready-to-eat items can be found at shops and markets that it is easy, not to mention enjoyable, to buy the makings of a feast—bread, cheese, charcuterie, quiches, crudités, pastries—and have yourself a merry little picnic on a bench, a patch of green (see page 234), or in your hotel room. If you're renting an apartment and have access to a kitchen, the advice is even simpler to heed.

CHECK THE MENU FROM OUTSIDE. Restaurants are required by law to display their menu so that it is visible from the street: this allows you to check the prices and see if they fit your budget before you step in.

BEWARE OF SPECIALS. Whether they are announced by the waiter or listed on a chalkboard, daily specials can come at a premium. Before you set your heart on them, make sure you know how much they cost, and check whether they're included in the fixed-price menu or formule you've chosen. And when you order from a menu-carte, pay attention to the *suppléments* ("+2€," "+5€") that may be charged extra for some of the dishes.

DRINK TAP WATER. It may have a slight aftertaste, but the water in Paris is fine to drink, and opting for *une carafe d'eau* (tap water in a carafe) rather than bottled water will save you a few euros.

LIMIT THE EXTRAS. Be prudent about the drinks you order on a whim, without checking how much they cost: Champagne, apéritifs, coffee, and digestive drinks can come at a higher price than you expect.

ORDER THE HOUSE WINE. Bistros and casual restaurants often have a wine of the month or a house wine that is served by the glass or the carafe (see page 90) at a moderate price. It is usually a modest wine that won't knock your socks off, but it will accompany your meal nicely and affordably enough.

COURSES

The concept of small plates is starting to catch on here and there, but most restaurant meals in Paris still unfold in the traditional French fashion: a starter (*l'entrée*) and a main dish (*le plat principal* or simply *le plat*), followed by cheese (*le fromage*) and/or dessert (*le dessert*).

It is not mandatory to order a full three-course meal, but at most restaurants, you are expected to order at least a main dish at lunch, and two courses at dinner—first and main, or main and dessert. Main courses typically take more time to prepare than first courses, so if you choose to skip the starter, expect to wait a little longer before your food is served.

Each dish comes with its own side, designed to complement its flavors, and chefs are reluctant to substitute one side for another. The average restaurant kitchen is understaffed and hence not very flexible, so if you have a change request, it should be made in a tone that suggests you realize you're asking for special treatment.

It is fairly common for diners to split dessert: it is then served on one plate, with as many spoons as you've asked for. Coffee is served after dessert, not with dessert, and the typical drink to order then is an espresso (see page 11).

At upscale restaurants, you will also be brought a light appetizer before the starter (*l'amuse-bouche*), a palate cleanser before dessert (*le pré-dessert*), and sweet miniature bites with coffee (*les mignardises*). You won't be charged extra for any of these; they are included in the price of the meal and the price of coffee.

1er arrondissement

Bioboa
Lunch, see page 79

L'Écume Saint-Honoré
Casual, Fish shop see page 242

La Ferme Opéra
Lunch, see page 79

Le Garde-Robe
Bar à vin / Wine shop / Brunch   VEG-FRIENDLY

This wine cellar focuses on natural wines (see page 262) made by independent French producers. Its cozy vintage space—exposed beams and stone walls are all the décor one needs, really—holds a scatter of wooden tables at which you can sit down for a sip and a bite, making this a fine rendezvous for a pre-dinner drink.

The well-sourced, no-cook edibles range from cured meats and smoked fish to well-aged cheeses and toasts of tapenade or white tarama. I like the *assiette mixte* (12€), which combines charcuterie (rosette, *saucisson,* and a kind of dry sausage produced on the Atlantic shore called *saucisson de la mer*) and cheese (Saint-Maur, Camembert, Saint-Nectaire), served with a slim baguette and pickled garlic. And if you prefer something warm, try the signature croque-monsieur (10€).

There is no wine list other than the shelves of bottles that line the wall and the brains of the young and friendly host, which can be picked for recommendations. Bottles start at 7€ (plus a 6€ corkage fee), and glasses of wine start at 4€. Brunch on weekends (18€).

41 rue de l'Arbre Sec, 1st. CROSS STREET: Rue Saint-Honoré. M° Louvre-Rivoli. PHONE: 01 49 26 90 60. Mon–Fri 8am–8pm; Sat 9am–7pm; Sun 10am–7pm.

Jean-Paul Hévin
Salon de thé / Chocolate shop, see page 181

Issé
Japanese   VEG-FRIENDLY

Because the bulk of Japanese restaurants in Paris focus on sushi and yaki-tori—it took long enough to educate the French palate, why look any further?—those of us who enjoy the breadth and wealth of Japanese cuisine are extra grateful for restaurants that explore paths less commonly traveled. Among them is Issé, a small but neat restaurant that subtitles itself "Tempura & Tapas."

The core of Issé's menu is composed of *agemono* (deep-fried dishes) and feather-light *tempura* (deep-fried seafood or seasonal vegetables), but also features an exciting variety of mini-dishes, from the classic (marinated tuna, *agedashi* tofu, seaweed salad) to the unusual (duck magret salad, sardine tartare with plums), which are meant to be ordered in tapas fashion and shared among diners. (About 15€ at lunch and 30€ at dinner.)

If the à la carte choices seem overwhelming, the lunch and dinner for-mules (starting at 10€ and 33.50€, respectively) take the stress out of ordering and provide a good tour of the chef's skills.

45 rue de Richelieu, 1st. CROSS STREET: Rue des Petits Champs. M° Pyramides or Palais Royal–Musée du Louvre. PHONE: 01 42 96 26 60. Mon–Sun 10:30am–3:30pm; Mon–Sat 6pm–midnight.

Le Jardin d'Hiver du Meurice
Salon de thé / Breakfast   VEG-FRIENDLY

For a sparkling afternoon tea experience, look no further than Le Meurice, the venerable *palace* hotel on rue de Rivoli. Under the Art Nouveau arcades of its winter garden, you will be served a divine French interpretation of the British teatime ceremonial.

The light-flooded room, the hugging armchairs, and the impeccable service make it a delicious way to feel pampered, and for 30€ you will get: tea or hot chocolate, finger sandwiches, scones with butter, jam, and clotted cream, and last but not least, your choice of three pastries from the groaning dessert cart—mille-feuille, chocolate fondant, pineapple tartlet, chestnut cake, macarons . . . (A smaller 19€ formule buys you tea and a pastry.)

Le Jardin d'Hiver du Meurice is open all day for breakfast (from 8:30am to 11am), light lunches, live jazz dinners, or drinks; the afternoon tea is served from 3:30pm till 6:30pm.

228 rue de Rivoli, 1st. CROSS STREET: Rue de Castiglione. M° Tuileries. PHONE: 01 44 58 10 10. WEB: www.meuricehotel.com. Mon–Sun 8:30am–10pm.

Lavinia
Bar à vin, see page 266

Willi's Wine Bar
Bar à vin   VEG-FRIENDLY

Their own vineyards have yet to gain international recognition, but the British have always had a keen appreciation for wine, and I find it refreshing that an Englishman, Mark Williamson, should be credited for opening the very first wine bar in Paris, in 1980.

Willi's is a warm and friendly place, equally suited to the enjoyment of a pre-dinner drink and a few nibbles at the shiny oak bar, or that of a full meal in the softly lit dining room. The wine list puts a strong focus on wines from France, and the Rhône region in particular, with additional finds from the Pays Basque, the Languedoc, and Bandol.

As for the food, it is a happy mix of French and Mediterranean: not exactly revolutionary, but reliably pleasing and wine friendly (three courses: 25€ at lunch, 34€ at dinner; lunch formules: 15€ and 19.50€). Many of the wines can be ordered by the glass (starting at 4€), which makes it easy for the sommelier to suggest individual pairings for the different dishes.

Willi's Wine Bar is a popular haunt for British, American, and Australian

LE QUARTIER JAPONAIS

Rue Sainte-Anne and its side streets are peppered with Japanese restaurants, authentic and affordable. Walk around and pick the one that looks the most appealing to you, or visit one of my favorites: **Kunitoraya** for all things udon (thick wheat noodles, 15 to 25€); **Kintaro** for ramen (10 to 20€); **Naniwa-Ya** for donburi, ramen, or katsu curry (breaded pork in curry sauce) at lunch, and a more varied, Osaka-style fare in the evening, including steamed vegetables, fried tofu, and octopus dumplings (12 to 20€). All three have very limited seating, so there is often a wait.

Kunitoraya. 39 rue Sainte-Anne, 1st. CROSS STREET: Rue Thérèse. M° Pyramides. PHONE: 01 47 03 33 65. WEB: www.kunitoraya.com. Mon–Sun 11:30am–10pm.

Kintaro. 24 rue Saint-Augustin, 2nd. CROSS STREET: Rue Monsigny. M° Quatre Septembre. PHONE: 01 47 42 13 14. Mon–Sat 11:30am–10pm.

Naniwa-Ya. 11 rue Sainte-Anne, 1st. CROSS STREET: Rue Thérèse. M° Pyramides. PHONE: 01 40 20 43 10. Mon–Sun 11:30am–10:30pm.

expats, but it is also frequented by locals, and the resulting Franglais vibe is a large part of its charm.

13 rue des Petits Champs, 1st. CROSS STREET: Rue Vivienne. M° Pyramides. PHONE: 01 42 61 05 09. WEB: www.williswinebar.com. Mon–Sat noon–2:30pm and 7pm–11pm; BAR SERVICE: noon–midnight.

~ Williamson also operates the restaurant next door, **Macéo**, where the food is more elaborate and the ambiance more upscale. Dinner à la carte costs around 45€, but formules range from 27€ (two courses at lunch) to 37€ (three courses at dinner); an all-vegetarian menu is available for 30€.

15 rue des Petits Champs, 1st. CROSS STREET: Rue Vivienne. M° Pyramides. PHONE: 01 42 97 53 85. Mon–Fri noon–2:30pm; Mon–Sat 7:30pm–11pm.

For your food shopping needs, you will find Japanese ingredients and ready-made dishes at either of these mini-marts: **Kioko** (widest choice but high prices), **Juji-Ya** (smaller, a bit cheaper, with a deli counter and seating space for a quick meal), and **Ace** (chiefly Korean with a Japanese aisle).

Kioko. 46 rue des Petits Champs, 2nd. CROSS STREET: Rue de Ventadour. M° Pyramides. PHONE: 01 42 61 33 66. WEB: www.kioko.fr. Tue–Sat 10am–8pm; Sun 11am–7pm.
Juji-Ya. 46 rue Sainte-Anne, 2nd. CROSS STREET: Rue des Petits Champs. M° Pyramides. PHONE: 01 42 86 02 22. Mon–Sat 10am–10pm; Sun 10am–9pm.
Ace. 63 rue Sainte-Anne, 2nd. CROSS STREET: Rue Rameau. M° Pyramides or Quatre Septembre. PHONE: 01 44 55 09 40. Tue–Sun 10:30am–8pm.

2ème arrondissement

A Priori Thé
Salon de thé / Breakfast / Brunch   VEG-FRIENDLY/OUTDOOR SEATING

When the turmoils of city life become too much to bear, it's time to duck inside the most beautiful of Paris's covered passageways and seek solace on the sheltered terrace of this tea salon, under the monumental arcades of the *galerie*. Or inside, if the terrace is too drafty.

A careful study of the pastry cart should help you decide between the seasonal tarts, cakes, and muffins, fine treats all of them, which can be downed with a cup of tea or a pitcher of hot chocolate. (Tea: 5€; pastries: 4 to 7€.)

A Priori Thé is also open for lunch on weekdays, when it serves an honorable, vegetarian-friendly fare of tarts and salads (about 15€), and for an opulent brunch on weekends (28€).

35 galerie Vivienne, 2nd. CROSS STREET: Rue Vivienne. M° Bourse.

PHONE: 01 42 97 48 75. BREAKFAST: Mon–Sat 9am–11:30am; LUNCH: Mon–Fri noon–3pm; BRUNCH: Sat–Sun noon–4pm; TEA: Mon–Fri 3pm–6pm and Sat–Sun 4pm–6:30pm.

Legrand Filles et Fils
Bar à vin, see page 259

LE CAVISTE, LE BAR À VIN ET LA CAVE À MANGER

A retailer of wine is called a **caviste**, a word that refers both to the shop and to the person who runs it. If a caviste wants to uncork his bottles and serve them to his customers, he needs a license to operate as a **bar à vin**. And because a bar license is difficult to obtain, many simply choose to serve food along with their wines: if the fare is more elaborate than peanuts and slices of *saucisson*—the typical wine bar nibbles—this activity makes them fall into the restaurant category, for which the license is somewhat easier to get.

This explains the boom of the **cave à manger** (a portmanteau of *cave*, wine cellar, and *salle à manger*, dining room), a versatile, casual place where you can buy your wine to go, stand at the counter to enjoy it with a few appetizers, or sit down to drink it with a full-fledged meal. In the latter two cases, a **droit de bouchon** (corkage fee) may be added to the retail price of the bottle.

If the fare is elaborate, the line between the cave à manger and the neo bistro (see page 46) can get blurry, but it boils down to the owners' approach, whether they serve food to go with their wine, or wine to go with their food.

Passage Jouffroy

Parigi and Damoiseau from
Le Valentin (page 89)

Chocolate hazelnut éclair
from Des Gâteaux et
du Pain (page 174)

Tablette mendiant from La Petite Rose (page 128)

Pork skin terrine
from Ribouldingue
(page 42)

VINS

Restaurant

à la Carte

Plat du Jour

Spécialité
de
Vins de Touraine

Liqueurs
de
1ères Marques

La Crêpe Dentelle
Casual, see page 32

Drouant
Chic OUTDOOR SEATING

Every fall, the world of French literature waits with bated breath for the most prestigious literary prizes to be awarded. Among them is the Prix Goncourt, for which the jury convenes at Drouant, near the Opéra.

This century-old restaurant was better known for its majestic Art Déco interior than for its culinary sparkle, but it resurfaced on the gastronome's map in 2005, when Antoine Westermann, an Alsatian chef of high repute, took over. He gave the dining room a face-lift and renovated the menu, keeping the *cuisine bourgeoise* spirit of the place but giving it stronger seasonal inflections.

As the diner soon realizes upon discovering the slightly cryptic menu, four is the magic number: appetizers come in sets of four small plates around a central theme (vegetables, fish, classics, world), main dishes (roasted lamb shank, skate with vinaigrette) are served with four side vegetables, and each dessert option will in fact get you four miniature ones. This is heaven if you love sampler packs, as I do, except that these preparations are so superbly executed you may wish you'd been served a bucketful of each.

Dinner will set you back 67€ (for a set of four appetizers, a main course, and a set of four desserts), but better deals are available at lunchtime on weekdays, when you can opt for the 20€ plat du jour or the 42€ three-course formule (chilled zucchini and cucumber soup, see recipe on page 28; braised shoulder of lamb; kirsch mille-feuille with almond ice cream—three options for each course).

Drouant has inherited the entire wine cellar of the gastronomic restaurant that Westermann used to run in Strasbourg, so the wine list is phone book thick and includes a number of rare vintages. On Saturdays, a vintner comes to present his wines, and a special lunch menu is designed around them (55€ for three courses and wine).

16 rue Gaillon, 2nd. CROSS STREET: Rue Saint-Augustin. M° Pyramides or Quatre Septembre. PHONE: 01 42 65 15 16. WEB: drouant.com. Mon–Sun noon–2:30pm and 7pm–midnight.

⌒ Westermann also owns **Mon Vieil Ami** on Île Saint-Louis, a small and classy neo bistro that serves classic French dishes with a focus on vegetables. (Three-course menu: 41€; plat du jour at lunchtime: 15€.)

69 rue Saint-Louis en l'Île, 4th. CROSS STREET: Rue Le Regrattier. M° Pont-Marie. PHONE: 01 40 46 01 35. WEB: mon-vieil-ami.com. Wed–Sun noon–2:30pm and 7pm–10:30pm.

Eat Me
Lunch, see page 79

Kintaro
Japanese, see page 18

Aux Lyonnais
Chic

Bouchons are to Lyon what bistros are to Paris, and this one first opened its doors in the late nineteenth century. For decades it held a special place in the heart of stranded Lyonnais and their hungry friends, and my dear uncle Jean-Paul, who was a regular in his twenties, still raves about the *saucisson chaud pommes de terre*.

But the advent of nouvelle cuisine was a severe blow, and Aux Lyonnais was on a downward slope when star-spangled chef and international businessman Alain Ducasse bought it in 2002. He had the breathtaking décor renovated (wood panels and tall mirrors, chandeliers, faience frescoes, and a stately mahogany staircase) as he lightened and spruced up the menu to better suit the modern palate.

Cervelle de canut (fresh cheese with herbs and garlic), *sabodet* (pig's head sausage), *quenelles de brochet* (plump pike dumplings in a crayfish sauce), pink praline tart . . . Beloved classics take on a definite air of elegance in this classy neo bouchon, but still manage to retain their soul and their comforting, down-to-earth appeal. Three-course formule: 30€; à la carte: about 45€. The selection of wines starts at 29€ by the bottle and 5€ by the glass.

32 rue Saint-Marc, 2nd. CROSS STREET: Rue de Richelieu. M° Richelieu-Drouot. PHONE: 01 42 96 65 04. Tue–Fri noon–2pm; Tue–Sat 7:30pm–11pm.

Le Mesturet
Casual / Breakfast   VEG-FRIENDLY

It may look like thousands of old Parisian bistros from the outside, yet the contemporary lettering on the awning should tip you off on the modernity of this one. But you haven't come all this way to study a logo, I imagine, so step inside and perch yourself on a stool in the comfy bar area for a quick lunch (plat du jour, sandwiches, onion soup) or find a table in the large but well-partitioned dining room for a more classic two- or three-course meal.

Regional dishes—*boudin noir* (blood sausage), snail puffs, *brandade de morue* (cod and potato mash), *blanquette de veau* (veal in cream sauce), beef cheek Bourguignon, rolled *tête de veau* (headcheese)—are joined by lighter preparations of fish and grilled meat, and even, rarity of rarities, a couple of vegetarian options.

The wine list is reasonably priced (bottles start at 19€) and offers an uncommonly wide choice of wines by the glass (4.10€); the service is kind and efficient. Because of its location near the Palais de la Bourse (the Paris stock exchange), Le Mesturet is busiest at lunch, and more quiet in the evening. Two courses: 19.50€; three courses: 25.50€; lunch formule (main course, wine, and coffee): 9.50€.

77 rue de Richelieu, 2nd. CROSS STREET: Rue Saint-Augustin. Mº Bourse. PHONE: 01 42 97 40 68. WEB: www.lemesturet.com. Mon–Sat noon–3pm and 7pm–10:30pm; BAR SERVICE: 7am–10:30pm.

Le Tambour

Casual   OUTDOOR SEATING

Located on the lower end of rue Montmartre (not to be confused with the Montmartre hill) in the trendy Montorgueil area, this fuss-free bistro attracts a young crowd with its bric-a-brac décor—part surreal métro station, part flea market—its buoyant ambiance, and its menu of gently priced brasserie dishes.

Burgundy snails, duck confit, *filet de bœuf Rossini* (beef steak topped with foie gras), chocolate cake, tarte tatin . . . By no means is it a display of culinary excellence, but the fare is hearty and honest, the wine is served *à la ficelle* (order a bottle and pay only for what you drink; see page 90), and the friendly staff likes to tease—all the ingredients you need for a casual dinner, Paris style. À la carte: about 20€.

One of the most distinguishing features of Le Tambour will benefit the night owl: the dinner service extends into the night until 3:30am, and the restaurant remains open even later, serving drinks and no-cook dishes until 6am.

41 rue Montmartre, 2nd. CROSS STREET: Rue Étienne Marcel. Mº Sentier or Étienne Marcel. PHONE: 01 42 33 06 90. WEB: restaurantletambour.com. Tue–Sat noon–3pm; Mon–Sun 6pm–6am.

LE RESTAURANT, LE BISTRO, LA BRASSERIE ET LE CAFÉ

Seasoned Parisian diners develop an instinct for recognizing what category a particular restaurant falls into, but few can explain precisely what the difference is between each. It is a fuzzy classification, indeed, but it can be broken down as follows.

Le restaurant, often shortened to *resto,* is the most generic term. It can be used for any business establishment where meals are served in exchange for payment, from the simplest neighborhood place (*un petit restaurant, un resto de quartier*) to the most upscale gastronomic restaurant (*un grand restaurant, un restaurant gastronomique*).

Le bistro, also spelled *bistrot,* is a small and unpretentious restaurant, often family owned, where a short menu of simple, comforting dishes is served in an informal ambiance. Bistros are typically open at mealtimes only, for lunch and/or dinner. The average bistro has modest gastronomic ambitions, but neo bistros (see page 46) set higher standards for themselves.

La brasserie was originally a restaurant that served beer—the literal meaning of *brasserie* is brewery—and a simple hearty fare, often of Alsatian inspiration. The term is now used, more broadly, for traditional restaurants that are larger than bistros and offer a longer menu served around the clock (*choucroute,* grilled meat, shellfish platters, etc.).

Le café is an establishment that is devoted to the serving of drinks all through the day (coffee, soft drinks, beer, wine), which you can either enjoy while seated at a table or standing at the bar; prices are a bit cheaper then. Most cafés serve croissants in the morning, and a basic food menu at lunchtime—salads, quiches, croque-monsieur, a plat du jour . . .

BREAKFAST AND BRUNCH

The breakfast habits of the average Frenchman are enough to make a nutritionist tear his hair out: many settle for a cup of coffee or a glass of juice, when they don't skip breakfast altogether.

But there are still those who love their *petit déjeuner* and wouldn't miss it for the world, a category I passionately belong to. Fresh bread or brioche with butter and jam, *viennoiseries*, a soft-boiled egg, a bowl of cereal, yogurt, fresh fruit or a compote, orange juice, a cup of coffee, café au lait, tea, or *chocolat chaud*—such are the usual suspects on the French breakfast table.

It is typically a private meal that's prepared and enjoyed at home. You can, however, go to any café in the morning and order a *café crème* (café-speak for a café au lait) with a croissant or a *tartine* (a split section of baguette served with butter and jam). And for something a little more elaborate, look for restaurants and bakeries marked BREAKFAST in this book, or visit any of the **Le Pain Quotidien** locations listed at right.

As for brunch, the concept started to appear in the early nineties, imported from North America, and has become increasingly popular since, as more and more restaurants and bars serve a brunch menu on Saturdays and/or Sundays, and Parisians get in line for their share.

The French interpretation is not always convincing: many restaurants happily use the brunch as a catchall for various leftovers and low-effort dishes, but some do a good job of it, and they're indicated by BRUNCH in this book. The brunch service usually operates under a no-reservations policy, so you should plan to arrive before noon, or expect a bit of a wait.

Le Pain Quotidien

18 place du Marché Saint-Honoré, 1st. CROSS STREET: Rue du Marché Saint-Honoré. M° Pyramides. PHONE: 01 42 96 31 70. WEB: www.lepainquotidien.com. Mon–Sat 8am–11pm; Sun 8am–7pm.

33 rue Vivienne, 2nd. CROSS STREET: Rue Feydeau. M° Bourse. PHONE: 01 42 36 76 02. Mon–Fri 7am–5pm; Sat–Sun 7am–6pm.

2 rue des Petits Carreaux, 2nd. CROSS STREET: Rue Saint-Sauveur. M° Sentier. PHONE: 01 42 21 14 50. Mon–Sun 7am–10:30pm.

18 rue des Archives, 4th. CROSS STREET: Rue Sainte-Croix de la Bretonnerie. M° Hôtel de Ville. PHONE: 01 44 54 03 07. Mon–Sun 8am–9:30pm.

Soupe Froide de Courgette et Concombre aux Herbes
Chilled Zucchini and Cucumber Soup with Herbs

Adapted from a recipe by Antoine Westermann, chef at Drouant (see page 21).

Pascale is one of the oldest friends I've made through Chocolate & Zucchini: she started her blog *C'est moi qui l'ai fait!* a few months after I did mine, we met at the Salon Saveurs (see page 280) soon after that, and we've been getting together regularly ever since, chatting over a nice meal, and comparing notes on our respective writing endeavors.

We once had lunch at Drouant and took advantage of the weekday *formule*, ordering different dishes for each course and switching halfway through, as good friends do. The entire meal was a springlike delight, but it is the chilled zucchini and cucumber soup that impressed us the most.

Enthusiastic cooks both of us, we tried to guess what went into it, analyzing each spoonful and deconstructing its vivid flavors, until a much simpler solution dawned on me: why didn't I just get in touch with the chef and ask? We nodded to each other and resumed our enjoyment of the soup.

FOR THE SOUP

1 large unpeeled cucumber or 2 medium, about 10 ounces (300 g)

Fine sea salt

1 tablespoon extra virgin olive oil

2 garlic cloves, crushed

1 large or 2 small yellow onions, about 12 ounces (340 g), finely minced

$^1/_3$ cup (80 ml) dry white wine

4 cups (1 liter) chicken or vegetable stock

1 teaspoon fresh thyme leaves (substitute $^1/_2$ teaspoon dried thyme)

1 tablespoon fresh tarragon leaves, loosely packed (substitute
   $1^1/_2$ teaspoons dried tarragon)

Freshly ground black pepper

4 small zucchini, about 2 pounds (1 kg), cut into thick slices

$^1/_2$ cup (120 ml) plus 2 tablespoons light whipping cream

A handful fresh mint leaves

A handful fresh sorrel leaves (substitute baby spinach or arugula)

Tabasco sauce or similar hot sauce, to taste

$^1/_2$ cup (120 g) fresh goat cheese

FOR THE CROUTONS

2 slices country-style bread, about 4 ounces (120 g), diced

1 tablespoon extra virgin olive oil

Serves 6
Chilling time: 2 hours

1. Quarter the cucumber lengthwise, carve out the seeds, and thinly slice. Transfer to a colander, sprinkle with $^1/_2$ teaspoon salt, toss to coat, and set aside to drain.

2. Heat the oil in a large soup pot over medium heat. Add the garlic and onions, and cook for 5 minutes or until the onions start to sweat, stirring regularly to avoid coloring.

3. Pour in the wine, scrape the bottom of the pan with a wooden spoon, and cook until the wine is entirely evaporated. Add the stock, thyme, tarragon, $^1/_4$ teaspoon pepper, and $^1/_2$ teaspoon salt. Cover and bring to a boil. Add the zucchini and simmer for 10 minutes, uncovered, until the zucchini is just tender.

4. Remove from the heat and let cool for a few minutes. Shake the colander that holds the cucumber to remove as much moisture as possible. Add the

$^1/_2$ cup (120 ml) cream and the cucumber to the pot, and purée until smooth with an immersion blender (or use a regular blender and work in batches). Transfer to a serving bowl, let cool to room temperature, about 30 minutes, cover, and refrigerate until chilled, about $1^1/_2$ hours. This can be prepared up to a day ahead.

5. Finely chop the mint and sorrel. Stir the herbs into the soup, season with Tabasco sauce, taste, and adjust the seasoning.

6. Prepare the croutons. Preheat the oven to the broiler setting. Combine the diced bread and olive oil in a medium bowl, sprinkle with a little salt and pepper, and toss to coat. Spread on a rimmed baking sheet and place under the broiler for a few minutes, until golden brown, watching closely to pre-vent burning and stirring the croutons regularly to ensure even browning. Set aside to cool.

7. In a small bowl, combine the goat cheese and the remaining 2 tablespoons of cream. Sprinkle with a little salt and pepper, and beat with a fork until smooth. Ladle the soup into soup plates. Place a rounded tablespoon of goat cheese in the center of each plate, sprinkle croutons in a circle around it, and serve immediately.

3ème arrondissement

Breizh Café

Casual   VEG-FRIENDLY

Bertrand Larcher was a man with a mission: his mission was to break the crêpe out of its rustic rut, shedding the obligatory Breton lace curtains and bulky sideboards to create the new, twenty-first-century crêperie. He opened the first one in Cancale, in his native Brittany (or *Breizh* in the Breton language), went to Tokyo with his Japanese wife to open a few more, then moved back to France to open this Parisian location in the Marais.

The menu makes equal room for time-proven classics (ham, egg, and cheese; andouille; butter and sugar; salted butter caramel) and modern creations (maki-style crêpe rolls served as an appetizer), all of them made with organic flour and artisanal ingredients. A chalkboard lists seasonal specials for both *galettes* (savory crêpes made with buckwheat flour) and crêpes (sweet ones made with wheat flour), and you can also sample oysters and cheese from Brittany. À la carte: about 20€.

When it comes to drinks, forget water and wine: order *lait ribot* (a lightly sparkling fermented milk, and one of my absolute favorite beverages) and hard cider or beer from Brittany, of which Breizh Café offers an unrivaled selection (bottles starting from 11€).

109 rue Vieille du Temple, 3rd. CROSS STREET: Rue du Perche. M° Saint-Sébastien-Froissart. PHONE: 01 42 72 13 77. WEB: www.breizhcafe.com. Wed–Sun noon–11pm; Closed Monday and Tuesday.

↝ Should you prefer a more traditional *creperie bretonne*, there are plenty to be found around Montparnasse, for this is where most workers from Brittany settled when they came to Paris in the twenties; **Ti Jos** is the most emblematic. I also recommend **La Crêpe Dentelle** in the Montorgueil area. In both cases, you will eat for about 20€.

Ti Jos. 30 rue Delambre, 14th. CROSS STREET: Rue du Montparnasse. M° Edgar Quinet or Vavin. PHONE: 01 43 22 57 69. Mon–Sat 11:30am–2:30pm; Wed–Mon

7pm–11:30pm; Closed for dinner on Tuesday and lunch on Sunday.

La Crêpe Dentelle. 8 rue Léopold Bellan, 2nd. CROSS STREET: Rue des Petits Carreaux. M° Sentier. PHONE: 01 40 41 04 23. Mon–Fri 11:30am–4pm and 7:30pm–10pm.

Café Suédois
Lunch / Salon de thé, see page 70

L'Estaminet
Bar à vin / Breakfast / Brunch   OUTDOOR SEATING

It would be easy to walk right by this minuscule restaurant, at the northern tip of the Marché des Enfants Rouges (see page 33), if two telltale barrels and a garland of vine didn't guard the entrance. The room is as fresh and bright as clean linens, and it is a most pleasant spot to down a glass of wine and simple French dishes.

The menu is short but gives you enough options to tailor a snack or a meal to the size of your appetite: a soup, a plat du jour (grilled frogs' legs, a mountain sausage with lentils, endives wrapped in ham), platters of artisanal charcuterie and cheese, assortments of smoked fish, Vendée oysters in season, homemade desserts . . . À la carte: about 15€; glasses of wine start at 3€.

L'Estaminet serves an 8.50€ breakfast formule every day until 11:30am (unfiltered apple juice, a croissant, *tartines* with jam, and a hot beverage) and a hugely popular 20€ brunch on Sundays. It belongs to the owners of the market's wine stall, Arômes et Cépages.

Inside the Marché des Enfants Rouges, on the right side, 39 rue de Bretagne, 3rd. CROSS STREET: Rue Charlot. M° Filles du Calvaire. PHONE: 01 42 72 34 85. WEB: www.aromes-et-cepages.com. Tue–Sat 9am–9pm; Sun 9am–2pm.

Au Fil des Saisons
Neo bistro

Au Fil des Saisons is the sort of restaurant that flies under the radar of the general public. It's not that it's doing anything wrong, quite the contrary, but it's not jumping through hoops or throwing confetti in your face, so it's easy to overlook. It doesn't help that it is buried on an anonymous side street off place de la République, or that its décor is somewhat lackluster.

However, it is worth finding that little street and turning a blind eye to the gilded chairs, in order to enjoy Stéphane Rocher's market-driven cuisine. Not only does the thirty-something chef follow the seasons as closely as a private eye would, but he takes the "everything homemade" philosophy to the point of baking his own rolls, little bundles of warmth that are brought to your table lined up on a skewer.

It is *cuisine bourgeoise* at its freshest that Rocher delivers—well-rounded, honest dishes such as a leek and scampi salad, a seven-hour duck confit, a sea bass with asparagus and white beans, or a port-roasted pigeon (game is prominently featured in the fall and winter), chased by an assortment of artisanal sorbets or a trio of *crèmes au chocolat* served in eggcups. Lunch formule: 17€ and 22€; dinner menu: two courses for 28€, three courses for 35€.

6 rue des Fontaines du Temple, 3rd. CROSS STREET: Rue du Temple. M° Temple or Arts et Métiers. PHONE: 01 42 74 16 60. Mon–Fri noon–2:30pm; Mon–Sat 7:30pm–10pm.

Le Marché des Enfants Rouges
Lunch
VEG-FRIENDLY/OUTDOOR SEATING

Les Enfants Rouges is the oldest covered market in Paris; it was created in the early seventeenth century and named in memory of a nearby orphanage, where the children wore a red uniform. Threatened with demolition in the mid-nineties, in 2000 it was saved *in extremis* by a neighborhood defense committee that campaigned for its renovation and reopening.

It is a small market that holds the classic stands for produce, cheese, meat, fish, or wine, but its distinguishing feature is that many of the vendors sell prepared dishes that can be taken home or eaten on the spot, at one of the picnic tables sprinkled throughout the market hall. I feel confident that this is as close to a food court as you will find in Paris.

Whether you're feeling like Moroccan, Mediterranean, Lebanese, Italian, French, or Japanese cuisine, it is a good lunchtime destination after a morning stroll through the Marais. Especially recommended are the Japanese stand **Chez Taeko** (bento box du jour: 12€) and the bucolic wine bar **L'Estaminet** (see page 32), which has indoor seating.

And as a postprandial nonedible treat, check out Fabien Breuvart's tiny photographer's studio, which specializes in old snapshots and family portraits.

39 rue de Bretagne, 3rd. CROSS STREET: Rue Charlot: M° Filles du Calvaire. Tue–Sat 8:30am–1pm and 4pm–7:30pm; Sun 8:30am–2pm.

4ème arrondissement

L'As du Falafel
Casual   VEG-FRIENDLY

Rue des Rosiers is the historical heart of Jewish Paris. The street is lined with kosher delis and bakeries, and the world-famous L'As du Falafel is a great spot to grab—you've guessed it—a falafel sandwich. Order the *spécial* (4.50€) from the window to the right, and collect it from the window to the left.

Sure, there is always a line, but this gives you time to observe the cook as he shapes little balls of chickpea batter and fries them with brio. Once done, the crisp, moist-hearted falafels snuggle up with their partners (crunchy cabbage, eggplant, sesame hummus, and optional hot sauce) between the warm sheets of the pita pocket. You are then free to walk away and bite in with delight, trying your best to shield your shirt from spills and squirts.

Alternatively, ask for a table inside and order your sandwich from there (4.50€). The service is hectic but friendly, and you'll be able to sample more of the house specialties: chopped liver, tahina, shawarma, etc. (Sampler plates: about 15€.)

34 rue des Rosiers, 4th. CROSS STREET: Rue des Écouffes. M° Saint-Paul. PHONE: 01 48 87 63 60. Sun–Thu noon–midnight; Fri noon–6pm; Closed on Friday night and Saturday.

◦ If the line at L'As du Falafel is too long or if you wish to give the underdog a try, turn around and go to Mi-Va-Mi, right there on the corner behind you, or walk a few steps farther down rue des Rosiers to Rami et Hanna: both have takeout windows and indoor seating, and their renditions of the falafel sandwich are similarly priced and just as good as that of their celebrity neighbor.

Mi-Va-Mi. 23 rue des Rosiers, 4th. CROSS STREET: Rue des Écouffes. M° Saint-Paul. PHONE: 01 42 71 53 72. Sun–Thu 10:45am–midnight; Fri 10:45am–5pm; Closed on Friday night and Saturday.

Rami et Hanna: 54 rue des Rosiers, 4th. CROSS STREET: Rue Vieille du Temple. M° Saint-Paul. PHONE: 01 42 74 74 99. Tue–Sun noon–midnight.

Berthillon
Salon de thé / Ice Cream Shop see page 197

Le Loir dans la Théière
Salon de thé / Brunch   VEG-FRIENDLY

Mismatched chairs and tables, leather benches and weathered armchairs, a mezzanine and a wooden staircase—the creaky antiques shop décor invites you to come in, pick a nook or a cranny that you like, shift and turn like cats do till they're comfortable, and relax.

While Le Loir dans la Théière is open for lunch on weekdays (salads, savory tarts, omelets, around 15€) and brunch on weekends (16.50€), I like it best in the hollow of the afternoon, when I can enjoy a glass of real iced tea, sweetened to my taste, and a generous serving of one of their home-style baked goods, be it a plum *clafoutis,* a strawberry tart, or my favorite, the walnut-apple cake. (Tea and pastry formule after 3pm: 9€.)

A book companion is the final touch of bliss—a Lewis Carroll, preferably, since the name of this *salon de thé* refers to Alice in Wonderland's mad tea party, which ends on the Mad Hatter and the March Hare trying to put the sleepy dormouse in the teapot.

3 rue des Rosiers, 4th. CROSS STREET: Rue Pavée. M° Saint-Paul.
PHONE: 01 42 72 90 61. Mon–Sun 9:30am–7pm.

Mi-Va-Mi
Lunch, see page 35

Mon Vieil Ami
Neo bistro, see page 22

Rami et Hanna
Lunch, see page 35

Le Trumilou
Casual

The rustic-kitsch décor of this Auvergnat bistro has seen better days (or at least, days when decorators thought sticking hay forks and copper pots to the walls was edgy), but its affordable cuisine and its location, scratching the back of the Hôtel de Ville and waving at Notre-Dame from across the river, make it a dining gem.

Traditional and unpretentious, generous and invigorating, the dishes on the menu include a tender *pounti* (a pork and Swiss chard terrine; see recipe page 97), well-seasoned snails, and an impeccable beef tartare. Grandmotherly desserts follow to tuck you in, and the *œufs en neige meringués* (a meringue-topped floating island) do so particularly well. And in lieu of a digestive, may I suggest a pinball session in the bar area? Three-course dinner formule: 19.50€; à la carte: about 25€.

84 quai de l'Hôtel de Ville, 4th. CROSS STREET: Rue de Brosse. M° Hôtel de Ville. PHONE: 01 42 77 63 98. Mon–Sun noon–3pm and 7pm–10:30pm.

5ème arrondissement

Le Café Maure

Salon de thé   OUTDOOR SEATING

Le Café Maure sits inside La Grande Mosquée de Paris, the oldest mosque in the city, founded in the aftermath of World War I. All white marble, mosaic fountains, and chirping birds, the patio is a haven of freshness and calm on a sweltering afternoon. If the weather is inclement, however, just retreat to the indoor room, plop yourself on a pouf, and admire the carved wood ceilings.

To complete the change of scene, a glass of honey-sweet mint tea or a cup of Moorish coffee (2€) is in order; a baklava (2€) won't hurt, either. Le Café Maure is open to all—although it is technically inside the mosque, it isn't a place of worship any more than the average Moroccan restaurant—and it is the perfect place to rest your feet after a walk through the nearby Jardin des Plantes, or to linger after a pampering session at the mosque's Turkish baths.

39 rue Geoffroy Saint-Hilaire, 5th. CROSS STREET: Rue Daubenton. M° Censier-Daubenton. PHONE: 01 43 31 38 20. WEB: www.la-mosquee.com. Mon–Sun 9am–midnight.

THE LANGUAGE BARRIER

Because Paris is visited by a large number of foreigners, one might imagine that the staff at restaurants and shops would speak at least some English, but that is not necessarily the case, and they may get defensive or annoyed if you assume they do.

If you don't speak French at all, I encourage you to try to find the time to memorize a few basic words and phrases before you visit; it really is the best investment you can make to prepare for your trip. I am not suggesting that all visitors should speak French fluently; the idea is simply to show that you're making an effort, trying to meet your interlocutor halfway.

And regardless of your language skills, you should always address a French person in French first. Say "*Bonjour*," or "*Bonsoir*" in the evening, smile, and ask, "*Vous parlez anglais?*" (This is the spoken version of the more formal "*Parlez-vous anglais?*" which sounds right out of a textbook.)

If they do switch to English, thank them, show that you're grateful for their efforts, and speak slowly (but not louder) to make yourself understood. If they don't speak English, keep smiling, and improvise with gestures and what little each of you knows of the other's language. Note that many Frenchmen *understand* a fair amount of English but lack the self-confidence to speak it, in which case they may reply in French to your English questions.

This may lead to a few misinterpretations, but it is all part of the adventure. You may occasionally be served a dish that's not at all what you had imagined, but it may turn out to be a pleasant surprise—and if it doesn't, well, think of the great story it'll make for the grandkids.

Les Délices d'Aphrodite

Greek   VEG-FRIENDLY/OUTDOOR SEATING

Greek cuisine is among the most shamelessly butchered the world over, but these Délices work hard to set the scales right. A few steps away from the chic and deservedly renowned Mavrommatis, this Hellenic bistro is run by the same team: it serves Greek classics to the same standards of refinement and authenticity, but in a more relaxed setting, and for a smaller bill.

Assortments of hot or cold *mezzedes* (appetizers) may constitute a whole meal, or else serve as a runway to the superb moussaka, char-crusty meat skewers, or stuffed calamari. Weekday lunch formules: 17.50€ and 19.50€; à la carte: 30€; wines start at 20€.

4 rue Candolle, 5th. CROSS STREET: Rue Daubenton. M° Censier-Daubenton. PHONE: 01 43 31 40 39. Mon–Fri noon–2pm and 7pm–11pm; Sat–Sun noon–3pm and 6pm–11pm.

Mavrommatis. 42 rue Daubenton, 5th. CROSS STREET: Rue Monge. M° Censier-Daubenton. PHONE: 01 43 31 17 17. WEB: www.mavrommatis.fr. Tue–Sat noon–2:15pm and 7pm–11pm.

⌒ **Mavrommatis** also operates a deli a block away, and has a concession stand at Lafayette Gourmet (see page 250).

47 rue Censier, 5th. CROSS STREET: Rue Monge. M° Censier-Daubenton. PHONE: 01 45 35 96 50. Mon–Sun 9:30am–9:30pm.

Les Papilles

Bar à vin / Wine shop   VEG-FRIENDLY/OUTDOOR SEATING

Part wine shop, part gourmet store, part restaurant, Les Papilles shows all the exterior signs of the *cave à manger* (see page 20) in a neat, well-lit space: a selection of natural wines on one wall, a zinc bar and a display case filled with cheeses and charcuterie on the other, and a bunch of tables huddled in between.

Get with the program by reading the day's menu on the chalkboard (four courses, no choices, a bargain at 28.50€) and browse the shelves to select the wine you'd like to drink with it. There is a 6€ corkage fee, but you will be sent home with the re-corked bottle if you have any left.

The menu is titled *Retour du marché* (back from the market) and lives up to the description by the freshness of the ingredients and such plainspoken, lively dishes as a cream of endive soup, a braised pork belly paired with *coco* beans (tiny white beans) and slow-roasted tomatoes, a brie de Meaux served with an apple compote, and an orange caramel blancmange, the French *panna cotta.*

TIPS FOR THE VEGETARIAN

Eating out as a vegetarian in Paris can be a challenge: France is a big meat-eating country and there aren't nearly as many vegetarians here as in North America, so restaurants have little experience catering to them. There are a few 100 percent vegetarian restaurants in Paris, but I've yet to find one that passes the taste bud test. I don't think one should lower one's standards just because a restaurant caters to the vegetarian niche, and this is why I haven't included them in this book.

I have, however, highlighted veg-friendly restaurants, those that offer vegetarian options or whose cuisine is so vegetable oriented you will find it easy to get by with a few adjustments. (See page 283 for a complete listing.)

In general, you won't have trouble finding a vegetarian starter on the menu, be it a salad, a soup, or a vegetable and cheese terrine. These may come with a nonvegetarian component (clams in the pumpkin soup, bacon chips on the endive salad), which you can just request not to be served. If you're a strict vegetarian, beware of the animal-based ingredients that may be hiding in a vegetarian-sounding dish, such as stock or gelatin; ask your waiter if he wouldn't mind double-checking with the chef.

Les Papilles serves the same copious menu for lunch and dinner; if you go at lunchtime, you may want to schedule a nap afterward. The downstairs room can be booked for private parties of six to fourteen.

30 rue Gay-Lussac, 5th. CROSS STREET: Rue Saint-Jacques. M° Luxembourg or Cluny-La Sorbonne. PHONE: 01 43 25 20 79. Mon–Sat noon–2pm and 7:30pm–10pm.

Main dishes are trickier: vegetables and grains are amply used in French cuisine, but they are still treated as a side, whose role is to flatter a piece of meat or fish, rather than the central focus of the dish. If there is no vegetarian main course on the menu, ask to be served two starters instead of a first and main course, or ask if the kitchen can put together a plate of sides for you.

Pescetarians—fish-eating vegetarians—will find it much easier to follow their diet, as a large majority of restaurants offer at least one seafood option. But some of the most meat-focused bistros don't serve fish at all, so it is best to check when you call to make your reservation.

Upscale restaurants—those in the "Chic" or "Gastronomic" categories—are happy to accommodate special requests, as long as you give them advance notice. Call ahead and ask if they can create a vegetarian menu for you; be sure to ask how much they'll charge for it.

And of course, let your waiter know that you're a vegetarian: don't expect him to be well informed on what does or doesn't qualify as vegetarian—a well-intentioned waiter was reported to have once asked, "How about foie gras; would that be okay?"—but if you work with him, he will help you make the right choices.

Le Pré Verre
Neo bistro

This contemporary bistro is located a few blocks from the Musée de Cluny (please go and bow to the beauty of the Lady and the Unicorn tapestries; I'll wait here till you return), in an area that is otherwise filled with restaurants that are so far below average they have to hire someone to stand on the sidewalk and talk you into stepping in, often in multiple languages.

Le Pré Verre is something else entirely: Philippe Delacourcelle is a maestro of herbs and spices, and he handles them with precision and flair: star anise murmurs through the chestnut soup, tamarind teases the bold flavors of the wild duck, and a dollop of lemon balm ice cream crowns the smooth chocolate cake.

The sound level is high and the service can get frantic, but the dinner menu-carte (three courses for 26.50€) and the lunch formule (13€) are as much of a delicious steal as you're going to find in this city.

8 rue Thénard, 5th. CROSS STREET: Rue du Sommerard. Mº Cluny–La Sorbonne. PHONE: 01 43 54 59 47. WEB: www.lepreverre.com. Tue–Sat noon–2pm and 7:30pm–10:30pm.

Ribouldingue
Neo bistro

Centering an entire menu on offal was a gutsy move, quite literally, but the gastronomic zeitgeist proved Nadège Varigny right. There is indeed an enthusiastic demand for underappreciated cuts of meat, especially when they're prepared with such a delicate hand as they are here: the pork skin terrine is silky on the tongue, fat capers shine over the pillow-like lamb's brains, and the emphatic veal kidney is tempered by a wholesome *gratin dauphinois*.

The list of wonders doesn't stop here: Ribouldingue is also the proper haven for fans of tripe, sweetbreads, head of veal, pork snout, beef tongue, cow udder, and even veal testicles, modestly referred to as *rognons blancs* (white kidneys) or *animelles*.

If you're not sure you can stomach an all-innards meal, however, or if your dining companions are more timid than you are, fret not. There are other, less challenging dishes to choose from: trout rillettes with cress, monkfish blanquette, or seared mackerels with caramelized turnips.

Desserts are offal free—to everyone's relief, I'm sure—and enchanting, such as a simple salad of *gariguettes* (a variety of strawberry) served with crème fraîche or a remarkable cilantro mousse with poached pineapple. The 27€ three-course menu is an excellent deal in the evening; it's a pity there is no smaller formule at lunchtime. The

wine menu features bottles from independent producers at gentle prices, starting at 16€. Ask to be seated in the cozy anteroom; it is less noisy than the main dining room.

(The name is a reference to *Les Pieds Nickelés,* a graphic novel from the early twentieth century that recounts the adventures of three small-time crooks named Croquignol, Filochard, and Ribouldingue; a few pages are wallpapered on the bathroom door.)

10 rue Saint-Julien le Pauvre, 5th. CROSS STREET: Rue de la Huchette. M° Saint-Michel or Cluny-La Sorbonne. PHONE: 01 46 33 98 80. Tue–Sat noon–2pm and 7pm–11pm.

～ If you're looking for a Right Bank alternative to Ribouldingue, head over to **Les Zingots,** a roomy bistro near Gare de l'Est that serves offal dishes among other brasserie staples. Lunch formules: 15€ and 17€; à la carte: about 40€; wine bottles start at 17€.

12 rue de la Fidélité, 10th. CROSS STREET: Boulevard de Strasbourg. M° Château d'Eau or Gare de l'Est. PHONE: 01 47 70 19 34. Tue–Fri noon–2pm; Tue–Sat 8pm–12:30am.

6ème arrondissement

L'Artisan des Saveurs
Salon de thé / Lunch   VEG-FRIENDLY

Quaintly decorated and cozy-chic, L'Artisan des Saveurs is a lovely teatime destination, where the pastries are fresh and delicate (pear charlotte, chocolate tart with candied kumquats, passion fruit blancmange, chocolate and grilled tea *macarons* [see page 166], 7 to 8€), the tea list extensive, and the hot chocolate voluptuous: it comes in five incarnations, including one with orange zest, and one flavored with betel leaves and amber rum (6.40€). Everything is made in-house, and Pascal Loustalot Barbé, the chef and owner, makes no compromise on the quality of his ingredients.

A range of his jams and confections—tea jelly, green tea marshmallows, *spéculoos* (a Belgian spiced cookie), macarons—can be purchased to go. L'Artisan des Saveurs is also open for lunch on weekdays and Saturdays

(main dishes around 16€, desserts: 8.20€).
Pastry classes on Thursday nights (60€); call
to inquire.

72 rue du Cherche Midi, 6th. CROSS STREET:
Rue de l'Abbé Grégoire. M° Sèvres-Babylone
or Vaneau. PHONE: 01 42 22 46 64. WEB:
www.lartisandesaveurs.com. LUNCH: Mon–Sat
noon–2:30pm; TEA: Mon–Fri 3pm–6:30pm and
Sat 3:30pm–7pm.

GAME

The official opening of the hunting season varies according to the type of animal and the region, but it extends roughly from September until January, and this is when a *gibier* bonanza appears on chalkboard menus.

Game meats have the reputation of being strong flavored and they are assertive ingredients indeed, but when adequately prepared (usually roasted, braised, or stewed), they make for richly flavorful, throaty dishes, precisely the sort that one yearns for in the heart of winter.

The varieties of game that most frequently appear on menus include:

- **Gibier à poil** (game with fur): *biche* (deer), *chevreuil* (venison), *lièvre* (hare), *marcassin* (young wild boar), *sanglier* (wild boar).
- **Gibier à plume** (game with feathers): *caille* (quail), *colvert* (wild mallard duck), *faisan* (pheasant), *palombe* (wood pigeon), *perdreau* (young partridge), *perdrix* (partridge).

NEO BISTROS

Once upon a time, in Paris, there was a generation of classically trained young chefs who decided that luxury hotels and gastronomic establishments were all good and well, but that independence probably tasted nice, too.

They each found a restaurant to call their own, taking over cheap-rent bistros in peripheral parts of the city, and started cooking, using the haute cuisine techniques they had long mastered, but applying them to more humble and more affordable ingredients.

Savvy diners were quick to catch on to this clever approach, which gave them the best of two worlds: the relaxed atmosphere of a bistro, the consistent quality of a gastronomic meal, and, as a bonus, the creativity of a chef who had to think out of the box to keep the food exciting and the prices low.

This was in the mid-nineties, and this neo bistro trend—also referred to as *bistronomie,* a portmanteau of *bistro* and *gastronomie*—is as strong as ever today: among these pioneering chefs were Christophe Beaufront (page 108), Yves Camdeborde (page 49), Thierry Breton (page 91), and Christian Etchebest (page 121), the latter three having worked under Christian Constant (page 63) at Le Crillon (page 64), and they are still among the most influential figures on the Parisian dining scene.

In fact, they have spawned a second generation of chefs who have walked in their footsteps and are now setting out on their own: Camdeborde has been particularly active in this mentoring role, as Stéphane Jégo (page 58) or Nadège Varigny (page 42) can attest.

Azabu

Japanese   VEG-FRIENDLY

Teppanyaki is a Japanese cooking technique that uses a wide griddle of smooth iron to sauté a variety of ingredients, and the chic Azabu specializes in this style of cuisine.

One of the most typical dishes thus assembled is the Osaka-style *okonomiyaki,* a thick eggy pancake filled with vegetables, fish, or meat. Azabu's are intensely flavorful, but shouldn't overshadow the rest of the dishes on the menu: a salad of lotus roots, miso-glazed eggplant, chicken with tofu, soft-shell crab, razor shell, scallops . . .

Aim for a seat at the bar, from which you can observe the chef as he assembles your meal with poise and a pair of spatulas. But if you prefer not to take the cooking smells home with you, ask to be seated downstairs. Weekday lunch formule: 18.50€; lunch bento box: 33€; dinner formules: 33 to 59€.

3 rue André Mazet, 6th. CROSS STREET: Rue Dauphine. M° Odéon.
PHONE: 01 46 33 72 05. Tue–Sat noon–2pm; Tue–Sun 7pm–10:30pm.

Le Bar à Soupes et Quenelles

Lunch, see page 101

Bread & Roses

Lunch / Salon de thé, see page 151

Le Caméléon

Chic

A dining landmark in this bourgeois part of the Montparnasse area, Le Caméléon had been on a slow and steady decline when it was taken over by Jean-Paul Arabian, an old-timer of the Parisian gastronomic scene. What used to be a bistro in the classic sense of the term has been propelled skyward on the scale of sophistication, but still retains a touch of dusty, nostalgic charm.

Likewise, the menu takes old favorites—leek and potato soup, garlic snails, skate with capers, thick-cut calf's liver—and casts a rejuvenating light on them, often with the aid of a well-chosen accessory—chicken lollipops in the soup, a parsleyed foam bath for the snails, or a macaroni gratin with the liver. Desserts are just as beguiling; go for the caramelized *pain perdu,* the original French toast, if it is in attendance.

Ask to be seated in the second dining room: it offers a view into the open kitchen, and from there you can blissfully ignore the flicker of the widescreen television (I don't know what possessed them to hang one there). Weekday lunch formules: 25€ for two courses, 30€ for three; à la carte: about 55€. Wine by the glass starts at 6€, bottles at 20€.

6 rue de Chevreuse, 6th. CROSS STREET: Boulevard du Montparnasse. Mᵒ Vavin or Raspail. PHONE: 01 43 27 43 27. Tue–Sat noon–2pm and 7pm–10pm.

Christian Constant
Salon de thé / Pastry shop / Chocolate shop / Ice cream

This tiny annex to Christian Constant's chocolate and pastry shop is where you should go for a textbook-perfect cup of hot chocolate—not too thick, not too thin, and just the right dose of sweetness—after a long walk around the Jardin du Luxembourg.

I like the classic Guanaja, but you can try the Spanish or the Mexican version for a nice change of pace. One pot easily serves two, and this leaves room for one of Constant's pastries, perhaps the *tarte fondante au chocolat,* the Sicilien (pistachio cream on a base of grilled almonds), or the Orphéo Négro (bittersweet chocolate and fresh strawberries with a heart of *praliné*). One would have wished for a bit more color and warmth in the décor, but the kindness of the service makes up for the charmless room.

Before you leave, drop by the shop next door and treat yourself to a box of elegantly flavored ganaches (ylang-ylang, verbena, ginger), unforgettably crisp *pralinés,* and faultless confections (candied fruits, fruit pastes, nougat, *guimauve*), or perhaps a *tablette* of single-origin chocolate (I favor the Venezuelan "bitter-plus," with 80 percent cocoa solids, which comes in super-thin sheets). Constant, man of many talents, also makes remarkable ice creams and sorbets: Tahiti vanilla, chicory, *fraise des bois*, white peach . . .

37 rue d'Assas, 6th. CROSS STREET: Rue de Fleurus. M° Rennes or Saint-Placide. PHONE: 01 53 63 15 15. SALON DE THÉ: Mon–Sun 11:30am–7pm; SHOP: Mon–Fri 9:30am–8:30pm and Sat–Sun 9am–8pm.

Le Comptoir du Relais
Neo bistro / Chic   OUTDOOR SEATING

Classically trained but independently minded, Yves Camdeborde is among the founding fathers of the neo bistro trend (see page 46). It is his first restaurant, the much lauded and perpetually packed La Régalade, that earned him this title, and he could have stayed there until retirement, sitting back and reveling in his well-oiled success, but no: his dream was to be an innkeeper. And so it is that after thirteen years of Régalade, Camdeborde and his wife, Claudine, bought the Relais Saint-Germain, a small seventeenth-century hotel in the Latin Quarter.

The restaurant downstairs, Le Comptoir du Relais, operates along two different modes: weeknight dinners involve a gastronomic five-course tasting menu (a terrine of cèpes, foie gras, and artichoke; a mousse of scrambled egg and sea urchin; beef fillet with bone marrow and heart of romaine; a cheese platter that gets passed around from table to table; saffron pears with a dollop of bittersweet ganache; all for a mere 45€), and the kitchen switches to brasserie-style à la carte dishes for lunch and on weekends.

Camdeborde's wild popularity makes it practically impossible to get a reservation for the gastronomic dinners—the restaurant is booked solid for months in advance—but the Basque-inspired brasserie menu is just as appealing (a platter of charcuterie from Camdeborde's brother's shop in Pau, red tuna *à la plancha*, Basque cake with sheep's milk ice cream, for an aver-

OFFAL VOCABULARY

The French word *abats* refers to those cuts of meat that are neither flesh nor muscle. Whether you adore or abhor them, this list of terms may come in handy:

Animelles: see *Rognons blancs.*

Cervelle: brain, generally of veal or lamb.

Cœur: heart, generally of beef or duck. Although the heart is technically a muscle, it is considered an abat.

Foie: liver, generally of veal or young cow (*génisse*). *Foie gras* is the liver of a fatted duck or goose.

Gésier: gizzard (a specialized stomach found in birds but not mammals), generally of duck or goose. The gizzard is technically a muscle, but it is considered an abat.

Joue: cheek, of pork or beef.

Langue: tongue, of pork or beef.

Museau: snout, of pork or beef.

Oreille: ear, generally of pork or veal.

Pied: foot, generally of pork or veal.

Queue: tail, generally of beef.

Ris: sweetbread (thymus or pancreas), generally of veal or lamb.

Rognon: kidney, generally of veal or lamb.

Rognons blancs or **animelles:** testicles, generally of lamb, ram, or ox.

Tête: head, generally of veal.

Tripes: tripe (stomach), generally of beef.

age tab of 30€) and the seating is first come first served, so you stand a good chance of securing a table if you get there early enough: at noon for lunch, or at 7:45pm for dinner.

9 carrefour de l'Odéon, 6th. CROSS STREET: Rue Monsieur le Prince. M° Odéon. PHONE: 01 44 27 07 97. BRASSERIE (NO RESERVATIONS): Mon–Fri noon–6pm and Sat–Sun noon–11pm; GASTRONOMIC DINNERS (SINGLE SERVICE, RESERVATION MANDATORY): Mon–Fri 8:30pm.

⌁ Staying at the Relais Saint-Germain hotel gives you access to an unforgettable breakfast spread assembled from first-rate ingredients—Spanish ham, farm-fresh eggs, Bordier butter and yogurt, Eric Kayser's bread . . . Camdeborde also runs the takeout shop next door, **La Crêperie du Comptoir,** selling crêpes, waffles, and sandwiches.

3 carrefour de l'Odéon, 6th. CROSS STREET: Rue Monsieur le Prince. M° Odéon. PHONE: 01 44 27 07 97. Mon–Sun 9am–midnight.

Da Rosa
Lunch, see page 201

Huîtrerie Régis
Casual, see page 242

Le Sensing
Chic

Here's a fact that a number of restaurant openings and makeovers have revealed over the past few years: once a classically trained chef gets to the height of his fame and recognition, he develops an itch to try new things, reach a different audience, and find some breathing room outside the golden cage of his gastronomic kitchen.

In the case of Guy Martin, of Grand Véfour fame, it meant creating Le Sensing around three basic ingredients: a sleek and modern interior design (in stark contrast to the Véfour's ornate eighteenth-century dining room, beneath the arches of the Palais Royal), one of his former sous-chefs, Rémi Van Peteghem, at the head of the kitchen, and a total bill that's about a third of what a meal costs at the mothership. Still not cheap, but affordable for a special occasion.

The short menu features contemporary and exciting dishes—mackerel and fennel tart (see recipe on page 56), red tuna stuffed with foie gras, Anjou pigeon in a muscovado sugar crust—that display an excellent balance of textures and flavors, and a true graphical talent in the plating.

CHEESE COURSE ETIQUETTE

In France, cheese is served after the main course and before (or in place of) dessert. When you order cheese in a restaurant, it may be brought to you as an *assiette de fromage*, already cut and plated. The proper way to eat cheese is this: tear off a bite-size piece of bread and hold it, crumb side up, with the fingertips of your left hand. Holding your knife in your right hand, cut a bite-size piece of cheese, pick or scoop it up with the tip of the blade, and deposit it on the prepared piece of bread, which you'll bring to your mouth using your left hand. Chew, moan, swallow, and repeat.

If, instead, a *plateau de fromages* (cheese platter) is brought to and left on your table, use the knife provided with the platter, and help yourself to three or four portions of moderate size. Wipe the blade discreetly on a piece of bread between cheeses, and cut each variety neatly, in such a way that every serving will have an equitable proportion of heart and rind. (Tiny cheeses are cut in halves or quarters, round or square cheeses are cut in tri-

Consider opening your meal with the platter of small bites, called *le snacking:* despite what the waiter may tell you, it can replace a starter (unless you haven't eaten in days) and it is a good way to explore the seasonal interests of the chef. And don't skip dessert, either: it would be a pity to forgo the pastry chef's generous take on the *baba au rhum* (a *savarin* sponge cake infused with rum and served with whipped cream) or his fiercely chocolaty ganache tartlet. Weekday lunch formules: 25€ and 55€; à la carte: about 65€.

19 rue Bréa, 6th. CROSS STREET: Boulevard Raspail. Mᵒ Vavin.

PHONE: 01 43 27 08 80. Tue–Sat noon–2:30pm; Mon–Sat 7:30pm–10:30pm.

angular wedges like a cake, cheese logs are cut in slices like slice-and-bake cookies, and long wedges of cheese are cut lengthwise in sticklike pieces, working your way up from the thinnest to the thickest end, where the rind is.) You are expected to help yourself swiftly and all in one go, so the platter can be passed around to another table.

At gastronomic restaurants, the wait staff wouldn't dream of letting you deal with the cutting and slicing, so cheese is served tableside, from a *chariot de fromages* (cheese cart) that is wheeled to your table—always an exhilarating moment. Take a few minutes to consider all the cheeses on offer, ask any question you may have about this or that variety—I like to have the waiter's opinion on which specimens he finds particularly remarkable—and set your heart on four cheeses or so; if you're irresistibly tempted by more varieties than that, you can push it to five or six. The waiter then slices the cheeses you've chosen—the portions tend to be too generous for my appetite, so I request small ones—and places them around the plate in the order in which they will best be enjoyed, from the mildest to the strongest.

Ze Kitchen Galerie
Chic

Fusion cuisine has taken such a bad rap over the past years that the term has become almost derogatory, and I shall resist the temptation to associate it with Ze Kitchen Galerie: William Ledeuil submits his cooking to a great many influences, yes, most notably from Southeast Asia, but they are intelligently combined to produce readable dishes that actually work.

The chestnut soup is flavored with galanga, the pheasant is marinated in ginger and cooked *à la plancha,* the white chocolate soup is spiked with wasabi and a scoop of litchi sorbet, and bite after bite, one hears the multitudinous chatter of the spices and herbs that lend uncommon depth to these preparations.

The décor has taken its cue from the contemporary art galleries that surround the restaurant—hence *ze* name—and the fish tank window at the back of the room is an improvement on the open kitchen idea: you get to observe the team at work without hearing the clatter, or smelling like a French fry when you get home.

The high ceilings make the room noisier than I like, and the two-top tables are quite close to one another, so if there's at least four in your party, request a round table when you call to reserve. Lunch formules: 23€ and 34€; à la carte: about 50€.

4 rue des Grands Augustins, 6th. CROSS STREET: Quai des Grands Augustins. M° Saint-Michel. PHONE: 01 44 32 00 32. WEB: www.zekitchengalerie.fr. Mon–Fri noon–2:30pm; Mon–Sat 7pm–11pm.

CRÊPES TO GO

Crêpes are among the few street foods that one finds in Paris: in well-frequented areas, sidewalk stands are practically climbing over each other to sell them to you, slathered with the spread of your choice. Before you indulge, stand by for a minute to check how good the ingredients look, and make sure the vendor will cook a fresh crêpe for you, rather than just reheat a pre-made one from the pile.

Good takeout crêpes, sweet or savory, can for instance be procured from **La Crêperie du Comptoir** (see page 51) and from the **Crêperie Bretonne** stand at the Président Wilson market on Saturday mornings, and the Convention market on Sunday mornings (see page 146 for market locations).

Tarte Fine Lisette et Fenouil
Mackerel and Fennel Tarte Fine

Adapted from a recipe by Rémi Van Peteghem, chef at Le Sensing (see page 51).

∼

A *tarte fine* is a thin individual tart, sweet or savory, that is assembled on a flat layer of puff pastry, with no raised edges. *Tartes fines* are most often round, but this one is a slender rectangle, along which pieces of marinated mackerel are aligned on a bed of fennel. It offers a sophisticated mix of flavors, the marinade taming the boldness of the fish, and the fennel blooming delicately underfoot.

Rémi Van Peteghem makes his tartlets with *lisette,* a smaller variety of mackerel. Fresh mackerel, which you may have sampled at your favorite sushi bar, has a rich and tender flesh, and a silky, edible skin that shimmers in hues of silver and blue. Should fresh mackerel prove difficult to find, these *tartes fines* can be made with fillets of fresh sardine, fresh herring, or fresh rainbow trout; in all cases, opt for small specimens that will yield thin fillets.

Flour for rolling out the pastry
1 sheet pre-rolled uncooked puff pastry, thawed according to package
    instructions if frozen
12 ounces (340 g) extra fresh Atlantic mackerel fillets, with skin (get the
    smallest specimens you can find, and let the vendor know the fish will
    be marinated, not cooked)
Juice of $1/2$ lemon
2 teaspoons soy sauce
3 tablespoons plus 1 teaspoon extra virgin olive oil
Freshly ground black pepper
1 garlic clove, finely minced
1 teaspoon fennel seeds
2 fennel bulbs , about 1 pound (450 g), trimmed, cored, and finely diced

Fine sea salt

4 dill fronds, for garnish

Serves 4 as a first course

1. Preheat the oven to 350°F (180°C) and line a rimmed baking sheet with parchment paper. Roll out or unfold the puff pastry on a lightly floured surface. Draw a rectangle on an index card or a piece of ordinary paper, about 2 1/2 by 5 inches (6 by 13 cm), snip it out, and use it as a guide to cut four rectangles of dough with a sharp knife; keep the remaining puff pastry for another use. Place the rectangles of dough on the prepared baking sheet, leaving a little space between them. Cover with a second sheet of parchment paper, spread baking weights or dried beans over the rectangles—this will prevent the dough from rising in the oven—and bake for 25 minutes or until golden brown. Remove from the oven and set aside.

2. As soon as you've slipped the dough in the oven, prepare the fish. Cut the fillets crosswise into rectangles, about 1 inch (2.5 cm) in width. In a medium bowl, whisk together the lemon juice, soy sauce, and the 3 tablespoons olive oil. Season with pepper. Add the fish to the bowl, stir gently to coat, cover, and leave in the fridge to marinate as you cook the fennel.

3. Heat the 1 teaspoon olive oil in a large skillet over medium heat. Add the garlic and cook for 2 minutes, stirring regularly to keep it from browning, until softened. Add the fennel seeds and toast for a minute, until fragrant. Add the diced fennel, season lightly with salt, and stir to combine. Cover and cook for 12 to 15 minutes, stirring every now and then, until cooked through but not too soft. Taste and adjust the seasoning.

4. Assemble the tarts: place the pastry rectangles on four serving plates and top each of them with a fourth of the fennel. Sprinkle with pepper. Drain the

fish thoroughly and divide the pieces among the four tarts, lining them up in a regular pattern, skin side up, over the fennel. Garnish each tart with a dill frond and serve immediately, with a handful of mixed greens; Rémi Van Peteghem serves his with a roasted fennel foam and a condiment of slow-roasted tomatoes, chopped finely with scallions and spiked with a dash of balsamic vinegar.

VARIATION: The fish may be seared briefly before you assemble the tarts. Set the cooked fennel aside, wipe the skillet clean, add a touch of olive oil, and cook the fish for 1 minute, skin side down, over medium-high heat.

7ème arrondissement

L'Ami Jean
Neo bistro

When Stéphane Jégo took over this Basque bistro after twelve years at Camdeborde's side (see page 49), he did not change the cramped décor by a single iota, and lovingly kept the old wooden bar, the tiny, naked tables, the braids of chile peppers dangling from the ceiling, and the kitschy memorabilia papering the walls.

In the napkin-size kitchen, however, a wind of youth and energy now blows full force, as the young chef revamps regional favorites (chiefly from Brittany, the Béarn, and the Basque country) with uncommon finesse and technical precision. Veal and foie gras terrine, squid and mackerel gratin, oxtail parmentier, skate with capers, old-fashioned *riz au lait*... The descriptions on the menu-carte (30€) are simple, and only heighten the diner's pleasure when the actual dishes arrive and the complexity of their flavors unfurls.

The atmosphere, rambunctious and decorum free, is the ideal environment in which to enjoy Jégo's warmhearted food, and the service is hectic but efficient. One final tip: if you visit during the hunting season, from September to January, the lip-smacking game dishes—stewed boar, roasted mallard, seared partridge—are entirely worth the splurge (30 to 40€). And in the spring and summer, picnic baskets can be ordered from L'Ami Jean (25€ per person).

27 rue Malar, 7th. CROSS STREET: Rue Saint-Dominique. M° Invalides.
PHONE: 01 47 05 86 89. Tue–Sat noon–2pm and 7pm–midnight.

Bellota-Bellota
Lunch, see page 204

Café Constant
Casual / Breakfast

Two doors down from his Violon d'Ingres (see page 63) was an unprepossessing corner bistro that Christian Constant acquired when the owner retired. In the unchanged 1950s décor, Constant's team serves comforting classics done deliciously right: *œufs mimosas* (deviled eggs), *terrine de campagne* (rustic pork terrine), *boudin blanc pommes en l'air* (a white sausage served with caramelized apples), *tête de veau sauce gribiche* (veal head served with a fresh herb and capers mayonnaise), *profiteroles* (vanilla ice cream puffs and chocolate sauce), *crème caramel* (caramel custard) . . .

The restaurant is small and doesn't take reservations, so come early or late to avoid the wait. À la carte: 27€. Café Constant is open all day, and also caters to those who just want a café-croissant in the morning, or a nightcap after dinner.

139 rue Saint-Dominique, 7th. CROSS STREET: Rue Augereau. M° École Militaire. PHONE: 01 47 53 73 34. Tue–Sat noon–2:30pm and 7pm–10:30pm.

Cuisine de Bar
Lunch / Breakfast   **VEG-FRIENDLY**

To the left of the Poilâne bakery (see page 152) is a Poilâne-owned annex that serves simple *tartines* (open-face sandwiches) assembled on toasted slices of Poilâne's world-famous *miche,* and served with a crisp salad—they have a heavy hand with the dressing, so be sure to ask for it on the side (*"La vinaigrette à part, s'il vous plaît"*).

The acoustics are terrible and the staff should really lighten up, but the ingredients are fresh and the tartines beyond reproach—I like the Crottin (goat cheese, tomato purée, and dry sausage) and the Poulet (chicken, anchovies, and capers).

The lunch formule buys you a tartine, a side salad, a drink, and coffee for 12.50€. You can also come in for breakfast and choose between three formules, from 4.50€ (toasted bread with butter and jam) to 8.70€ (toasted bread, a croissant, an orange juice, and coffee or tea). Cuisine de Bar doesn't take reservations, but the wait isn't usually very long.

8 rue du Cherche Midi, 7th. CROSS STREET: Rue de Sèvres. Mᵒ Saint-Sulpice or Sèvres-Babylone. PHONE: 01 45 48 45 69. Tue-Sat 8:30am-7pm.

Délicabar
Lunch / Salon de thé / Brunch   **VEG-FRIENDLY/OUTDOOR SEATING**

When the fashionista is out shopping, finding lunch can be a hassle, forcing her to lug her purchases around and waste precious time and energy, all for a sad and hasty salad. The department store Le Bon Marché kindly solves this agonizing problem by offering a restaurant on one of its fashion floors, so you can shop till you drop, recuperate, and shop again, all without leaving the store.

The interior design is sleek and pop-modern with bright spots of color, and the food is largely up to par, thanks to young Sébastien Gaudard, a former head pastry chef at Fauchon. His fresh and colorful creations focus on vegetables, fruits, and chocolate, and the menu hops playfully between the sweet and the savory, with main dishes constructed as desserts (smoked salmon mille-feuille, endive and almond milk tartlet) and vice versa (chocolate and caramel soup, citrus and *pain d'épice* salad). It can be a bit puzzling at first, but the color-coding helps.

The outdoor patio is an oasis of chic for summertime lunches (about 20€ à la carte; the restaurant does not take reservations, so try to arrive before 12:30pm to beat the lunch rush), but the Délicabar is just as lovely in the morning or the afternoon, to relax in the company of a cup of tea and a croissant or one of Gaudard's glossy pastries, which can also be bought to go.

38 rue de Sèvres, first floor of Le Bon Marché, 7th. CROSS STREET: Rue du Bac. M° Sèvres-Babylone. PHONE: 01 42 22 10 12. WEB: www.delicabar.fr. Mon, Tue, Wed, Fri 9:30am–7pm; Thu 10am–7pm; Sat 9:30am–8pm.

Les Fables de La Fontaine
Neo bistro

This elegant pocket bistro, which focuses on all things marine, is the third star in the Christian Constant constellation (see Le Violon d'Ingres on page 63 and Café Constant on page 59). Originally operated by Constant himself, it is now in the hands of two of his former protégés from Le Violon d'Ingres.

There is no set menu here, just a handful of dishes created around the day's catch: a beautiful but chilly December day might bring such starters as a half-dozen oysters, a crawfish tartare in clear broth, or an aspic of *tourteau* crab, to be followed by a seared fillet of *lieu* (pollack) paired with Jerusalem artichokes and chestnuts, or a braised *dorade* (John Dory) served with *gratin dauphinois* and a heart of *sucrine* lettuce.

Save some appetite for dessert, especially if the kitchen has baked the signature *gâteau basque* (an almond cake stuffed with black cherry jam). The room is tiny—twenty-two covers, tops—so reservations are indispensable. À la carte: about 45€. (The name is a double reference to the location of the restaurant, whose arcades face a pretty fountain, and the work of French fabulist Jean de La Fontaine.)

131 rue Saint-Dominique, 7th. CROSS STREET: Rue Augereau. M° École Militaire. PHONE: 01 44 18 37 55. Mon–Sun noon–2:30pm and 7:30pm–10:30pm.

Les Ombres
Chic, see page 72

Les Ormes
Chic

It is the sort of restaurant in which it would be easy, once settled in the faintly faded dining room, to sit back and forget which decade you're in, for Stéphane Molé, the thirty-something chef and owner of Les Ormes and one of Joël Robuchon's disciples, has chosen to apply his skills to the preservation and celebration of the classic French repertoire.

And he interprets it with a respect and passion that come across in each forkful: the menu shifts every few weeks to account for the change of seasons, but may include a foie gras rubbed with spices and crowned with candied pistachios, a pan-seared skate served with capers and caramelized fennel, and a knock-your-socks-off *jarret de veau à la cuiller,* a veal shank that is braised for hours until the meat is so tender it could be eaten with a spoon (see recipe on page 267).

The dessert menu is no less pleasing—Molé also worked closely with pastry chef Christophe Felder at Le Crillon—and ranges from a thin tart of Solliès figs with a black currant sorbet, to a rich ganache of Guanaja chocolate served with French-toasted *pain d'épice* and a scoop of chicory ice cream.

Molé's attention to detail is also evident in the quality of the ingredients he procures: the vegetables are handpicked by Joël Thiébault (see page 215), the bread is baked by Jean-Luc Poujauran, and the cheese is provided by Philippe Alléosse (see page 229). Three-course lunch formule on weekdays: 38€; three-course menu-carte at dinner: 49€; carte blanche tasting menu: 65€.

22 rue Surcouf, 7th. CROSS STREET: Rue de l'Université. M° Invalides. PHONE: 01 45 51 46 93. WEB: www.restaurant-les-ormes.fr. Tue–Sat 12:45pm–2pm and 7:45pm–10pm.

Le Violon d'Ingres
Chic

After working in luxury hotel kitchens for thirty years and godfathering the neo bistro trend (see page 46), Christian Constant left Le Crillon (see page 64) in the late nineties to open his own restaurant in the posh 7th. His numerous admirers followed him excitedly to this new venue, a sixty-cover operation called Le Violon d'Ingres.

In 2006, after eight years of success, Constant decided to give his Violon a new coating of varnish. The dining room was redecorated (it is now a more contemporary shade of chic) and the prices went on a diet (the average tab was divided by three), while the cuisine stayed true to Constant's unanimously acclaimed neoclassical style: technical yet intuitive, impressive without ostentation.

The almond-crusted fillet of sea bass from Saint-Malo with Sicilian capers (see page 244) shows perfect balance in the textures and the seasoning, the *cassoulet* from Montauban—Constant's hometown—is what all cassoulets aspire to be, and few desserts are as delicately indulgent as the warm vanilla soufflé, into which a sauce of salted butter caramel is ladled tableside. Three courses: 45€; two courses: 32 to 36€. Tasting menu: 60€; bottles start at 22€; wine by the glass starts at 5€.

(Although both make a fine chocolate tart, this Christian Constant is not to be confused with the pastry chef and chocolatier on page 48. The restaurant is named in honor of Jean Auguste Dominique Ingres, a neoclassical painter who was born in Montauban in the late eighteenth century; the French expression *un violon d'Ingres* also means a hobby, for Ingres played the violin in his spare time.)

135 rue Saint-Dominique, 7th. CROSS STREET: Rue Augereau. M° École Militaire. PHONE: 01 45 55 15 05. WEB: www.leviolondingres.com Tue–Sat noon–3:30pm and 7pm–11pm.

⁓ Constant runs or oversees three more restaurants on rue Saint-Dominique: Café Constant (see page 59), Les Fables de La Fontaine (page 61), and a more recent addition, **Les Cocottes de Christian Constant**, an all-day, every-day snack shop where one can sit at the counter and eat breakfast for 9€, or three courses for 25€. (No reservations.)

135 rue Saint-Dominique, 7th. CROSS STREET: Rue Augereau. M° École Militaire. No telephone. Mon–Sun 8am–10:30pm.

8ème arrondissement

Les Ambassadeurs
Gastronomic / Brunch

The *palace* hotel on place de la Concorde, Le Crillon, is home to one of the most exciting gastronomic restaurants in the city. The thirty-something and exceptionally gifted Jean-François Piège directs the kitchen, and his scintillating style dances between the classic French repertoire and his own modern inventions. In striking contrast to the showy ballroom where diners are seated, the menu is pared down and simple, and the descriptions of the dishes read like so many haikus.

Precise flavors, luxurious pairings, and artful presentations, Piège's cuisine is all about capturing the essence of the ingredients and revealing them in the most palate-pleasing and eye-catching way. The 75€ lunch formule (weekdays only) gets you three seasonal courses (scallops with black truffle, a fillet of sea bass paired with a cabbage-stuffed buckwheat crêpe, a pineapple and coconut *vacherin* in a cage of meringue; two choices for each course) plus an outstanding cheese platter; it is my favorite way to experience the magnificence of Les Ambassadeurs without having to call my banker (dinner costs around 200€ à la carte).

And if you feel hungry and opulent on a Sunday morning, consider treating yourself to the Pantagruelian brunch: it is an avalanche of the finest breakfast treats (*viennoiseries,* an assortment of bread, raw milk butter by Jean-Yves Bordier, jams by Christine Ferber, *œuf cocotte,* Spanish ham, Norwegian smoked salmon, fruit salads, pastries), and a memorable way to spend 70€.

10 place de la Concorde, 8th. CROSS STREET: Rue Royale. M° Concorde. PHONE: 01 44 71 16 16. WEB: crillon.com. Tue–Sat 12:30pm–2pm and 7:30pm–10pm; Sun noon–3pm.

Boulangépicier
Lunch / Bakery / Breakfast VEG-FRIENDLY/OUTDOOR SEATING

Owned and operated by restaurant shogun Alain Ducasse, Boulangépicier is, as you may have guessed from the portmanteau name, a bakery and a gourmet store all rolled into one, which regulars just call "Be." A selection of fine foods (truffles, oils, condiments, jams) lines one wall, but the real attraction here is the artisanal and naturally leavened bread that is baked fresh on the premises. Try the sourdough *tourte,* the buckwheat flour bread, or the one that's studded with chocolate chips and dice of orange peel; it is what they serve for breakfast in heaven.

Luxurious sandwiches are assembled on these fine loaves and garnished with top-notch ingredients, and I have been known to go out of my way to snatch a Brochette Riviera (a sampler of three mini-sandwiches pricked on a skewer), or a sardine and tomato sandwich on olive baguette.

Such quality does have a price (the brochette costs 7.50€, the sardine sandwich 8€), but if you're a serious sandwich aficionado, you won't regret shelling out the dough. Salads, soups, and desserts round out the selection;

much recommended are the mango and passion fruit compote (see recipe on page 73) and the *visitandine*, a small almond cake. All items can be enjoyed in the seating area at the back, or bought to go.

73 boulevard de Courcelles, 8th. CROSS STREET: Rue des Renaudes.
M° Courcelles. PHONE: 01 46 22 20 20. WEB: www.boulangepicier.com.
Mon–Sat 7am–8pm.

Alternate location:

Le Printemps de la Maison—3rd floor, 74 boulevard Haussmann, 9th.
CROSS STREET: Rue du Havre. M° Havre-Caumartin. Mon–Wed and Fri–Sat
9:35am–7pm; Thu 9:35am–10pm.

Le Bristol

Gastronomic   OUTDOOR SEATING

Stepping inside a Parisian *palace* hotel does strange things to your body: as soon as you're past the revolving doors, the outside world vanishes, your gait slows down, your spine straightens, and you find yourself walking in a confident stride as if you were an heir or heiress, quite blasé about all that glitter and gold.

At Le Bristol, you have the entire hall to practice before you reach the restaurant, where Eric Fréchon works his magic. His cuisine is a sure-footed mix of brilliance and humility, of French tradition and carefully chosen foreign influences, of haute-cuisine techniques and respectfully handled, spectacular ingredients.

A sea bass poached in a mussel broth and paired with chanterelles and smoked eel, a roasted wood pigeon (cooked rare, as it should be) served with an earthy trio of cèpes, offal cake, and corkscrew-shaped potatoes . . . Each dish is a plate-size painting that the diner feels compelled to study and admire, each forkful uncovering a tasty detail, a sensory find.

Dessert can sometimes be a letdown in such gastronomic establishments, but it is not the case at Le Bristol, where the pastry team delivers sweet creations with a talent that largely matches Fréchon's, as illustrated by the thin

CHALKBOARD MENU

While some restaurants stick to the classic menu format—a printed list that is handed to each diner once seated—many have adopted the chalkboard approach, which allows the chef to update the menu every day and make last-minute changes: just before the beginning of service, the menu choices are handwritten on a blackboard (*ardoise*) that the waiter props up on a chair by your table, or directly on your table. Granted, it forces you to crane your neck and the writing isn't always legible, but it also makes for a convivial moment, as all the members of your party—and sometimes those of neighboring tables—look in the same direction and join forces to decipher the squiggles. Once you've placed your order, the board gets passed around to another table, and reappears when it is time to make dessert decisions.

chocolate cookie with preserved lemons and tonka bean sorbet, or the buttery French-toasted brioche served with flambé *mirabelle* plums and caramel-flecked vanilla ice cream.

Depending on the time of year and the weather, you may be seated in the winter salon, in the garden-view summer dining room, or on the blissful terrace. 90€ lunch formule every day (three courses; two choices for each); à la carte: 120 to 220€.

112 rue du Faubourg Saint-Honoré, 8th. CROSS STREET: Avenue Matignon. M° Miromesnil or Saint-Philippe du Roule. PHONE: 01 53 43 43 40. WEB: hotel-bristol.com. Mon–Sun 12:30pm–2pm and 7:30pm–10pm.

Café Jacquemart-André
Lunch, see page 70

Eric Kayser
Lunch / Bakery, see page 149

Naked
Lunch, see page 79

Olsen
Lunch, see page 209

Les Saveurs de Flora
Chic

A welcome oddity in an area that's dubbed the "Golden Triangle" for the high prices and matching pretensions of its restaurants, Les Saveurs de Flora holds its own in terms of elegance, but is neither intimidating nor outrageously priced.

The namesake chef, Flora Mikula, is a child of Provence who's done her share of traveling, and this results in a modern Mediterranean cuisine with a view on Asia. Although the menu holds inspired à la carte dishes, it is the thriftier menu-carte that gets my vote: 36€ will buy you three courses (a soup of root vegetables topped with house-smoked foie gras, a swordfish skewer in satay sauce, a poached pear served with beer sorbet and a rye waffle; several choices for each course), bookended by an *amuse-bouche* and a plate of *mignardises*. (At lunchtime, you can order two courses from the same menu for 28€.)

The froufrou preciousness of the dining room ("So *this* is what it feels like to sit inside a ball of cotton candy!") may make you wary of similar mannerisms from the kitchen, but have no fear: Mikula's cooking is playful and sassy, yes, but never affected.

Service is uneven, but the chef's smile isn't, when she comes out on her round of meet-and-greet at the end of the shift. Laurent Dubois (see page 228) and Joël Thiébault (see page 215) respectively supply the cheese and vegetables on the menu.

36 avenue George V, 8th. CROSS STREET: Rue Pierre Charron. M° George V.
PHONE: 01 40 70 10 49. WEB: www.lessaveursdeflora.com. Mon–Fri noon–2pm
and 7pm–11pm; Sat 7pm–11pm.

La Table du Lancaster
Gastronomic   OUTDOOR SEATING

Set inside a nineteenth-century miniature *palace* hotel just off the Champs-Élysées, La Table du Lancaster boasts an inspired menu created by Michel Troisgros, owner of the eponymous gastronomic restaurant in Roannes, an hour from Lyon. The chef's passion for bright and acidulated flavors translates here into a contemporary and sparkling French cuisine, infused with colors and spices from afar.

The dishes are organized by flavor themes—the éclat of citrus, the vivacity of vinegar, the piquant of spices—among which you may find a grapefruit-scented turbot, a lacquered suckling pig served with green mango in a light vinaigrette, or sautéed frogs' legs spiked with tamarind. The dessert menu is just as well traveled, from the aerial coconut soufflé with piña colada sorbet to the crisp chocolate mille-feuille, served with bergamot granita.

Dinner costs around 100€ à la carte, unless you opt for the eight-course 120€ tasting menu; more accessible is the three-course lunch formule (52€; no choices), which can be enjoyed in the Zen-inspired courtyard garden.

7 rue de Berri, 8th. CROSS STREET: Avenue des Champs-Élysées. M° George V.
PHONE: 01 40 76 40 18. WEB: www.hotel-lancaster.fr. Mon–Fri 12:30pm–2pm
and 7:30pm–10pm; Sat–Sun 7:30pm–10pm.

EATING IN MUSEUMS

Just because you're feeding your soul doesn't mean you won't get hungry for real food; the following museums house restaurants for that very purpose.

Café Suédois @ Centre Culturel Suédois
VEG-FRIENDLY/OUTDOOR SEATING

The Swedish cultural center is set in a sixteenth-century *hôtel particulier* in the Marais, L'Hôtel de Marle. The permanent collection delineates the artistic exchanges between Sweden and France from the seventeenth to the twentieth centuries, and temporary exhibitions display the work of contemporary artists and designers. House-made sandwiches, soups, and Swedish pastries are served at the charming Café Suédois and its courtyard terrace.

11 rue Payenne, 3rd. CROSS STREET: Rue du Parc Royal. M° Saint-Paul or Chemin Vert. PHONE: 01 44 78 80 11. WEB: www.ccs.si.se. Tue–Sun noon–6pm.

Café Jacquemart-André @ Musée Jacquemart-André
BRUNCH/VEG-FRIENDLY/OUTDOOR SEATING

It's not every day that you're invited to tea in a nineteenth-century private mansion: this one belonged to a couple of art collectors, Nélie Jacquemard and Édouard André, whose living quarters have been transformed into a museum, and their dining room into a *salon de thé*. I'm sure you'll enjoy the visit as much as I do—especially the tour of the grand kitchen—and when you're done, you can have lunch or tea beneath the Tiepolo fresco, or out in the courtyard. The catering is provided by Stohrer (see page 164). Lunch formule: 15.50€; tea and pastry formule: 8.60€; Sunday brunch: 25€.

158 boulevard Haussmann, 8th. CROSS STREET: Rue de Téhéran. M° Miromesnil. PHONE: 01 45 62 11 59. WEB: www.musee-jacquemart-andre.com. Mon–Sat 11:45am–5:30pm; Sun 11am–3pm.

Tokyo Eat @ Palais de Tokyo VEG-FRIENDLY/OUTDOOR SEATING

Inside the museum of contemporary art is a trendy, urban design restaurant of huge proportions, where you'll be served an eclectic but fresh world cuisine under UFO-like lamps—unless you opt for the splendid terrace. (Plat du jour at lunch on weekdays: 12€; à la carte: 40€.) **Tokyo Idem** is a smaller, cafeteria-like space where you can have a snack and a drink. Don't miss the edgy gift store, either.

13 avenue du Président Wilson, 16th. CROSS STREET: Rue de la Manutention. M° Iéna. PHONE: 01 47 20 00 29. WEB: www.palaisdetokyo.com. Tue–Sat noon–3pm and 8pm–11:30pm.

Le Jardin @ Musée de la Vie Romantique
VEG-FRIENDLY/OUTDOOR SEATING

The neoclassic mansions of the Nouvelle-Athènes neighborhood were home to a thriving crowd of writers, musicians, painters, and actors in the nineteenth century, and this particular house belonged to a Dutch artist named Ary Scheffer. It is now a museum devoted to Romanticism, where you can see Scheffer's paintings and workshop, documents and memorabilia about his friend George Sand, and temporary exhibitions featuring the work of Romantic artists. Between May and October, a *salon de thé* is set up in the adorable garden, amid the flowerbeds and under the glass ceiling of the greenhouse. Lunch formule: 9.50€; a pot of loose-leaf tea and a slice of cake add up to 7.50€.

16 rue Chaptal, 9th. CROSS STREET: Rue Henner. M° Blanche or Saint-Georges. PHONE: 01 55 31 95 67. WEB: vie-romantique.paris.fr. Tue–Sun 11:30am–5:30pm.

Ziryab @ Institut du Monde Arabe

The mission of the Arab World Institute is to foster cultural exchanges between France and Arabic countries. Three floors of the glass-curtained building—designed by Jean Nouvel in the late eighties—are devoted to artifacts that document Arab civilization from the prehistoric era to the early twentieth century, and temporary exhibitions are organized each year. On the very top floor is a gastronomic restaurant named Ziryab: mealtime prices are rather steep (42 to 50€), but in the afternoon, from 3 till 6:30pm, you can simply sit down for tea (5€) and baklava (8€), and enjoy the sweeping view of the city, from Notre-Dame to La Bastille.

1 rue des Fossés Saint-Bernard, 5th. CROSS STREET: Boulevard Saint-Germain. M° Sully-Morland or Cardinal Lemoine. PHONE: 01 53 10 10 16. WEB: www.yara-prestige.com. Tue–Sun 3pm–6:30pm.

Les Ombres @ Musée du Quai Branly OUTDOOR SEATING

The museum of primary arts, devoted to the indigenous civilizations of Africa, Oceania, Asia, and the Americas, caused quite a controversy when it opened: some objected to the papier-mâché look of the exhibition rooms and what they perceived as a condescending approach. I do recommend a visit, however, if only to make up your own mind, admire the architecture of the building (Jean Nouvel again), and have lunch at Les Ombres, the museum's classy rooftop restaurant. The view of the Eiffel Tower is stunning, especially from the terrace, and the menu offers fresh, if pricey, modern French fare. (Three-course menu at lunch: 37€; à la carte in the evening: 50 to 70€; reservation mandatory.) **Café Branly,** located in the garden of the museum, serves good salads and sandwiches (about 12€).

27 quai Branly, 7th. CROSS STREET: Avenue Rapp. M° Pont de l'Alma or Alma-Marceau. PHONE: 01 47 53 68 00. WEB: www.lesombres-restaurant.com. Mon–Sun noon–2:15pm and 7:30pm–10:15pm.

Compote de Mangue aux Fruits de la Passion
Mango and Passion Fruit Compote

Adapted from a recipe by Dominique Saugnac, chef at Boulangépicier (see page 65).

For months after I first discovered Boulangépicier, the sandwiches were enough of a treat for me that I didn't feel the need to explore the dessert selection. It took a conversation with my neighbor Patricia, who at the time worked nearby and was hooked, too, to draw my attention to the unassuming tubs of bright orange compote, a silky preparation of mango and passion fruit that's as flamboyant in color as it is in flavor.

3 fresh ripe mangoes, about 3 pounds (1.4 kg)
1 organic lime
$^1\!/_2$ cup (100 g) sugar
1 vanilla bean, split lengthwise (substitute 1 teaspoon pure vanilla extract)
2 fresh purple passion fruits (see Note 1)

Serves 4

1. Core, peel, and dice the mangoes into $^1\!/_3$-inch (1-cm) cubes (see Note 2). Finely grate the zest of the lime and squeeze its juice.

2. In a medium saucepan, combine half of the mango flesh with the lime zest, lime juice, sugar, vanilla bean, and 3 tablespoons water. Set over low heat and cook for 1 hour, stirring regularly to prevent the mixture from browning, and crushing the fruit with a wooden spoon, until the mixture forms a thick marmalade. Remove from the heat and let cool for a few minutes. *(continued)*

3. Fish out the vanilla bean, if using, and scrape the seeds with the tip of a knife. Return the seeds to the marmalade and discard the bean (or: rinse, let dry completely, and slip in a jar of sugar or a bottle of olive oil to flavor it).

4. Add the marmalade to the remaining mango flesh, stir to combine, and let cool completely. (This can be prepared up to a day ahead. Cover and refrigerate until 30 minutes before serving.) Ladle the compote into four serving cups. Halve the passion fruits, top each cup with the flesh, seeds, and juice from half a passion fruit, and serve immediately.

NOTE 1: Purple passion fruits are egg-shaped fruits with a thick, dark purple skin, and a golden, sweet-tart flesh with tiny edible seeds. They are available from Latin markets and gourmet grocery stores; choose fragrant specimens with a firm but wrinkled skin. If you can't find any, top each cup with a handful of blackberries or raspberries.

NOTE 2: To dice a mango, start by slicing through it vertically on either side of its large, flat pit using a sharp knife, running it as close to the pit as you can. Score the flesh of each half in a crisscross pattern, running the knife all the way to the skin, but without cutting through it. Flip each half inside out, slice off the cubes of flesh, and discard the skin. Use a knife to scrape the remaining flesh from around the pit.

9ème arrondissement

Autour d'un Verre
Bar à vin   OUTDOOR SEATING

Mari and Kevin, the Finnish-American couple who run Autour d'un Verre, have managed to create a wine bar where customers feel right at home: the ambiance is laid-back, the cooking is simple and served on flea market dinnerware, and the (well-behaved) cat and dog roam around freely.

The daily menu is composed of humble, heartwarming dishes of French inspiration (a country terrine, a broth of peas and scallions, fillets of *rouget* [red mullet] and mashed potatoes, a butter-soft chocolate cake with berry coulis), to be enjoyed with a bottle of natural wine from the impressive chalkboard list, which the owners will help you navigate. Three-course menu-carte: 17.50€ at lunch and 21€ for dinner. Wines start at 16€.

21 rue de Trévise, 9th. CROSS STREET: Rue Richer. M° Cadet.

PHONE: 01 48 24 43 74. WEB: www.autourdunverre.net.

Mon–Fri noon–2:30pm; Tue–Sat 8pm–11pm.

Cantina Clandestina
Italian, see page 86

Carte Blanche
Neo bistro

The residential neighborhood and ordinary décor may not seem very promising, but a closer look at the chalkboard menu should restore your confidence that you're in for an exciting ride: humble ingredients join forces with luxurious ones (the veal kidney is sautéed with chanterelles, the blood sausage and the lobster cohabit on a thin tart) in seasonal preparations that range from bistro classics to fanciful creations.

Entertaining plating touches abound (the marinated sardines are served in a can, the *sot-l'y-laisse* skewers appear at the table on a miniature barbecue grill, the caramel and ginger mousse is layered in a ball jar), but there is nothing gimmicky about the clear, refreshing flavors of these dishes. The service is professional yet friendly, the wine list full of interesting choices (all of them available by the glass), and the menu-carte reasonably priced (three courses: 35€).

6 rue Lamartine, 9th. CROSS STREET: Rue de Rochechouart. Mᵒ Cadet.
PHONE: 01 48 78 12 20. Mon–Fri noon–2:30pm; Mon–Sat 7pm–10:30pm.

Casa Olympe
Neo bistro

On a side street of La Nouvelle-Athènes (see page 71), chef Olympe Versini cooks impeccable bistro dishes under Provencal and Corsican influences. The seasonal menu changes regularly and a chalkboard announces daily specials. Offal enthusiasts will dart upon such delights as calf brain fritters or crispy sweetbreads with Pantarella capers, while the others may be more tempted by a fresh herb flan in a scampi broth, or the fillets of *rouget* (red mullet) served over a scallion tartlet.

Desserts are simple yet satisfying, whether you opt for the berry blanc-mange (a French almond milk version of the Italian *panna cotta*) or the se-lection of homemade ice creams. The service is a little stiff-necked, but there is kindness to be found when you scratch the surface. Two-course lunch for-mule: 29€; three-course menu-carte: 38€.

48 rue Saint-Georges, 9th. CROSS STREET: Rue Saint-Lazare. Mᵒ Saint-Georges or Notre-Dame de Lorette. PHONE: 01 42 85 26 01. Mon–Fri noon–2pm and 8pm–11pm.

Chartier
Casual

It is not so much the gourmet as the romantic in you who will delight in the Chartier experience: I, for one, feel grateful that what started out in 1896 as a *bouillon*—a soup kitchen for blue-collar workers—has lived through so many decades and is still standing now, churning out hundreds of meals a day to a mixed crowd of locals and tourists, nostalgic or penniless or both.

The fare is extremely simple and the prices, though not as dirt-cheap as they once were, remain among the lowest in the city: if you choose wisely, you can make up a three-course meal for less than 15€. The menu is as long as the line outside—Chartier doesn't take reservations but the turnover is brisk—yet it is best to stick to the basics: half a dozen snails or a hard-boiled egg with mayo, followed by roast chicken with fries or a grilled *andouillette*, and, to conclude the meal, raspberries and cream or a wedge of Camembert.

It is the staff's job to keep things moving along, and they do a stunning impression of the stereotypical Parisian waiter, scribbling your order on the paper tablecloth with barely a grunt, avoiding eye contact, and snatching your dishes away when it looks like you're about done. It is part of the brusque charm of the place, and legend has it that one of them cracks a smile every few years.

Vast as a railroad terminal and just as clamorous, the dining room offers plenty of features to gawk at—mirrored walls, glass ceilings, globe chandeliers, and neat little drawers in which regulars were once allowed to keep their personal napkin. (And no, you can't, so don't even ask.)

7 rue du Faubourg Montmartre, 9th. CROSS STREET: Boulevard Montmartre. M° Grands Boulevards. PHONE: 01 47 70 86 29. WEB: www.restaurant-chartier.com. Mon–Sun 11:30am–3pm and 6pm–10pm.

⌁ Across town is another *bouillon* from the 1920s that was quite popular with the workers from the nearby automobile factories. Now called **Le Café du Commerce**, the majestic, three-level restaurant remains a feast for the eye, with its retractable glass roof, mezzanines, and greenery. It operates all day, serving a typical brasserie fare: goat cheese salad, Limousin beef, grilled pork foot . . . Weekday lunch formule: 15€; three-course dinner menu: 28€.

51 rue du Commerce, 15th. CROSS STREET: Rue du Théâtre. M° Avenue Émile Zola or Commerce. PHONE: 01 45 75 03 27. Mon–Sun noon–3pm and 7pm–midnight.

Cojean
Lunch / Breakfast / Brunch   VEG-FRIENDLY

The opening of the first Cojean restaurant was a turning point in the life of hasty Parisian lunchers. Before then, the choices were limited: yes, you could buy a sandwich from a bakery, or a café, or one of the many chain *sandwicheries*, but the bread was rarely stellar, the filling usually contained more mayo than all the other ingredients put together, and this made for neither a healthful nor a satisfying meal.

But then Cojean descended from the sky and filled the void, introducing quick lunch options that are good for you *and* your taste buds, to be enjoyed in a bright and Zen-inspired space. Salads, sandwiches, soups, desserts—everything is fresh from the morning, the recipes are inventive and seasonally sound, and the staff is unusually friendly for such a busy place.

Some of the goods are displayed on self-service shelves, while the others—hot soups, savory tarts, freshly mixed fruit or vegetable juices, pastries—must be ordered from the counter. Personal favorites include the vegetarian grilled sandwich (6.20€), the Gonzague salad (grilled chicken, Mimolette cheese, radicchio, chervil, almonds, and grapes, 6€), and the *Dix Heures du Soir en Été* juice (pineapple, strawberry, and orange, 4.50€; literally, "10pm on a summer night").

Order your lunch to go (*à emporter*) and eat it on the sunny steps of the nearby Madeleine church, or sit down to eat it *sur place,* if you can find a stool to squeeze onto.

4 rue de Sèze, 9th. CROSS STREET: Boulevard de la Madeleine. M° Madeleine. PHONE: 01 40 06 08 80. WEB: cojean.fr. Mon–Fri 8am–6pm; Sat 9am–7pm.

Alternate locations:

3 place du Louvre, 1st. CROSS STREET: Rue de l'Amiral Coligny. M° Louvre-Rivoli or Pont Neuf. PHONE: 01 40 13 06 80. Mon–Sun 9am–6pm. (Brunch on Sundays.)

17 boulevard Haussmann, 9th. CROSS STREET: Rue du Helder. M° Chaussée d'Antin. PHONE: 01 47 70 22 65. Mon–Fri 8am–7pm; Sat 10am–7pm.

24 rue de Sèvres, basement of Le Bon Marché, close to the bookstore, 7th. CROSS STREET: Rue du Bac. Mº Sèvres-Babylone. PHONE: 01 42 22 81 60. Mon–Sat 11am–7pm.

～ Cojean's success has inspired the creation of similar self-service eateries in the city, concentrated in the 1st, 2nd, 8th, and 9th arrondissements, where there is a local—and mostly female—office crowd to cater to:

Bioboa is all about organic chic: white walls and designer furniture are warmed up by flower arrangements and a colorful mural of tropical birds. The lunch formules—from 8 to 13€—allow you to sample a fresh and flavorful fare of fruit cocktails, soups, salads, and sandwiches, including a veggie burger and a few "detox" items.

3 rue Danielle Casanova, 1st. CROSS STREET: Avenue de l'Opéra. Mº Pyramides. PHONE: 01 42 61 17 67. Mon–Sat 11am–6pm.

Eat Me and **Naked**—don't give me that look, I didn't pick the names— explore the concept from the same angle, offering healthful and appetizing edibles in artfully designed spaces, respectively in the Montorgueil and the Champs-Élysées areas. As an icing on the flourless cake, the former provides nutritional information for all its menu items (lunch formules: 10 to 13€), while the latter boasts a vertical interior garden that purportedly purifies the air you breathe (lunch formules: 8.50€ and 9.50€).

Eat Me. 38 rue Léopold Bellan, 2nd. CROSS STREET: Rue Montmartre. Mº Sentier. PHONE: 01 42 36 18 28. WEB: www.eatme.fr. Mon–Fri 9am–7pm.

Naked. 40 rue du Colisée, 8th. CROSS STREET: Avenue Franklin Roosevelt. Mº Franklin Roosevelt. PHONE: 01 43 59 03 24. Mon–Fri 8:30am–4pm.

La Ferme Opéra and its cute bovine logo put a farmyard spin on the idea of virtuous but tasty fast food. Sandwiches on naturally leavened baguette, organic vegetable soups, funky salads (a cauliflower "couscous" with fava beans and pesto), golden *tourtes* (savory pies), soft-boiled eggs with buttered toast, and vegetarian-friendly hot dishes—all of these can be bought to go, or eaten in the low-ceilinged but comfy room in the back, washed down with an artisanal fruit juice, farmhouse milk, or a freshly brewed coffee-based drink. Sandwiches and salads cost around 5€; lunch formules: 9 to 11€.

55 rue Saint-Roch, 1st. CROSS STREET: Avenue de l'Opéra. M° Pyramides.

PHONE: 01 40 20 12 12. Mon–Fri 8am–8pm; Sat 9am–7pm; Sun 10am–7pm.

Corneil
Casual ·

Much roomier on the inside than it appears from the outside, Corneil is a corner restaurant that blends into the street décor so well it would be easy to miss. Such an oversight would be a pity, however, for this is a jewel of a contemporary bistro where the atmosphere is warm and friendly, the service attentive and professional, and the food unpretentious and delectable.

My ideal meal at Corneil begins with the split bone marrow, served with toasted country bread and *fleur de sel,* and moves on to the humongous *côte de bœuf* (rib steak) for two, grilled to perfection and served with a salad and a bowl of thumb-size garlic-roasted potatoes (52€ for two, with a first course or a dessert each).

Other worthy choices—subject to seasonal changes—include a haddock carpaccio, a rustic homemade terrine, a grilled sea bass served with root vegetables, or a lamb saddle rolled with goat cheese and herbs and baked in a crisp shell of phyllo dough. À la carte: about 20€ for lunch and 32€ for dinner.

18 rue Condorcet, 9th. CROSS STREET: Rue Lentonnet. M° Anvers or Poissonnière. PHONE: 01 49 95 92 25. Tue–Fri noon–2:30pm; Mon–Sat 8pm–midnight.

Jean
Chic

The owner and maître d' used to work at Taillevent and the chef trained at Bristol (see page 66). But when they took over this neighborhood restaurant at the foot of the Montmartre hill, these two were very clear about the cocktail they wanted to mix—casual-chic ambiance and modern gastronomic fare.

The renovated dining room has kept its brasserie-like allure—wood paneling, floor tiles, handsome staircase—and, although spacious, it doesn't seat more than thirty-five diners, which means that each of them benefits from a reasonable amount of elbow room, a rare commodity in this city.

Chef Benoît Bordier's playful creativity is immediately apparent when you peruse the menu, from the witty names of the dishes (Monsieur Cochon, Parc Floral, Choc des Générations) to the daring pairings (asparagus and blood sausage, beef with spinach and cocoa, mussels and cinnamon, clementines with fennel and milk chocolate). And the kitchen actually keeps the promises that the menu holds, delivering acrobatic dishes that hijack the classics of French cuisine and fly them right over to the twenty-first century.

The lunchtime *menu du marché* gets you three courses (no choices) for 45€. Three courses chosen à la carte cost around 65€, and you can pick one of the two surprise tasting menus: five dishes for 65€; seven for 85€. The service, as presided over by Jean-Frédéric Guidoni, is smooth and friendly.

8 rue Saint-Lazare, 9th. CROSS STREET: Rue Bourdaloue. M° Notre-Dame de Lorette. PHONE: 01 48 78 62 73. Mon–Fri noon–2:30pm and 8pm–10:30pm.

LEARNING THE MOVES

Taking a cooking, baking, or wine tasting class is a great way to learn new skills and meet like-minded enthusiasts. The following cooking schools offer quality teaching in pleasant environments. In all cases, reservations are mandatory; visit the Web sites well in advance to check the schedules and rates.

L'Atelier des Chefs

At this modern-minded cooking school, classes last from thirty minutes (a midday class during which you cook your lunch and eat it, too) to four hours, and cost from 15 to 140€. All classes are hands-on and conducted by young professional chefs who teach in French, but can accommodate non-French speakers. Four locations in Paris.

10 rue de Penthièvre, 8th. CROSS STREET: Rue de Miromesnil. M° Miromesnil. PHONE: 01 53 30 05 82. WEB: www.atelierdeschefs.com.

Alternate location:

27 rue Péclet, 15th. CROSS STREET: Rue Lecourbe. M° Vaugirard. PHONE: 01 56 08 33 50.

L'Atelier de Fred

In the congenial atmosphere of his tiny, baby blue workshop, Frédéric Chesneau teaches groups of five how to cook an inventive three-course meal without losing their minds (60€ for a three-hour class). Although classes are in French, Chesneau's English is good enough that he can make sure non-French speakers follow. Wednesday afternoons are devoted to classes for kids from seven to twelve (35€ for a two-hour class). L'Atelier de Fred can be reserved for a custom-made cooking class; call to inquire.

Passage de l'Ancre, 223 rue Saint-Martin, 3rd. CROSS STREET: Rue Chapon. M° Arts et Métiers. PHONE: 01 40 29 46 04. WEB: www.latelierdefred.com.

La Cuisine de la Fraîch'Attitude

The food art gallery Fraîch'Attitude (see page 282) hosts themed cooking classes in its bright and colorful *cuisine*. The classes focus on easy yet stylish recipes using fresh produce—the gallery is run by Aprifel, a grower-funded agency that promotes the consumption of fruits and vegetables—and are taught by chefs and food writers, in French only. A two-hour session costs only 12€ and attendance is limited to ten, so classes fill up quickly.

60 rue du Faubourg Poissonnière, 10th. CROSS STREET: Rue de Paradis. M° Poissonnière or Bonne Nouvelle. PHONE: 01 49 49 15 15. WEB: www.cuisinefraichattitude.com.

École Lenôtre

In addition to a professional cooking school outside of Paris, Lenôtre also offers hands-on cooking or baking classes for the home cook. These are held at the recently refurbished Pavillon Élysées, and cover a large array of topics, from the great classics of French pastry (macarons, opéra, croissants) to themed menus (bistro, finger food, mushroom). Classes are held in French. Prices range from 115 to 160€ for a three-and-a-half-hour class in groups of eight.

10 avenue des Champs-Élysées, 8th. CROSS STREET: Avenue de Marigny. M° Champs-Élysées-Clemenceau. PHONE: 01 42 65 97 60. WEB: www.lenotre.fr.

Ô Chateau

The young French sommelier Olivier Magny hosts English-language wine appreciation classes in a loft in the Oberkampf neighborhood. In his energetic and amicable style, this anti–wine snob walks his students through the different wine regions of France and the basic techniques of wine tasting, before uncorking a selection of bottles for the class to taste. Three formules from 20 to 65€ per person; custom tasting sessions can be organized.

PHONE: 01 44 73 97 80. WEB: www.o-chateau.com. *(continued)*

David Witter

Witter's goal is to help his students enjoy their wine more. For his tasting classes, held in a Marais apartment, he selects six French wines to taste, serves matching nibbles, and explains about regions, grape varietals, and food and wine pairings. The classes are conducted in English, they last for two to three hours, and cost 40€ per person. Sign up online to receive the list of upcoming classes; Witter organizes custom classes for groups of four and up.

WEB: davidinparis.com.

Some restaurants or shops organize cooking classes and demonstrations: **L'Artisan des Saveurs** (see page 44), **Spring** (see page 88), **Pousse-Pousse** (see page 210), and **Goumanyat** (see page 220). Some wine shops offer tasting classes as well, such as **Lavinia** (see page 266), **Legrand Filles et Fils** (see page 259), and **Le Vin en Tête** (see page 128), and many more host free tasting sessions, which are excellent occasions to learn about wine in an informal way. **Le Parti du Thé** and **Le Palais des Thés** (see pages 255 and 252) give tea-tasting classes.

J'Go
Casual

Creative cuisine can be exciting and all, but when you feel like simple, wholesome food, it's nice to have restaurants like J'Go to turn to. The menu, which changes at the turn of each season, focuses on the culinary—and mostly carnivorous—treasures of Gascony, a former province in the southwest of France: this is your chance to enjoy Quercy lamb (the name of the restaurant, roughly pronounced as jee-go, is a play on the word *gigot,* meaning leg of lamb), Bigorre black pork, or Gers poultry in generous, well-executed dishes.

Start your meal with a shredded pork terrine (a house specialty called Lou Pastifret), a warm lentil salad served with a confit of pig's ears and pork snout, or a bowl of the day's soup. And as a main course, you can either have a single order of your favorite cut of meat, or, and this is by far the most convivial option, order a whole rotisserie piece that you will share, family style, with your dining companions.

All dishes come with sides of white beans from Tarbes, homemade fries, seasonal vegetables, and country bread, to mop up the juices. This may leave you with little room for dessert, but sweets aren't the strong point of the menu anyway. (Lunch formules: 16€ and 21€; dinner formule: 22€; à la carte: about 30€.) The all-red wine list takes you on a tour of the southwestern wine countries, with high- and low-road choices from each winery.

One caveat: the open kitchen is fun to watch, but be prepared to take the smells home with you. The service is friendly and efficient even when the restaurant is packed, which happens often; reservations are strongly advised. If you haven't booked your table, however, having a drink and a few tapas (foie gras, cheese, dry-cured ham, mini-skewers, around 5€ each) in the downstairs bar area is an equally pleasurable option.

4 rue Drouot, 9th. CROSS STREET: Boulevard Montmartre. M° Richelieu-Drouot. PHONE: 01 40 22 09 09. WEB: lejgo.com. Mon–Sat noon–3pm and 7pm–12:30am; NONSTOP BAR SERVICE from noon to 12:30am.

Musée de la Vie Romantique
Salon de thé, see page 71

La Paninoteca / Pizza Da Carmine
Italian / Lunch   VEG-FRIENDLY/OUTDOOR SEATING

Parisians are nowhere near as opinionated about their pizza as New Yorkers are, but many of us do have a favorite joint that we swear by, of which we dream at night, and where we could eat every single night if other temptations didn't beckon. La Paninoteca holds that place in my heart and stomach.

It was a ten-seat hole-in-the-wall in its first incarnation, but years of happy customers have allowed Carmine, the owner, to buy the space next door and grow into a two-room restaurant with a larger wood-burning oven. Regulars turned mozzarella-white with fear: would this expansion be the downfall of the Paninoteca? But relief washed over them as they realized that the pizzas were just as good as before (my favorite is the Parma, with mozzarella, Parma ham, and arugula) and that more tables meant a shorter wait.

The portions are generous (consider splitting an antipasti plate and a pizza with a friend), but there is no need to save room for the uneventful desserts. The atmosphere is like the service, joyful and exuberant, and on warm days, absolute bliss is within reach if you can snatch a table on the sidewalk terrace. All pizzas are available to go, as are the delectable panini on home-baked bread. Pizzas 10 to 16€; panini 5 to 6€.

61 rue des Martyrs, 9th. CROSS STREET: Avenue Trudaine. M° Pigalle. PHONE: 01 48 78 28 01. Tue–Sat noon–2pm and 8pm–11pm.

⤳ In a strange case of statistical oddity, two more great pizzerias have sprouted within a block of La Paninoteca: the similarly inspired **Cantina Clandestina** and the more trendy **La Pizzetta**, both of which serve thinner crusted pizzas than La Paninoteca, but with equal standards of quality.

Cantina Clandestina. 17 rue Milton, 9th. CROSS STREET: Rue Manuel. M° Notre-Dame de Lorette. PHONE: 01 53 21 05 16. Mon–Fri 11:30am–2:30pm; Mon–Sat 7:30pm–10pm.

La Pizzetta. 22 avenue Trudaine, 9th. CROSS STREET: Rue Lallier. M° Pigalle. PHONE: 01 48 78 14 08. Mon–Sun 12:30pm–2:15pm; Mon–Thu 7:30pm–11pm; Fri–Sat 7:30pm–midnight.

Pousse-Pousse
Lunch, see page 210

Rose Bakery

Lunch / Salon de thé / Breakfast / Brunch   VEG-FRIENDLY/OUTDOOR SEATING

Rose Bakery was created by an Englishwoman, Rose, and her French husband, Jean-Charles. After operating a fine foods store in London for a few years, the couple hopped across the Channel to open this restaurant-cum-pastry shop in a stark, corridor-like space that used to be a *chartil*, a sort of garage where produce vendors parked their carts.

Their philosophy is simple: they serve healthful, tasty dishes that focus on vegetables and grains, and an array of sensational pastries, chiefly British inspired (sticky toffee pudding, date and oat slice, fresh ginger cake, shortbread, about 2 to 4€), that make a reasoned use of sugar and fat.

Rose Bakery is open for breakfast, lunch, and tea, but it is at noon that I rush there most eagerly, for the square savory tarts, the freshly made soups and risotti, the ploughman's lunch (a platter of cheese, bread, and salad), or my absolute favorite, the daily assortment of salads (13€). You will no doubt notice them to your right as you step in through the wrought-iron door: half a dozen bowls filled with, say, broccoli salad in a peanut dressing, roasted potato salad with chorizo, caramelized fennel salad, chickpea and eggplant salad, beet and Cheddar salad, and curried cauliflower salad, all of them masterfully prepared and bursting with flavor.

The bread is made by Poujauran (one of the best bread bakers in the city, who used to have a *boulangerie* but sells wholesale now), the cheese comes from the famed London creamery Neal's Yard Dairy, and the ingredients used in the kitchen are organic and locally sourced wherever possible. The front of the restaurant doubles up as a mini-store, where you can buy British goods, cheese, organic vegetables, and any dish or pastry to go. My only complaint concerns the sketchy and inexplicably austere service. Weekday lunch formule: 13.50€; à la carte brunch on weekends.

46 rue des Martyrs, 9th. CROSS STREET: Rue de Navarin. M° Notre-Dame de Lorette. PHONE: 01 42 82 12 80. Tue–Sun 10am–6pm.

Spring
Neo bistro

Daniel Rose is the man behind this intimate sixteen-cover restaurant, located in the rapidly rising part of the 9th arrondissement that journalists have dubbed SoPi—south of Pigalle—without quite succeeding in making the nickname stick.

The thirty-something Chicagoan came to France to study philosophy, but he changed his mind along the way and opted for culinary school instead. After a few years of *stages* here and there, he renovated a derelict bistro on a quiet street, hired a waitress, and started serving his nightly seasonal menu—four courses, no choices, 36€—inspired by the day's market and his mood.

Curried cream of celeriac, marinated swordfish with raw beets, roasted pigeon with parsnips and peas, rosemary baked apple: Rose's dishes are artfully simple and delightfully executed, with a spontaneity that springs up at you from the plate—no pun intended.

The sincerity of his cooking, the pleasant atmosphere of his open-kitchen dining room, and the exceptional value of his menu were quickly recognized as such, and the restaurant is now very popular, which makes it difficult to score a reservation without a bit of forethought. Cooking classes and private dinners are held on Saturday nights. Call to inquire.

28 rue de la Tour d'Auvergne, 9th. CROSS STREET: Rue Rodier. M° Anvers or Cadet. PHONE: 01 45 96 05 72. Tue–Fri 8:30pm; Single service, by reservation only.

Tienda Nueva
Colombian / Specialty shop

Behind the dusty window is a tiny, unlikely enclave of Colombian spirit, part general store, part cantina, that serves as a popular hangout for the city's Latin American community, and provides a lovely escapist experience for the rest of us.

The store half holds all the groceries Colombian expats might miss (corn flour, *arepa* mix, jarred cactus, *dulce de leche*) and a selection of records—edgy, I'm told—by South American artists. On the restaurant side you'll find home-style Colombian specialties—*empanadas, arepas, tamales*—to be consumed at the bar or taken home.

A few daily dishes round out the menu—a hearty soup of beef, corn, and plantains, or a chicken stew with vegetables and rice, to be washed down with an exotic fruit juice. The service is kind and full of smiles. Daily formule: 9.90€.

57 rue Rodier, 9th. CROSS STREET: Avenue Trudaine. M° Anvers.
PHONE: 01 45 26 11 80. Mon–Thu 11am–6pm; Fri–Sat 11am–10pm.

Le Valentin

Salon de thé / Pastry shop / Breakfast   VEG-FRIENDLY

Hidden from the boulevard bustle in a nook of the passage Jouffroy (one of three covered passageways that connect rue Saint-Marc to rue du Faubourg Montmartre), Le Valentin transports you instantly to a small town in Lorraine, the owner's region of birth.

The décor is a bit tired, but the pastries and confections are charmingly old-fashioned, featuring warm, spice-rich flavors of eastern French inspiration. Among the house specialties are the Parigi (a chocolate and orange tartlet under a crackled macaron crust), the Damoiseau (a moist blueberry cake with almonds and honey), or the Mirabelle de Lorraine (a bite-size candied plum stuffed with marzipan), but the classics are just as worthy of your taste buds: the linzer torte, the *nonettes* (pucks of *pain d'épice*), the *bugnes* (doughnuts from Lyon), the homemade nougat, or the dainty petits fours.

Buy pastries to go (around 4€ each), or eat them on the premises (add 1€ per pastry), with a cup of tea or *chocolat chaud à l'ancienne* (4.50€).

30 passage Jouffroy, 9th. CROSS STREET: Boulevard Poissonnière. M° Grands
Boulevards. PHONE: 01 47 70 88 50. Mon 9:30am–7:30pm; Tue–Sat
8:30am–7:30pm; Sun 10am–7pm; LUNCH SERVICE: 11:30am–3pm.

LA FILLETTE, LE POT, LA FICELLE ET LE COMPTEUR

The most common way to order wine is by the bottle or by the glass, but a few options may be offered by the **pichet** or **carafe**: you then have a choice between a 25-centiliter carafe (the equivalent of two glasses) or a 50-centiliter carafe (the equivalent of four glasses). The former is referred to as **un quart**, the latter as **un pot lyonnais** or **une fillette**.

Some restaurants and wine bars also serve wine **à la ficelle** or **au compteur**: you are brought a full bottle, but at the end of the meal, you are only charged for what you've poured. The wines offered *à la ficelle* are often of higher quality than those served by the carafe, but be warned: once the bottle is uncorked and set on the table, few resist the temptation of drinking the whole thing.

10ème arrondissement

Café Panique
Neo bistro

The main reason why Café Panique doesn't draw in throngs of eager diners is that it is in a neighborhood that's near absolutely nothing at all, on a side street with zero foot traffic, and with no storefront to speak of: the door is at the end of what looks like an apartment building's entryway. But once you've gotten through these minor hurdles, you're in for a treat: the room, a converted workshop, is high-ceilinged and skylight-bright, the atmosphere is one of unstuffy elegance, and although diners are shielded from the cooking smells and the clatter by a glass pane, the kitchen is in full view.

And this open kitchen reveals a fact that's uncommon enough to emphasize: the chef and owner is a woman, a self-taught and indubitably talented one, Odile Guyader. Her cuisine is seasonally inspired and sparklingly fresh—if you happen to linger until the last drop of the evening, you may hear her place order calls to her suppliers for the next morning—and the dishes she produces show a balance and vibrancy not frequently tasted elsewhere: ginger marinated haddock with diced vegetables on a Parmesan cracker, lamb saddle rolled with mint and cumin under a drizzle of olive juice, and a delectable caramel tiramisù.

The lunch formule is a particularly good deal (two courses, wine, and coffee for 19€), but the dinner menu (three courses for 31€) remains an excellent value.

12 rue des Messageries, 10th. CROSS STREET: Rue du Faubourg Poissonnière. M° Poissonnière. PHONE: 01 47 70 06 84. WEB: cafepanique.com. Mon–Fri noon–2pm and 7:30pm–10pm.

Chez Casimir
Casual, see page 92

Chez Michel
Neo bistro

Chez Michel belongs to the first wave of neo bistros that opened in the nineties in low-rent parts of the city (see page 46), and sure enough, it is plopped on a rather dull street, a few blocks from the Gare du Nord.

The chef, Thierry Breton, hails from Brittany, a fact that translates to his name as well as his cuisine, in which ingredients from land and sea cohabit splendidly. He handles scallops, tuna belly, and black sea bass just as well as he does pork, poultry, or game, with the sort of talent that makes his neo-traditional preparations seem effortless, and taste spectacular.

The three-course menu-carte is an excellent deal at 30€, but if you are, understandably, tempted by the market suggestions scribbled on the chalkboard (a terrine of foie gras, hare, and chocolate; a papillote of mussels and clams; partridge with wild mushrooms), be aware that most will add not-negligible *suppléments* to your tab.

10 rue de Belzunce, 10th. CROSS STREET: Rue Saint-Vincent de Paul. M° Gare du Nord. PHONE: 01 44 53 06 20. Tue–Fri 11:45am–2pm; Mon–Fri 6:45pm–midnight.

﹏ Two doors down from Chez Michel is **Chez Casimir**, a restaurant run by the same team. Cheaper (lunch formules: 22 to 26€; dinner: 29€ for three courses and cheese) and more classic (cod *brandade*, braised lamb shank with *coco* beans [tiny white beans], rice pudding with orange marmalade), Casimir is a good plan B if Michel is booked full.

6 rue de Belzunce, 10th. CROSS STREET: Boulevard de Magenta. M° Gare du Nord. PHONE: 01 48 78 28 80. Mon–Fri 11:45am–2:30pm and 6:45pm–10:30pm.

STREET FOOD

The French don't have much of a street food culture: with the exception of a few specific foods that they customarily eat on the run (sandwiches, croissants, crêpes, ice cream, roasted chestnuts), they usually sit down to eat.

It's a question of manners—it's difficult to eat tidily as one walks, and it's rude to impose the sight of one's chewing on random passersby—as well as culture: the act of eating is not to be taken lightly, and one should take the time to enjoy food respectfully.

If you go against this unspoken rule, you may get funny looks that range from simple curiosity to tutting disapproval. Shrug them off if you don't care what people think, or just find a bench to sit on before you dig in.

As a final note on this subject, I will add that the métro, as an enclosed space where a large number of human beings share the same breathing air and very little elbow room, is not a suitable eating environment.

Pleine Mer
Casual, see page 242

Le Réveil du Xème
Casual   VEG-FRIENDLY

There was a time when most Parisian bistros were operated by *bougnats*—
an old-fashioned colloquialism for someone who comes from the Auvergne
region—and Le Réveil has stayed true to its roots, from the yellowing memorabilia on the walls, to the rustic, fuss-free dishes on the menu.

Regional specialties—*pounti* (a pork and Swiss chard terrine, see recipe
on page 97), *tripoux auvergnats* (tripe), stuffed cabbage, *truffade* (a cheese
and potato mash)—share chalkboard space with copious salads, beef from
Salers, and platters of charcuterie or cheese, to be enjoyed with one of the
many Beaujolais on the wine list. Homey treats await on the dessert tray,
such as goat *faisselle* (fresh cheese) with honey or jam, *flognarde aux pommes*
(a sort of apple flan), or a puffy rhubarb cake.

Add to that a kind and welcoming staff, a dining room full of longtime
regulars, and you'll wish you lived next door and had ready access to this
warmhearted time machine. About 20€ for two courses. No-cook plates can
still be ordered in the afternoon when the kitchen is closed.

(The name should be read as *le réveil du dixième:* X is the Roman nu-
meral for ten, the arrondissement's number.)

33 rue du Château d'Eau, 10th. CROSS STREET: Rue Bouchardon. M° Jacques
Bonsergent or Château d'Eau. PHONE: 01 42 41 77 59. Mon–Fri 7:30am–1am;
Sat 10am–4pm; LUNCH: Mon–Sat noon–3pm; DINNER: Mon–Fri 7:30pm–10:30pm.

Urbane
Neo bistro / Brunch

Run by a French-Irish couple who used to own a similar operation in
Belfast, Urbane strikes a rare chord between the trendy and the cozy: yes, it
is located in a shabby-but-clearly-on-the-rise area of the 10th arrondisse-

ment, a stone's throw from the Canal Saint-Martin; yes, the loft-like space is decorated by the work of a few artist-friends; and yes, the menu plays the world cuisine game, with Anglo, French, and Asian influences.

But what could result in one more affected, concept-loaded restaurant is, instead, turned into an inviting neo bistro by the grace of a bright young chef whose enthusiasm leaps out from the inventive dishes he assembles, and a discreetly warm wait staff.

The lunch service revolves around a short daily formule (two courses for 15€, three for 19€, two options for each) that may unfold into a celeriac and cilantro soup, a fillet of cod in a spiced sesame crust with hash browns, and a lemon cookie tart.

In the evening, the menu is fleshier (four options for each course), and flashier: warm crawfish with lemongrass and seaweed, scallops from Erquy with a green curry foam, braised lamb shank with a mash of root vegetables, buckwheat blinis with a rhubarb ginger compote . . .

A touch of mannerism occasionally rears its head in the menu descriptions and the plating, but the fault is easily forgiven, for the cooking is earnest, the flavors clear-spoken, and the prices gentle. (Two courses for 24€; three for 29€; add cheese for 6.50€; 16€ brunch on Sundays.)

12 rue Arthur Groussier, 10th. CROSS STREET: Avenue Parmentier.
M° Goncourt. PHONE: 01 42 40 74 75. WEB: myspace.com/urbaneparis.
Tue–Fri noon–3pm; Tue–Sat 7:30pm–11pm; Sun 11:30am–3pm.

Le Verre Volé

Bar à vin / Wine shop   VEG-FRIENDLY

When Cyril Bordarier opened Le Verre Volé in the early nineties, his idea was to create a wine cellar-cum-bistro, a place where you could buy natural wines, taste them, and sit amid the shelves and boxes to down your bottle with a few simple dishes. The space he found on the banks of the Canal Saint-Martin had no kitchen to speak of—just enough room for a minus-

LE QUARTIER INDIEN

Indian

Paris's Little India is made up of two clouds of boutiques and restaurants on either end of rue du Faubourg Saint-Denis: to the south, gravitating around rue de Jarry and the passage Brady covered passageway, is the Pakistani community; to the north, the area outside the métro station La Chapelle is the turf of a Tamil community that hails mostly from Sri Lanka. It is in this micro-*quartier* that one finds the most authentic Indian restaurants (try **Dishni** or **Muniyandi Vails**), and a multitude of grocery stores, the largest being **V.T. Cash & Carry**, for all one's spice, rice, and produce needs. It is also where the Ganesh festival is flamboyantly celebrated every year, on the first or second Sunday of September.

Dishni. 25 rue Cail, 10th. CROSS STREET: Rue du Faubourg Saint-Denis. M° La Chapelle. PHONE: 01 42 05 44 04. Mon–Sun noon–11:30pm.

Muniyandi Vilas. 207 rue du Faubourg Saint-Denis, 10th. CROSS STREET: Boulevard de la Chapelle. M° La Chapelle. PHONE: 01 40 36 13 48. Mon–Sun 10:30am–midnight.

V.T. Cash & Carry. 11 rue Cail, 10th. CROSS STREET: Rue Philippe de Girard. M° La Chapelle. PHONE: 01 40 05 07 18. Tue–Sun 9am–7pm.

cule counter and a toaster oven—so he decided to focus on ingredients so splendid they would require minimal transformation.

Fifteen years later, the concept is as fresh as ever, and Le Verre Volé is the perfect illustration of the wine bar that works. The hospitable Bordarier has a knack for discovering talented vintners and confidential vintages, and his selection is remarkable. Likewise, the plates are assembled from artisanal goods provided by trusted suppliers—terrines and charcuteries by Joël Meurdesoif (see page 233), Spanish ham and smoked anchovies by Philippe Poulachon (see page 204), greens from Annie Bertin's garden in Brittany, perfectly ripe cheeses, AAAAA-certified *andouillette* from Troyes . . .

The appetizers run from 6 to 9€, the mains around 12€, and all can be shared. Eight wines are offered by the glass; bottles run from 5€ to much higher, so if the wine is a recommendation from the wait staff, don't forget to ask how much it costs; a 7€ corkage fee is added if you drink it on the premises. The room seats sixteen diners at the most, so reservations are indispensable.

67 rue de Lancry, 10th. CROSS STREET: Quai de Valmy. M° Jacques Bonsergent. PHONE: 01 48 03 17 34. Mon–Sun 10:30am–2am; LUNCH: noon–2:30pm; DINNER: 7:30pm–10:30pm.

Alternate location (wine shop only):

38 rue Oberkampf, 11th. CROSS STREET: Rue de la Folie-Méricourt. M° Oberkampf or Parmentier. PHONE: 01 43 14 99 46. Tue–Sat 10am–1pm and 4pm–8:30pm.

Les Zingots
Neo bistro, see page 44

Pounti Auvergnat
Pork and Swiss Chard Terrine

~

This terrine of pork and Swiss chard, bright with fresh herbs and subtly sweetened by prunes, is a specialty from Auvergne, a mountainous region in the center of France. Originally a poor man's dish assembled from the previous day's
leftovers, it was served for supper, hot or cold, conveniently combining meat,
vegetables, and fruit in a single dish.

I tasted it for the first time a few years ago, having purchased a slice from a
charcuterie stall at the Marché Beauvau (see page 145), and was immediately taken
with its rich flavors and comforting texture, filling yet not heavy. I order it every
chance I get—it is likely to appear on the menu wherever Auvergne cuisine is
served—and make my own, too, for simple dinners, buffets, and portable lunches.

20 good-quality prunes (sometimes marketed as dried plums), about
    9 ounces (250 g)
Unsalted butter for greasing
4 large eggs
^{1}/2 cup (120 ml) milk
1^1/4 cups (150 g) all-purpose flour
14 ounces (400 g) lean ground pork
1 small yellow onion, about 6 ounces (170 g), finely chopped
One slice day-old country bread, about 2 ounces (60 g), crust removed
    and crumb roughly crumbled
^{1}/2 teaspoon salt
^{1}/4 teaspoon freshly ground black pepper
3 large leaves Swiss chard (keep the stalks for a stir-fry), finely chopped
^{1}/3 cup (loosely packed) fresh flat-leaf parsley leaves, roughly chopped
^{1}/4 cup (loosely packed) fresh tarragon leaves, roughly chopped
6 leaves fresh sage, finely chopped

Serves 6 to 8 as a first course or light main course

1. Place the prunes in a medium heatproof bowl, cover with boiling water or hot tea, and set aside to plump up. Preheat the oven to 350°F (180°C) and grease a 4-cup (1 liter) ceramic terrine dish or loaf pan with butter; grease the lid of the dish, too, if there is one.

2. In a large bowl, whisk together the eggs and milk. Sift in the flour and whisk until combined. Add the meat, onion, bread crumbs, salt, and pepper, and mix with a wooden spoon. Fold in the chard and herbs, and mix again until combined.

3. Drain the prunes, pat them dry, and pit them. Transfer a third of the meat mixture to the prepared dish and pack it into an even layer. Arrange half of the prunes over it in a regular pattern. Cover with another third of the meat, well packed, top with the rest of the prunes, and add the rest of the mixture. Even out the surface with a spatula.

4. Cover with the lid of the dish if it has one, or a double layer of foil if it doesn't, and bake for 1 hour, until the juices run clear and an instant-read thermometer inserted in the center registers 160°F (70°C). Switch the oven to the broiler setting, remove the lid or foil, and return the terrine to the oven for 5 to 8 minutes, keeping a close eye on it, until the top is nice and golden.

5. Transfer the dish to a cooling rack and let the terrine settle for 15 minutes before unmolding. Serve warm, at room temperature, or cold, cutting the terrine in thickish slices with a serrated knife. The slices can also be cut into cubes and served as an appetizer. Leftovers should be wrapped tightly in foil and refrigerated until the next day; slices can then be sautéed in a hot skillet, greased with a touch of olive oil.

11ème arrondissement

Astier
Casual

This legendary bistro had lost some of its sparkle in recent years, but it is now back in the game thanks to a new team, who has infused it with a fresh energy without sacrificing its historical aura. Great favorites from the French grandmotherly repertoire (marinated herring and warm potatoes, rib steak with bone marrow toast, *baba au rhum* and whipped cream) are executed with flair, and the occasional wink of modernity.

The printed menu is augmented by chalkboard-scribbled specials, and a fun thematic selection of dishes that is renewed every few weeks. "The Pig, from Head to Toe," for instance, worked its way down the animal with a different cut for each day of the week, from fried pig's ears on Monday to pork foot carpaccio on Sunday.

At lunchtime, you will get two courses for 19.50€ or three for 25.50€; the 29.50€ dinner menu is a real bargain, buying you three courses plus a large platter of cheese that is passed around from table to table. The wine list includes four hundred references, ten of which can be poured by the glass; the passionate sommelier is happy to advise on wine pairings. Seating is a little cramped, in true Parisian bistro fashion.

44 rue Jean-Pierre Timbaud, 11th. CROSS STREET: Rue de Nemours.
M° Parmentier. PHONE: 01 43 57 16 35. WEB: www.restaurant-astier.com.
Mon–Sun 12:15pm–2:30pm and 7pm–10:30pm.

Babylone
Jewish   VEG-FRIENDLY

Paris is crawling with dingy little stands that sell falafel and shawarma sandwiches—broadly referred to as *sandwichs grecs*—under the most inauspicious hygienic conditions, but Babylone, a stylish stamp-size restaurant on a side street of the swarming Bastille area, could not be further from that class.

One foot in the door, and already you can tell it isn't just any old kebab joint. The pitas stacked on the counter look supple and plump, the meat rotating on the skewer is actually identifiable as such, and the short-haired, bespectacled owner—who could try a smile once in a while, just to see if it fits—is assembling sandwiches with meticulous concentration. Walk to the back to hang your coat and you'll catch a glimpse of the pantry, where happy heads of cabbage and glossy bulbs of eggplant further assure you that the key word here is "fresh."

My favorite item on the menu is La Grande, a sampler plate that combines all the house preparations: bite-size falafels, caramelized shavings of meat, dollops of hummus, tahini, and tarama, and little hills of cabbage salad, eggplant caviar, and parsleyed cucumbers (9.50€). The rest of the menu offers various combinations of the same elements, a vegetable soup of the day, a few simple desserts (*fromage blanc* with homemade jam, artisanal sorbets, baklava), and micro-brewed beers.

Sandwiches can be ordered to go or eaten at the counter—Le Mixte combines falafels, shawarma, and all the fixings for 5.50€. No reservations necessary unless you're a large group.

21 rue Daval, 11th. CROSS STREET: Rue de la Roquette. M° Bastille.
PHONE: 01 47 00 55 02. Mon 5pm–midnight; Tue–Sat 10am–midnight.

La Bague de Kenza
Pastry shop / Salon de thé, see page 171

Le Bar à Soupes
Lunch   VEG-FRIENDLY

Inspired by the soup bars she had discovered in London in the late nineties, Anne-Catherine Bley opened the first such venue in the city, to the hand-clapping delight of health-conscious, veggie-loving Parisians.

The six daily soups (including chilled ones in the summer) are prepared on the premises every morning, using fresh and seasonal produce. The recipe repertoire spans several continents around time-proven classics (pumpkin and chestnut, leek *velouté,* cauliflower and cumin) and the owner's sprightly creations (tomato, apple, and ricotta; carrot, pineapple, and ginger; spinach and avocado).

The salted butter chocolate cake is just as delicious, and will effectively cancel out the benefits of that good-for-you soup. Your meal can be purchased to go, or eaten at a table in the no-frills dining room. Formule: 9.50€.

Some of Anne-Catherine Bley's recipes have been published in book form, and you can sign up to receive the weekly soup menu by e-mail—a valuable source of inspiration for your own soup-making endeavors.

33 rue de Charonne, 11th. CROSS STREET: Rue des Taillandiers. M° Ledru-Rollin. PHONE: 01 43 57 53 79. WEB: lebarasoupes.com. Mon–Sat 12pm–3pm and 6:30pm–11pm.

∽ A few years after the opening of the pioneering Bar à Soupes, a few similar soup bars have followed in its footsteps.

First came **Le Bar à Soupes et Quenelles,** a tasting room of sorts for the Giraudet company, which has been producing quenelles (spoon-molded dumplings flavored with chicken, pike, squid ink, morels, rye or chestnut flour . . .) in Bourg-en-Bresse since 1910. Seven soups are available each month (fava bean and cumin, sardines and cilantro, beets and balsamic vinegar, lobster bisque . . .), to be enjoyed with a puffy quenelle in lieu of bread.

Dessert can take the form of a soup, too, mixing apricots and almonds, strawberries and mint, or chocolate and chestnuts. Seating is limited, so get there early or take your lunch to go. Lunch formule: 11.50€. A block further from the rue Princesse location is the **Maison Giraudet** boutique, where you will find the full range of their products: soups, sauces, prepared dishes, and, of course, wonderful quenelles.

5 rue Princesse, 6th. CROSS STREET: Rue du Four. M° Mabillon. PHONE: 01 43 25 44 44. WEB: giraudet.fr. Mon–Fri 10am–3:30pm; Sat 10am–7pm.

Alternate location:

Lafayette Gourmet, 40 boulevard Haussmann, 9th. CROSS STREET: Rue de Mogador. M° Auber or Chaussée d'Antin. Mon–Wed and Fri–Sat 9:30am–8:30pm; Thu 9:30am–9pm.

Maison Giraudet. 16 rue Mabillon, 6th. CROSS STREET: Rue Guisarde. M° Mabillon. PHONE: 01 43 25 53 00. Tue–Sat 10am–1pm and 3pm–7:30pm.

And in the Belleville neighborhood is another delightful soup bar named **Zoé Bouillon** (see page 137).

Bistrot Paul Bert
Casual

If one wanted to capture the spirit of today's Parisian bistro and bottle it for generations to come, Bistrot Paul Bert would be a good place to start: a typical, ageless décor, a crowded room, a hurried yet friendly service, and an unfussy cuisine that never disappoints.

Scallops are seasoned with kari Gosse (a secret mix of spices invented and patented in the late nineteenth century by an apothecary in Brittany) and roasted in the shell, a golden thigh of *Coucou de Rennes* (a heritage poultry)

is paired with a creamy sauce of yellow wine and morels, and homemade mashed potatoes are brought forth in an earthenware dish, for the whole table to share.

If you and one of your dining companions are in a carnivorous mood, consider sharing the 2½-pound rib steak for two (35€ each): it comes in the only two acceptable shades (rare and very rare), with a green salad and thick fries.

Keep in mind, however, that this won't leave you with much room for dessert, and you may regret it when the Paris-Brest (a ring of choux pastry filled with praline-flavored buttercream and sprinkled with sliced almonds and confectioners' sugar—you'll like it) and the pink praline floating island are served to still-hungry diners near you.

The owner is quite the wine connoisseur and his cellar is filled with gems; ask for advice or take your pick among the chalkboard suggestions. Weekday lunch formule: 16€; three-course menu-carte: 32€; bottles start at 20€.

18 rue Paul Bert, 11th. CROSS STREET: Rue Chanzy. M° Faidherbe-Chaligny. PHONE: 01 43 72 24 01. Tue–Sat noon–2pm and 7:30pm–11pm.

Le Chateaubriand
Neo bistro

The world first caught wind of Iñaki Aizpitarte's talent when he was cooking at La Famille (see page 131). Once everyone had learned his name and more or less how to pronounce it (in-yah-kee eye-spee-tart), he took off to apply his creative energies elsewhere. After a brief but much noticed flyover at the restaurant of a contemporary art museum in the southern suburbs, he settled at Le Chateaubriand, a handsome 1930s bistro in a slipshod but fast gentrifying part of town.

These successive career hops have benefited the young Basque chef: his untamed cooking style—full of ideas, contrasts, and bursts of energy—has gained definition without losing any of its exciting qualities.

Le Chateaubriand is open for lunch (Basque-style tapas from 4 to 10€; 14€ two-course formule), but it develops its full potential at dinnertime, when each dish in the daily tasting menu (five mini-courses, no choices: 40€) tickles the mind and surprises the palate: oyster soup with beets and berries, glazed mackerel with nori and glasswort, lamb saddle with smoked eel, basil tapioca with berries . . .

Two caveats: don't go if your list of dislikes is long, or if you are ravenous: servings are on the small side. The service is casual—sometimes overly so— and the wine list a good panorama of independent vintners.

129 rue Parmentier, 11th. CROSS STREET: Rue du Faubourg du Temple. M° Goncourt. PHONE: 01 43 57 45 95. Tue–Fri noon–2pm; Tue–Sat 8pm–11pm.

Dong Huong
Vietnamese, see page 136

L'Écailler du Bistrot
Neo bistro

A refreshing sea breeze blows on this annex to Bistrot Paul Bert (see page 102). As its name implies—*un écailler* is someone who shucks and sells oysters—the menu puts a strong focus on these live delicacies (Belon, Utah Beach, Fine de Claire, of pristine freshness and served at optimal temperature) but makes ample room for quality fish and shellfish in pleasingly straightforward dishes: house-smoked salmon, wild sea bass with mashed potatoes, roasted scallops . . . Three-course lunch formule: 16€; à la carte: about 40€. Seafood platters can be ordered to go.

22 rue Paul Bert, 11th. CROSS STREET: Rue Chanzy. Mº Faidherbe-Chaligny.
PHONE: 01 43 72 76 77. Tue–Sat noon–2:30pm and 7:30pm–11pm.

Chez Ramulaud
Neo bistro   OUTDOOR SEATING

A neo bistro of the most unpretentious kind, Ramulaud just lets the warmth of the 1930s décor and the sincerity of the cuisine speak for themselves.

A chalkboard of daily suggestions is added to the seasonal menu-carte, and the unfortunate consequence is that it may take you a while to reach a decision, as you ponder the respective appeal of the *boudin blanc* (white sausage) with morels in chicken broth and that of the cabbage stuffed with snails and mushrooms, or discuss the merits of the cod on a pastis-scented fennel fricassée and the poached Bresse chicken served with polenta fingers in a chocolate-coffee sauce.

Desserts are less memorable, so if neither the chocolate *panna cotta* nor the quince compote calls your name, just opt for the trolley of farmhouse cheeses, or skip directly to coffee. Lunch formule: 17€; menu-carte: 29€.

Wine is infinitely more than a sidekick to food here, a fact that's immediately apparent when you notice the pyramids of wooden crates in every corner and sample a bottle from the extensive and competitively priced wine list.

269 rue du Faubourg Saint-Antoine, 11th. CROSS STREET: Rue Roubau.
M° Faidherbe-Chaligny or Rue des Boulets. PHONE: 01 43 72 23 29.
Mon–Fri noon–2:30pm; Mon–Sat 8pm–11pm.

Le Réfectoire
Casual / Brunch

The name of this trendy Oberkampf restaurant refers to the dining hall of French school cafeterias, a good illustration of the atmosphere of a place that plays the nostalgia note with a tongue-in-cheek spirit.

Unless you entertain misinformed fantasies about what French kids are ordinarily fed at school, you will be relieved to hear that the food at Le Réfectoire flies hundreds of miles above that—a salad of tomatoes, figs, and mozzarella, a crusty steak of tuna cooked nice and rare, and a caramel mousse flavored with Carambar, the legendary candy to which all French children owe at least one cavity.

Lunch formules: 14€ and 17€; dinner menu-carte: 28€; Sunday brunch: 20€. Good wine list with a focus on artisan vintners. Le Réfectoire is run by the same owners as La Famille (see page 131).

80 boulevard Richard Lenoir, 11th. CROSS STREET: Rue Saint-Sébastien.
M° Richard Lenoir or Saint-Ambroise. PHONE: 01 48 06 74 85. Mon–Sat
noon–2pm; Mon–Sun 8pm–10:30pm; BRUNCH: Sun noon–4pm.

Saigon Sandwich
Vietnamese

On a little street off the general hullabaloo of boulevard de Belleville hides a Vietnamese sandwich joint called Saigon Sandwich: barely larger than my kitchen, it is the workshop of a sandwich-making artist, a man who takes immense pride—and justifiably so—in the quality and freshness of his subs, assembled to order throughout the day.

For those unfamiliar with the Vietnamese sandwich (*bánh mì*), it is a deceptively simple combination of meat, crudités (cucumbers, carrots, daikon, onions, cilantro, chiles), and some sort of dressing (most often mayonnaise, garlic chile sauce, Maggi sauce, or a combination thereof) on a piece of baguette, a souvenir of the French colonization during the nineteenth and twentieth centuries.

He offers just three sandwiches, from 2.50€ to 2.80€: the Classique involves sliced pork (*jambonneau*) and Vietnamese salami; the Spécial adds headcheese (*fromage de tête*) and sliced meatballs; and my favorite, the extraordinarily flavorful Poulet, is garnished with marinated steamed chicken. Any of these take kindly to the company of soy or coconut juice, and can be eaten while sitting on the miniature plastic stools or, if you find the space too cramped (I wouldn't blame you), purchased to go.

8 rue de la Présentation, 11th. CROSS STREET: Rue Louis Bonnet. M° Belleville. No telephone. Mon–Sat 10am–6pm; Sun 10am–2pm.

Le Temps au Temps
Neo bistro   OUTDOOR SEATING

It is a shoebox of a restaurant with all the right accessories: a bar that takes up half the space, a few tables crowded together for warmth, and a sign that has to be put on the door nightly, informing hopeful but unrealistic diners that the place is *complet*—fully booked.

Le Temps au Temps is a four-hand recital, in the age-old tradition of small French restaurants: the young Sylvain Sendra mans the stove, while his wife, Sarah, glides between the tables and handles the seating, the ordering, the pouring, the serving, and the clearing, never departing from her smile.

And the customers certainly don't seem to complain as they dig into the chef's imaginative back-from-the-market dishes, which tap into his regional

French heritage—crispy head of veal drizzled with foie gras vinaigrette, honey-rubbed duck magret, rice pudding with salted butter caramel—or jazz it up with cleverly applied foreign influences: a cream of pumpkin soup made meaty with baby clams and flavored with *kumbawa* (a Thai citrus), a fillet of *lieu jaune* (a type of cod) in a green-tea crust, or a farmhouse Saint-Nectaire served with spiced crackers.

Menu-carte: 30€; weekday lunch formule: 16€. (The name of the restaurant refers to the French maxim, *"Il faut laisser le temps au temps"*: Time will make things right if you just let it.)

13 rue Paul Bert, 11th.

CROSS STREET: Rue Chanzy.

M° Faidherbe-Chaligny. PHONE: 01 43 79 63 40. WEB: www.temps-au-temps.com. Tue–Sat noon–2pm and 8pm–10:30pm.

12ème arrondissement

La Ruche à Miel
Salon de thé, see page 172

13ème arrondissement

L'Avant-Goût
Neo bistro

Barely a block away from the rackety place d'Italie, Christophe Beaufront's restaurant is a superb illustration of the neo bistro concept (see page 46). His style is innovative yet never puzzling, enthusiastic but never gushing, and his pairings and seasonings show a real knack for harmonious contrasts.

The chalkboard menu-carte (31€) shifts every day to reflect the chef's whims and market finds, but a typical fall meal may unfold into a thin tart of leeks and duck liver, slow-cooked pork cheeks with pumpkin risotto, and a pear and chestnut crumble. At lunchtime, the 14€ formule is a true bargain that will get you the soup and plat du jour (perhaps a leek and coconut *velouté* followed by roasted fillets of *julienne* [European ling], with spiced rice and a saffron vinaigrette), plus a glass of wine and coffee.

The red-and-gold dining room is always packed—reservations are indispensable—and correspondingly noisy. The owners also run the wine shop across the street, L'Avant-Goût Côté Cellier (see page 264).

26 rue Bobillot, 13th. CROSS STREET: Rue du Moulin des Prés. M° Place d'Italie or Corvisart. PHONE: 01 53 80 24 00. Tue–Sat 12:15pm–2pm and 7:45pm–10:45pm.

Le Petit Pascal
Casual   VEG-FRIENDLY/OUTDOOR SEATING

At first glance, there isn't much that distinguishes Le Petit Pascal from hundreds of other bistros in the city, but a closer inspection soon reveals what the neighborhood crowd cherishes: the neatness of the dining room, the kind efficiency of the service, and the quality of the food.

The menu options take a few moments to study, sprawled as they are on several chalkboards around the room: shareable platters of Cantal charcu-

MEAT COOKING STAGES

If you order seared meat at a restaurant, you will be asked how you want it cooked. Here's the full vocabulary, from the shortest to the longest cooking time:

- For **beef** and, incidently, red tuna: *bleu* (very rare); *saignant* (rare); *à point* (medium-rare); *bien cuit* (well-done).
- For **duck** or **lamb**: *rosé* (rare); *à point* (medium-rare); *bien cuit* (well-done).

Keep in mind that what the French call rare is rarer than what would be served as such in North America. But saignant really is considered the optimal stage at which to enjoy the flavor and texture of meat, so I encourage you to give it a try.

terie served with *cornichons* (I am especially fond of the veal terrine called *fricandeau*) or well-aged farmhouse cheeses (Morbier, Cantal, Saint-Nectaire . . .), copious salads (including a few vegetarian options), and a collection of bistro classics done right: a grilled steak with Roquefort sauce, an herb-roasted rack of lamb, or a duck confit, homemade and particularly tasty.

Desserts are just as comforting—profiteroles, chocolate mousse, stewed fruits—and the wine list, which leans heavily toward southern France, offers good value wines by the glass, pichet, or bottle.

33 rue Pascal, 13th. CROSS STREET: Boulevard de Port Royal. Mᵒ Les Gobelins. PHONE: 01 45 35 33 87. Mon–Fri noon–2:30pm and 7:30pm–10pm.

LE QUARTIER CHINOIS

The main Parisian Chinatown stretches its dragon wings along the double spine of avenue d'Ivry and avenue de Choisy, in the outreaches of the 13th arrondissement. Not the most picturesque from an architectural point of view, it is nonetheless the largest such neighborhood in Europe, a vibrant multicultural mix of immigrants from China, Vietnam, Laos, Cambodia, and Thailand. It is *the* place to be for the Chinese New Year celebrations—in late January or February, depending on the lunisolar calendar.

Le Quartier Chinois is home to the colossus of Asian food retail, **Tang Frères**—a gigantic store in which you could get lost for days but never starve—and its eternal rival, **Paris Store,** a bit smaller but less crowded. Both offer cheap prices on produce, fish, meat, and otherwise hard-to-find exotic ingredients.

Restaurants and noodle joints abound along the avenues and side streets; I go to **Tricotin** for dim sum, **Thieng Heng** for Vietnamese sandwiches (especially the *spécial maison* and the lemongrass beef), **Pho Mui** for pho, **Sinorama** for Cantonese cuisine, **Rouammit** for Laotian, and **Sukhothai** for Thai.

And if you'd like to chase your meal with something sweet, drop by **Pâtisserie de Choisy** or **Pâtisserie de Saison** for Asian-style pastries: steamed coconut balls, mooncakes, custard tartlets, tapioca shakes, etc.

Paris's other Chinatown is located in **Belleville** (see page 136).

Tang Frères. 48 avenue d'Ivry, 13th. CROSS STREET: Rue de la Pointe d'Ivry. M° Porte d'Ivry. PHONE: 01 45 70 80 00. Tue–Fri 9am–7:30pm; Sat–Sun 8:30am–7:30pm.

Paris Store. 44 avenue d'Ivry, 13th. CROSS STREET: Rue de la Pointe d'Ivry. M° Porte d'Ivry. PHONE: 01 44 06 88 18. Tue–Sun 9am–7pm.

Tricotin. 15 avenue de Choisy, 13th. CROSS STREET: Boulevard Masséna. M° Porte de Choisy. PHONE: 01 45 84 74 44. Mon–Sun 9am–11:15pm.

Thieng Heng. 50 avenue d'Ivry, 13th. CROSS STREET: Jardin Baudricourt. M° Porte de Choisy. PHONE: 01 45 82 92 95. Mon–Sun 8am–7pm.

Pho Mui. 97 avenue d'Ivry, 13th. CROSS STREET: Rue Baudricourt. M° Tolbiac. PHONE: 01 45 83 70 68. Mon–Sun 8am–10:30pm.

Sinorama. 135 avenue de Choisy, 13th. CROSS STREET: Rue Toussaint Féron. M° Tolbiac. PHONE: 01 44 24 27 81. Mon–Sun noon–3pm and 7pm–1am.

Rouammit. 103 avenue d'Ivry, 13th. CROSS STREET: Rue Baudricourt. M° Tolbiac. PHONE: 01 45 85 19 23. Tue–Sun noon–2:30pm and 7pm–10:30pm.

Sukhothai. 12 rue du Père Guérin, 13th. CROSS STREET: Rue Bobillot. M° Place d'Italie. PHONE: 01 45 81 55 88. Tue–Sat noon–2:30pm and Mon–Sat 7pm–10:30pm.

Pâtisserie de Choisy. 62 avenue de Choisy, 13th. CROSS STREET: Rue de la Vistule. M° Maison Blanche. PHONE: 01 45 82 80 70. Thu–Tue 9:30am–7pm; Closed on Wednesday.

Pâtisserie de Saison. 65 avenue d'Ivry, 13th. CROSS STREET: Jardin Baudricourt. M° Porte d'Ivry. PHONE: 01 45 84 37 70. Mon–Sun 9:30am–8:30pm.

APÉRITIFS

If you're the first of your party to arrive, or once the menus have been dealt around the table, the waiter or sommelier asks if you'd like a pre-dinner drink. I like to inquire whether the restaurant has a house apéritif (*"Vous avez un apéritif maison?"*) and see what quirky beverage turns up, but if none is proffered, here are a few suggestions of what can be ordered:

- **Pineau des Charentes** (*blanc* or *rosé*), a sweet wine made from Cognac brandy and unfermented grape juice
- **Lillet** (*rouge* or *blanc*), a blend of Bordeaux wine and citrus liqueurs
- **Suze,** a bittersweet apéritif distilled from gentian roots
- **Pastis,** the emblematic aniseed-flavored apéritif from Marseille
- **Martini** (*rouge, rosé,* or *blanc*), an Italian vermouth
- **Kir,** a mix of white Burgundy and *crème de cassis* (black currant liqueur); it can be made with other fruit liqueurs, or with Champagne instead of ordinary white wine, in which case it is called *kir royal.*

If you prefer to stick to a lower alcohol content, any white wine, dry or sweet, is considered appropriate, as are Champagne and its more affordable cousins, Crémant d'Alsace, Crémant du Jura, or Crémant de Bordeaux. Tomato juice is the typical alcohol-free alternative.

14ème arrondissement

Le Bis du Sévéro
Neo bistro, see page 115

La Cerisaie
Neo bistro

In another incarnation of the couple-owned, miniature bistro that the Parisian diner relishes so (see Le Temps au Temps, page 106), the young Cyril Lalanne and his missus play the culinary cards of their native French southwest: Basque ham and tomato French toast, goose magret with roasted pears, black pig from Bigorre with sweet peppers from Anglet, roasted wood pigeon on a foie gras ravioli, swordfish on a bed of *piperade* (a vegetable omelet) . . .

Lalanne's is a rigorously technical yet spirited cuisine that places first-rate ingredients at the front of the stage, and lets them speak for themselves. And at 30€ for three courses, it's not hard to find an audience who will listen, a good glass of Cahors in hand.

I find La Cerisaie to be best suited to evening meals, when you can roll right home and into bed after dinner, and when the dim lights cast a more forgiving eye on the charmless dining room.

70 boulevard Edgar Quinet, 14th. CROSS STREET: Rue du Montparnasse.
M° Edgar Quinet or Montparnasse-Bienvenüe. PHONE: 01 43 20 98 98.
Mon–Fri noon–2pm and 7pm–10pm.

Le Sévéro
Neo bistro

When an ex-butcher trades his cap for a toque to open a micro-bistro, you can't blame him for letting meat take over the entire menu, especially when said meat is so well sourced, and aged by the expert himself: a colossal *côte de bœuf* to share (cooked as it should be—crusty on the outside, rare on the inside—75€ for two), a thick, flavorsome rib steak of veal, or a tartare seasoned to zesty perfection, served with thick-cut and high-flying *frites maison.*

Simple salads, terrines, and charcuteries—including an outstanding blood sausage from Auvergne—fight for your attention at starter time, and artisan bottles from the Caves Augé (see page 261) make up the bulk of the wine list, to which an entire chalkboard wall is devoted. Cheese and acceptable dessert classics (*crème caramel,* chocolate mousse) can close your meal, but I doubt you'll have room.

Le Sévéro's popularity promptly outgrew its twenty seats, and encouraged the owner to open a twin location a block further down the street, **Le Bis du Sévéro.** Same spirit, same size, same meat, but because the chef there has a different background (he's Japanese, for one thing), one or two seafood dishes exercise passive resistance to the carnivorous invasion.

A meal at either address costs between 30€ and 50€ depending on your selection and your appetite, and bottles start at 18€. Le Bis du Sévéro offers weekday lunch formules at 19€ and 23€.

Le Sévéro. 8 rue des Plantes, 14th. CROSS STREET: Rue Sévéro. M° Alésia. PHONE: 01 45 40 40 91. Mon–Fri noon–2:30pm and 7:30pm–10:15pm.

Le Bis du Sévéro. 16 rue des Plantes, 14th. CROSS STREET: Rue de la Sablière. M° Alésia PHONE: 01 40 44 73 09. Tue–Sat noon–2pm; Mon–fri 7:45pm–10pm.

Ti Jos
Casual, see page 31

Salade Toute Violette
All Purple Salad

Adapted from a recipe by Sébastien Gaudard, chef at Délicabar (see page 60).

Sébastien Gaudard's monochromatic salads are among the most popular dishes he has created for Délicabar, the restaurant he runs inside the Bon Marché department store. This simple idea—seasonal compositions around a single color—translates into countless variations that are just as flavorful as they are attractive: *salade toute verte, salade toute orange, salade toute blanche . . .*

I am especially fond of his *salade toute violette;* it combines fresh figs and cured beef on a bed of red-leaf lettuce, with the non-purple yet delectable addition of buffalo mozzarella and toasted almonds. The fig vinaigrette can also be used on its own, to jazz up a simple salad of arugula.

FOR THE FIG VINAIGRETTE

3 medium dried black Mission figs, about 2 ounces (60 g), preferably unsulphured, stems removed

$1/2$ teaspoon fleur de sel or kosher salt

$1/4$ teaspoon freshly ground black pepper

2 tablespoons sherry or balsamic vinegar

$1/2$ cup (120 ml) extra virgin olive oil

FOR THE SALAD

1 large head red-leaf lettuce or *lollo rosso* lettuce (substitute 8 packed cups mixed greens, about 8 ounces, or 230 g, from a mix that includes some red leaves)

8 medium ripe black Mission figs, about 18 ounces (500 g), stems removed (one of the figs will be used for the vinaigrette)

10 ounces (300 g) fresh mozzarella, preferably buffalo mozzarella

7 ounces (200 g) thinly sliced air-dried cured beef, such as *bresaola*
   from Italy or *cecina de León* from Spain
^{2}/3 cup (50 g) sliced almonds, toasted

Serves 6 as a first course or light main course
Resting time: 20 minutes

1. Prepare the vinaigrette. Place the dried figs in a small heatproof bowl, cover with boiling water, and set aside to plump up for 20 to 30 minutes. Drain, pat dry, and finely chop.

2. Combine the plumped dried figs and 1 fresh fig, quartered, in a mortar, and grind to a paste with the pestle. (Alternatively, this can be done in a small food chopper, or in a bowl, using a flat-bottomed spice jar as a pestle.) Add the salt, pepper, and vinegar, and keep grinding the mixture as you drizzle in the olive oil. Taste and adjust the seasoning.

3. To prepare the salad, core the lettuce and separate it into individual leaves. Rinse and spin dry. Cut the remaining fresh figs into sixths and dice the mozzarella in ^{1}/2-inch (1.5-cm) cubes.

4. Divide the slices of beef among six salad bowls, placing them all around the rim of each bowl, half in, half out, so you can fold them back over the contents of the bowl later.

5. Place the salad and mozzarella in a large salad bowl, drizzle with the vinaigrette, and toss gently to coat, preferably working with your hands.

6. Divide the salad among the serving bowls, top with fresh figs and almonds, and fold the slices of beef back over the salad. Serve immediately, with fresh crusty bread or focaccia (see page 161).

15ème arrondissement

L'Arbre de Sel

Korean · VEG-FRIENDLY/OUTDOOR SEATING

This family-owned restaurant provides an authentic taste of Korea, fresh, homemade, and MSG-free. Start with *man doo* (grilled ravioli) or *kimchi jeon* (a chewy crêpe of fermented vegetables), before you move on to the *bibimbap* (vegetables, beef, and an egg served over rice, a specialty from the city of Jeonju) or the *bulgogi*, the famous Korean barbecue, cooked at your table and served with *banchan*, an assortment of condiments. And don't forget to try the sticky rice cake or the jellied chestnuts for dessert.

Weekday lunch menus start at 9.50€; weeknight dinner menus (Monday through Thursday) start at 12.50€; à la carte: about 26€. Good tea and sake list. There is a 10 percent discount on dishes purchased to go.

The dining room, simply and tastefully decorated, also serves as a miniature cultural center, regularly hosting readings by Korean writers and exhibitions of Korean artists' paintings and photography.

138 rue de Vaugirard, 15th. CROSS STREET: Avenue du Maine. M° Falguière. PHONE: 01 47 83 29 52. WEB: arbredesel.com. Mon–Sat noon–3pm and 7pm–11pm.

Le Bélisaire

Neo bistro

As a food writer, it is vital for me to have a network of friends who live or work in different parts of the city, and who make it their duty to alert me to local gems that might otherwise have slipped under my radar. Case in point: this excellent bistro, located in a residential part of the 15th arrondissement, near Maxence's office, and where he and his coworkers like to treat themselves to lunch every once in a while.

The 20€ lunch menu-carte is of unparalleled value, buying you three courses from the long chalkboard list: an unctuous risotto with Brittany lobster and wild asparagus, a crunchy-smooth salad of endives and slow-cooked pigeon thighs, roasted fillets of mackerel in a citrus butter sauce, a tripe stew with spring vegetables served in an individual cast-iron cocotte, and finally, a cherry *clafoutis* or a *panna cotta,* served with mango coulis and a warm madeleine.

The dinner menu reveals similarly inspired, market-driven options and remains a very good deal: 25€ for two courses, 30€ for three. The comfortable dining room is in pure bourgeois style—antique sideboard, starched tablecloths, and striped wallpaper. The mustachioed maître d' is kind and wine savvy, and the young chef likes to spring from the kitchen like a jack-in-the-box to greet his sated customers at the end of the service.

(Curious about the name? Impress your friends by explaining that Flavius Belisarius was a Byzantine general in the sixth century, and the main character of a censored novel published in 1767 by philosopher Jean-François Marmontel, after whom the street is named.)

2 rue Marmontel, 15th. CROSS STREET: Rue Yvart. M° Vaugirard.
PHONE: 01 48 28 62 24. Mon–Fri noon–2pm; Mon–Sat 8pm–10:30pm.

Le Café du Commerce
Casual, see page 77

La Cave de l'Os à Moelle
Bar à vin / Wine shop

If you've never eaten at a *table d'hôte* before, La Cave de l'Os à Moelle shall be a great introduction to the concept—a large table that you share with perfect strangers, family style, for the duration of the meal. This can be good or bad news, depending on the strangers you happen to commune with, but it makes for a fun experience in all cases, and if you're with a large group of friends, it is the ideal format for everyone to sit together.

La Cave is the wine bar annex to the neo bistro L'Os à Moelle (literally, "marrow bone") across the street, and the food served here is prepared there. The simple, brilliant formule is as follows: an assortment of starters awaits on the table when you arrive. Salads and pickled vegetables, marinated sardines or herring, pâtés and terrines with *cornichons,* and a basket of rustic bread all get passed around from guest to guest.

The soup and main course of the day—a frothy cream of celeriac, and amber-roasted quails, perhaps—are simmering away on a stove at the back, and diners get up with their vintage and mismatched plates to help themselves. A cheese platter follows, before the sweet-toothed can turn their attention to the bountiful dessert buffet that seems to have taken ten grandmothers to produce: *crème caramel,* apple compote, cherry *clafoutis,* chocolate mousse, prunes in spiced wine . . .

To accompany your meal, take a moment to explore the natural wines that line the wall, and pluck the bottle of your choosing; it will be charged at store price (starting from 8.20€) with no corkage fee.

La Cave de l'Os à Moelle is open for lunch and dinner (two seatings at 7:30pm and 9:30pm) and in both cases, the do-it-yourself service keeps the prices low (20€). Reservations are indispensable for the seated meals, but La Cave is equally enjoyable to down a glass of wine and a few side nibbles (terrines, Spanish ham) at the bar. All bottles are available to go.

181 rue de Lourmel, 15th. CROSS STREET: Rue Vasco de Gama. M° Lourmel. PHONE: 01 45 57 28 28. Tue–Sun 10am–midnight; LUNCH: noon–3pm; DINNER: 7:30pm–10:30pm.

∾ The owners of La Cave de l'Os à Moelle have opened a similar wine bar called **Les Symples de l'Os à Moelle** in Issy-les-Moulineaux, just outside the city limits but easily accessible by métro.

18 avenue de la République, Issy-les-Moulineaux. CROSS STREET: Rue Kléber. M° Mairie d'Issy. PHONE: 01 41 08 02 52. Mon–Fri 12:30pm–2:30pm; Mon–Sat 7:30pm–10:30pm.

Le Troquet
Neo bistro

Christian Etchebest has pinpointed the formula for the perfect Basque bistro: a dining room that has "rustic charm" written all over it—old tiles, stained mirrors, and heavy tables of carved wood, no two of which are alike—an atmosphere of low-key elegance, and finger-licking dishes.

It is *terroir* food with a delicious twist, when superb ingredients meet their fate in tasteful pairings and precisely administered cooking; when the curdled goat cheese comes with *piquillos* and chanterelles, and the beef skirt with spiced butter and a foie gras mac 'n cheese; when the *rascasse* (scorpion fish) is stewed with clams in a brawny broth, and black cherry jam is spooned over a vanilla soufflé.

In line with its Basque pedigree, Le Troquet is a fine place to sample southwestern wines, such as Irouléguy or Coteaux de Chalosse. Lunch formules: 24€ and 28€; dinner menu-carte: 30€; six-course tasting menu: 40€.

21 rue François Bonvin, 15th. CROSS STREET: Rue Miollis. M° Ségur or Sèvres-Lecourbe. PHONE: 01 45 66 89 00. Tue–Sat noon–2pm and 7:30pm–11pm.

16ème arrondissement

L'Astrance
Gastronomic

From his antipodean work experiences, Pascal Barbot has brought back a passionate curiosity for rare seasonings and a talent for casting them in crisp, aerial dishes that reinvent the classic French repertoire. His cuisine is imaginative and brilliant without being showy, and he excels at composing minimalist tableaux that appear to be simple juxtapositions of ingredients at first, but turn out to sublime flavors and textures, giving new depth to

Curnonsky's maxim, *"La cuisine, c'est quand les choses ont le goût de ce qu'elles sont"* (Cuisine is when things taste like themselves.)

Sitting down for a meal at L'Astrance means embarking on a blindfolded ride: the only option is a surprise tasting menu—thirteen dishes for dinner, seven at lunch—and the experience is bound to leave you starry-eyed, having put under your belt such singular dishes as a multilayered cake of thinly sliced mushrooms and verjuice-marinated foie gras; a slow-cooked fillet of sea bass with clams and mussels in a frothy curried sauce; a velvety celeriac soup topped with Parmesan cream and paper-thin petals of black truffle; or a veal loin with *cocos de Chambord* (tiny white beans) and chorizo coulis.

The sweet-toothed should not expect more from the dessert course than a refreshing final movement, three mini-dishes woven around fruity and acidulated notes, followed by a jasmine-scented *lait de poule* (the French eggnog) served in an eggshell, Barbot's signature chaser.

The restaurant barely seats thirty in a slate gray room, and the two-table mezzanine is ideal for lovebirds, especially those who seek a vantage point from which to observe the perfectly choreographed service. Reservations should be made at least a month in advance; lunch menus: 70€ (one of the best lunch deals ever) and 120€; dinner menu: 170€. For an extra 40€ at lunchtime and 100€ at dinnertime, the friendly sommelier will pour you a series of wines as your meal progresses.

4 rue Beethoven, 16th. CROSS STREET: Avenue de New York. M° Passy.
PHONE: 01 40 50 84 40. Tue–Fri 12:15pm–3:15pm and 8:15pm–9:15pm.

Le Pré Catelan

Gastronomic   OUTDOOR SEATING

When I was little, my family often took bike rides to the Bois de Boulogne, a large park that used to be a hunting ground to the kings of France, on the western rim of Paris. One of our favorite spots was the Pré Catelan, a landscaped garden close to the great lake. And whenever we went, we would make a point of riding around to the gastronomic restaurant of the same name, to peer at the gold-gilded dining room, study the menu, and giggle at how expensive the dishes were in contrast to their simplistic names: "*la carotte*," "*l'agneau*," or "*la pomme*."

Now that I am old enough to have a bank account rather than a piggy bank, I still think the à la carte prices are steep, but I am now privy to the fact that the lunch formule (weekdays only, no choices) is a more affordable 75€. And I have been given to taste enough gastronomic meals to know that this one provides an exceptional price/quality ratio, introducing you to Frédéric Anton's brilliant, ethereal cuisine.

For that price, you get three courses (scallops with cider, walnuts, and French caviar; calf sweetbread with cinnamon celeriac and a tempura of edible flowers; banana and peanut tartlet), coffee, and your choice from the jaw-dropping cart of *mignardises*.

Another reason why I think Le Pré Catelan is best enjoyed at lunchtime has to do with the escapist experience of walking away from the city and into the park, of reaching the beautiful Napoleon III pavilion and, from late spring to early fall, of savoring your luxurious lunch on the terrace, beneath century-old trees.

À la carte: around 180€; seasonal tasting menus: 140€ and 180€. Wine by the glass starts at 12€, by the bottle at 50€. To get to the restaurant, take the

SOLO DINING

You should feel entirely comfortable dining on your own in Paris, whether you're a man or a woman.

Solo eaters are a much more common sight at lunchtime, when it is assumed that they're in the city on business, than in the evening, when eating out is more of a social occasion. But that doesn't mean you can't treat yourself to dinner: you may arouse people's curiosity and get a few covert looks, but they will be intrigued and mildly admiring glances, not pitying ones.

Experience has shown that one tends to get better service when eating alone, because it is easier to establish a rapport with the wait staff then. This is especially true at upscale restaurants, where they figure that if you're here on your own, you must really be serious about your food, so they go out of their way to make your experience memorable.

To keep myself busy between courses I usually bring a book, a magazine, or a notebook—sharing a meal with oneself seems to be particularly conducive to creative thinking—but I often find that observing the activity of the restaurant is entertainment enough, and I set aside whatever I'm doing when the food is served.

The key is to feel—or at least act—confident and comfortable, and to enjoy yourself and your own company. You will likely end up in conversation with the diners around you—if such is your wish—and in all cases, you will notice that you're more attuned to the dining experience, because you're free to devote all your senses to the ambiance and the flavors.

métro to Porte Dauphine, and walk along route de Suresnes into the Bois de Boulogne, until you reach Le Pré Catelan. It is a twenty-minute walk and signs will point you in the right direction. Alternatively, a taxi can drive you to the restaurant.

Route de Suresnes, 16th. м° Porte Dauphine. phone: 01 44 14 41 14. web: www.precatelanparis.com. Tue–Sat 12am–2pm and 7pm–10pm; lunch: Sundays in the spring and summer.

Tokyo Eat
Casual, see page 71

17ème arrondissement

Caïus
Chic

The wood-paneled room looks like a British gentlemen's club, but it is Jean-Marc Notelet's contemporary French cuisine that is outlined on the daily chalkboard menu, jazzed up by flavors he's plucked along the spice route: roasted whelk salad with annato seeds (a lipstick-red spice from South America), lamb shank and oriental herb compote, and wok-seared raspberries served with a coconut milk ice cream.

Attention to detail shows everywhere, from the sophisticated plating and the professional service, down to the signature coffee-time treat, a tin box of *spéculoos* cookies swimming in whole spices so they may absorb all the flavors. Upon request, the knowledgeable sommelier will select a series of wines by the glass to pair with your meal. Two-course lunch formule: 23€; three-course menu-carte: 38€; wine by the glass starts at 3.50€.

6 rue d'Armaillé, 17th. cross street: Rue des Acacias. м° Argentine or Ternes. phone: 01 42 27 19 20. Mon–Fri noon–2:30pm and 7:30pm–10:30pm.

L'Entredgeu
Neo bistro

Before L'Entredgeu opened, I never had any reason to go to this featureless area of the 17th, except to attend the Salon Saveurs food show (see page 280) or to go bowling when the urge struck, about once a year.

But word-of-mouth travels fast about energy-filled bistros such as this one, and gourmands from several arrondissements away now flock in, eager to partake of the 30€ menu-carte—a very good deal if you steer clear of the handful of dishes that add a *supplément* to your tab.

From Philippe Tredgeu's kitchen—he cooks, while his wife, Pénélope, manages the front of the house—emerges a joyous parade of French classics, masterfully done and quietly glowing. A pressed terrine of beef jowls and foie gras, roasted oysters with parsnips, a caramelized pork belly served on a fluffy mound of polenta, seared fillets of *rouget* (red mullet) on a bed of asparagus, or glorious game dishes (see page 45) in the fall and winter.

Because you are requested to order your dessert up front, these dishes may well be chased by a rice pudding crowned with a crisp layer of caramel, or a vanilla custard served with miniature madeleines, regardless of how sated you feel. Tredgeu is, fortunately, light-handed in his use of sugar.

Just be aware of the string that is attached to success for such a small place: the dinner service is organized in two jam-packed seatings, and the wait staff sometimes loses its cool and forgets to smile.

The drinks list includes plenty of options for the natural wine aficionado, with bottles starting around 18€. Two-course lunch formule: 22€.

83 rue Laugier, 17th. CROSS STREET: Boulevard Gouvion Saint-Cyr. M° Porte de Champerret. PHONE: 01 40 54 97 24. Tue–Sat noon–2pm and 7:30pm–10:30pm.

L'Épicerie Verte
Lunch, see page 227

TURNING TABLES

Most Paris restaurants have small dining rooms and, to make their business economically viable, some choose to organize the evening service in two seatings—the first around 8pm, and the second around 10pm. You should be alerted to this when you call to make your reservation.

Both seatings have their pros and cons. The restaurant will be less crowded during the first—Parisians eat late—but you'll have to relinquish your table in time for the second service. If you pick the second seating, you may have to wait a bit for your table to free up, the atmosphere will be more bustling—most diners will have downed an apéritif or two before coming—and you will have as long as you like to linger over your meal. The choice is yours.

Oh Bigre!
Bar à vin   VEG-FRIENDLY

Some wine sellers manage to squeeze a few dining tables right in the middle of their shop, but the team at Le Vin en Tête decided to develop their wine bar activities in a separate location, right around the corner from their original wine shop.

Oh Bigre! is a warmly lit, shabby-chic place that's open from early evening, just in time for the apéritif, till two in the morning, when most Parisian bars close. In the meantime, a large number of glasses will have been served, alongside simple but eloquent platters of vegetables, cheeses, French or Spanish charcuterie, terrines, or oysters (in season), each option listed alongside the name of its provider.

Don't look for a written wine list; there is none. Just explain the sort of wine you'd like to drink, and the staff will come up with something from the cellar to make you happy (wine by the glass starts around 4€).

Oh Bigre! is very popular with the trendy Batignolles crowd, and the room gets quite noisy as the evening progresses. Le Vin en Tête organizes wine tasting classes; check the Web site for details.

4 rue Bridaine, 17th. CROSS STREET: Rue Lamandé. M° Rome. PHONE: 01 44 90 05 04. WEB: www.levinentete.net. Tue–Sat 6pm–2am. **Le Vin en Tête** 30 rue des Batignolles, 17th. CROSS STREET: Rue La Condamine. M° Rome. PHONE: 01 44 69 04 57. Mon 4pm–9pm; Tue–Sat 10am–9pm; Sun 10:30am–1:30pm and 4:30pm–8pm.

La Petite Rose
Salon de thé / Pastry shop   VEG-FRIENDLY

A dollhouse in shades of powder pink and cocoa brown, this boutique is yet another proof that French pastries and a Japanese approach make for a winning combination (see Sadaharu Aoki on page 165). The chef here is Miyuki Watanabe, a Japanese woman who was trained in Tokyo, came to Paris to work for Gérard Mulot, then set up her own shop a few steps from rue de Lévis.

Her picture-perfect entremets cater principally to the chocolate fan, who will swoon over the Valentin (chocolate and raspberry), the Marius (chocolate and chestnut), or the Délice (chocolate and orange), as the others delight in the lemon tartlet, the Paris-Brest, or the assorted macarons, all of which are reasonably priced for such high quality (pastries: about 4€).

Have your purchases wrapped in the signature pink box and improvise a sweet picnic in the nearby Parc Monceau, or take a seat in the *salon de thé* area and pair your pastries with a pot of green tea (4€) or hot chocolate (5€). La Petite Rose also sells freshly made filled chocolates (6.40€/100g) and chocolate bars; I especially enjoy the *tablette mendiant,* a bittersweet beauty in an embroidered gown of caramelized hazelnuts, almonds, and pistachios.

11 boulevard de Courcelles, 17th. CROSS STREET: Rue de Miromesnil. M° Villiers. PHONE: 01 45 22 07 27. Thu–Tue 10am–7pm; Closed on Wednesday.

Le Stübli

Salon de thé / Lunch / Pastry shop / Breakfast / Brunch   **VEG-FRIENDLY**

A bubble of Viennese spirit in Paris, this fifty-year-old pastry shop and tea salon is the ideal spot to indulge in the sweetest of German and Austrian specialties, made fresh daily, and delicious as can be.

Internationally acclaimed confections (apple or sour cherry strudel, poppy seed cake, Sachertorte, Linzetorte, Black Forest cake) share the display case with lesser-known pastries (a caramelized walnut and honey tart, a moist yogurt-based brioche, a fluffy lemon roll), and a happy parade of seasonal treats when Advent rolls around (cinnamon stars, spiced fruit cakes, gingerbread).

All of Le Stübli's pastries can be purchased to go, but I can't imagine who wouldn't want to sit down in the quaint little room upstairs, to eat a pastry with a pot of tea and a side of whipped cream—an actual item on the menu (2.20€).

Le Stübli also operates as a restaurant at lunchtime, and the savory menu then presents such classics as grilled sausages, *Koulibiac* (a salmon pie), or *Fleischstrudel* (a ground beef strudel), along with salads and sampler plates of regional specialties. Pastries: 4 to 6€; lunch formule: 15.50€.

11 rue Poncelet, 17th. CROSS STREET: Rue Saussier Leroy. M° Ternes.
PHONE: 01 42 27 81 86. WEB: stubli.com. SALON DE THÉ: Tue–Sat 9am–6:30pm
and Sun 9am–12:30pm; LUNCH SERVICE: Tue–Sat noon–3pm; SHOP: Tue–Sat
9am–7:30pm and Sun 9am–1pm.

18ème arrondissement

La Cave des Abbesses
Bar à vin, see page 264

Chéri Bibi
Casual, see page 131

Coquelicot
Bakery / Lunch, see page 157

La Famille
Neo bistro

When it opened a few years ago in the heart of Montmartre, this miniature loft of a restaurant gained instant popularity, thanks to its bohemian-chic atmosphere and the innovative cooking style of Iñaki Aizpitarte, who churned out unpredictable creations from the pocket kitchen downstairs.

When the young Basque chef packed his knives and rode off into the sunset (see page 103), his departure could have signed the death warrant of La Famille, but the two owners found a more than worthy replacement in Bruno Viala: his dishes not only demonstrate an equal level of creativity—jellied oysters and seaweed-cilantro cappuccino, pressed duck confit and juice ravioli, coconut chocolate cake and lime-pineapple compote—but also the levelheadedness that's necessary to keep his inventions on track.

The menu is short and sweet—just four options for each of the three courses—and the riddling descriptions usually require an explanation from the wait staff, but that's part of the fun. The wine list holds exciting gems by lesser-known, artisanal vintners. Three-course menu-carte: 35€; six-course tasting menu: 50€.

41 rue des Trois Frères, 18th. CROSS STREET: Rue de La Vieuville. M° Abbesses. PHONE: 01 42 52 11 12. Tue–Sat 8pm and 10pm (two seatings).

✍ The two cousins who own La Famille also run **Le Réfectoire** in the Oberkampf neighborhood (see page 105), and have opened another restaurant at the foot of the Sacré-Cœur, **Chéri Bibi**, where they serve a mix of comfort food (whelks with homemade mayonnaise, a roasted thigh of partridge with mashed potatoes) and travel-inspired dishes (lemongrass marinated salmon, a beef stew with cocoa) in a comfortable dining room furnished with flea market finds. Two courses: 19€; three courses: 24€.

15 rue André del Sarte, 18th. CROSS STREET: Rue Charles Nodier. M° Anvers. PHONE: 01 42 54 88 96. Tue–Thu 8pm–11:30pm; Fri–Sat 8pm–midnight.

L'Homme Tranquille
Casual   VEG-FRIENDLY

"Warmth" is the first word that presents itself beneath my fingertips, wagging its tail in its eagerness to describe this long-standing Montmartre restaurant. Small wooden tables fill a room that is dimly lit by low lamps and candles, and wallpapered from floor to ceiling with a random pattern of art and movie posters, plastered one on top of the other over the decades.

It is a family operation—the mother and grandmother manage the kitchen while the son, Antoine, handles the service with the occasional help of his wife—that delivers a reliably comforting, home-style fare: a *salade de saison* with goat cheese and cilantro (a dream of freshness), a honey-roasted chicken served with mashed potatoes, a duo of Comté and Morbier from the father's cheese farm in the Doubs, a spiced prune soup with vanilla ice cream . . .

Dishes spring up from the downstairs kitchen on an old-fashioned service lift that keeps me endlessly entertained, and they are brought to the table with a bright smile and a few words of kindness. The menu reflects the seasons through daily specials, but it changes little from year to year; the regulars complain otherwise. Menu-carte: 26€.

81 rue des Martyrs, 18th. CROSS STREET: Rue d'Orsel. M° Abbesses or Pigalle. PHONE: 01 42 54 56 28. Tue–Sat 7:30pm–11pm.

Le Mono
Togolese   VEG-FRIENDLY

Named after one of Togo's largest rivers, Le Mono is a family-owned restaurant devoted to the cuisine of this small western African country. It is a no-frills, buoyant place that's especially packed on weekend nights, when the chef prepares the house specialty: a meltingly tender suckling pig.

The other dishes are just as wholesome—*djenkoumé* chicken (with bananas and a tomato sauce), *gombo fetri* (a stew thickened with okra), braised fish, spinach *mafé* (spinach in peanut sauce)—and the variety of sides will send the starch lover into a tap dance: grilled plantains, fried yams, a manioc mash named *foufou,* a steamed corn bread . . .

The portions are generous and the prices reasonable: about 18€ for two courses, which may be enjoyed with a Flag, the Togolese beer.

40 rue Véron, 18th. CROSS STREET: Rue Aristide Bruant. M° Blanche or Abbesses. PHONE: 01 46 06 99 20. Thu–Tue 7pm–midnight; Closed on Wednesday.

Pulcinella
Italian   VEG-FRIENDLY/OUTDOOR SEATING

It is uncannily difficult to find an authentic and unpretentious Italian restaurant in Paris: most are either mediocre or horrendously overpriced, but Pulcinella, with its seasonal Neapolitan cuisine and affable service, is just the kind I like.

The dining room is cozy, and the market-fresh dishes du jour are advertised on a few chalkboards that get passed around from table to table—a handful of antipasti (marinated vegetables, octopus salad, carpaccio) that can be ordered in small or large format, four or five pasta dishes (spaghetti with lobster, asparagus and scamorza ravioli, mezzi rigati with veal ragù), and a few main courses (veal scallop, braised salmon), all of them simple but impeccable.

The wine list highlights mostly Italian wines, with affordable choices and pitcher options. And if you're up for dessert, good luck deciding between the exemplary *panna cotta* and the indulgent *cantuccio,* a sort of tiramisù that involves whipped cream and caramelized almonds.

Two-course lunch formule: 13€. At dinner, three courses cost around 30€.

17 rue Damrémont, 18th. CROSS STREET: Rue Steinlen. M° Lamarck-Caulaincourt. PHONE: 01 46 06 46 94. Mon–Sat noon–2:30pm; Mon–Sun 7:30pm–11:30pm.

Chouquettes
Sugar Puffs

~

When we were little, my sister and I sometimes spent the afternoon with my grandmother, who was then in her mid-seventies yet had more vitality than all her grandchildren combined. I remember playing dominoes, sifting through boxes of black-and-white family photographs, spending hours in the toy section of department stores, and, when it was time for a snack, dropping by the bakery to buy a bulging paper bag of *chouquettes*, sugar-studded puffs that Céline and I would devour, down to the last grains of pearl sugar that had gathered at the bottom.

Baking your own chouquettes is about as easy as it is fun. They can be served with tea in the afternoon, for breakfast and brunch, or for dessert, to escort a cup of ice cream. The same choux pastry is used, minus the sprinkled sugar, to make éclairs, *religieuses*, Paris-Brest, and profiteroles.

6 tablespoons (75 g) unsalted butter, diced
$^1/_4$ teaspoon fine sea salt
2 tablespoons (25 g) sugar
1 cup (140 g) all-purpose flour, sifted
4 large eggs, at room temperature
Pearl sugar for sprinkling (see Note)

Makes about 40
Resting time: 30 minutes

1. Make sure you have all the ingredients measured out before you start. Combine the butter, salt, sugar, and 1 cup (240 ml) fresh water in a small saucepan, and bring to a simmer over medium heat. Remove from the heat,

add the flour all at once, and stir quickly with a wooden spoon until well blended. Return the pan to medium-low heat and keep stirring until the mixture forms a smooth ball that pulls away from the sides of the pan.

2. Let cool for 3 minutes. Add the eggs one by one, stirring well after each addition. Cover and refrigerate for 30 minutes, or up to a day; you have just made choux pastry.

3. Preheat the oven to 400°F (200°C) and line a baking sheet with parchment paper. Remove the batter from the fridge and use two teaspoons—or a piping bag fitted with a plain tip—to form small balls of batter, about the size of a walnut, that you will plop on the prepared sheet, leaving an inch of space between them. Sprinkle with pearl sugar.

4. Bake for 20 minutes, until puffed up and golden (never ever open the oven door during the first 10 minutes of baking). Turn off the oven, open the door just a crack, and leave the chouquettes in for another 5 minutes to prevent a temperature shock, which would cause them to deflate.

5. Transfer to a rack and let cool completely before serving. Keep any leftovers in an airtight container at room temperature, and reheat for 5 minutes in a 300°F (150°C) oven to restore the original texture.

NOTE: Pearl sugar—*sucre perlé* in French, and available at G. Detou (see page 200)—comes in coarse, lentil-size nuggets that remain crunchy when baked. It sometimes goes by the name of nib sugar, and can be purchased wherever cake-decorating supplies are sold, in Scandinavian shops (the Swedish call it *pärlsocker*), or online. If you can't find it, crush sugar cubes in a sturdy food storage bag using a rolling pin or a meat mallet; you may find this quite relaxing. Alternatively, use a coarse sugar, such as Demerera or turbinado, chopped caramelized nuts, or chocolate chips.

19ème arrondissement

BELLEVILLE

Asian

Belleville used to be a North African neighborhood, but its population changed gradually in the eighties to become chiefly Asian: a few cafés, hallal butchers, and kosher shops are still holding their ground, but most of the territory has been annexed by this Right Bank Chinatown.

It is a smaller *quartier chinois* than the one in the 13th (see page 110), but it still holds plenty of little food shops, grocery stores, and authentic dining options: I go to **Le Pacifique** for dim sum, **Krung Thep** and **Lao Siam** for Thai cuisine, **Dong Huong** for pho, and **Saigon Sandwich** (see page 105) for the best Vietnamese sandwiches in the city.

Le Pacifique. 35 rue de Belleville, 19th. CROSS STREET: Rue Rampal. Mº Belleville. PHONE: 01 42 49 66 80. Mon–Sun 11am–midnight.

Krung Thep. 93 rue Julien Lacroix, 20th. CROSS STREET: Rue Lesage. Mº Pyrénées. PHONE: 01 43 66 83 74. Mon–Sun 8pm–10pm.

Lao Siam. 49 rue de Belleville, 19th. CROSS STREET: Rue Rampal. Mº Belleville. PHONE: 01 40 40 09 68. Mon–Sun noon–3pm and 7pm–11:30pm.

Dong Huong. 14 rue Louis Bonnet, 11th. CROSS STREET: Rue de la Présentation. Mº Belleville. PHONE: 01 43 57 18 88. Wed–Mon noon–10:30pm; Closed on Tuesday.

La Boulangerie par Véronique Mauclerc
Lunch / Bakery / Salon de thé, see page 159

Chapeau Melon
Bar à vin, see page 265

Zoé Bouillon
Lunch

VEG-FRIENDLY

A winding street with a village-like feel, a dining room with café tables and checkerboard tiles, and behind the counter, a friendly staff who ladles out freshly made soups—here are the ingredients that make up Zoé Bouillon.

Each soup in the daily rotation of six comes with its matching topping—herbed croutons, chopped scallions, toasted seeds—and may be paired with your choice of accompaniment among the seasonal side salads and the moist quick breads (called *cake* in French), perfect for dipping.

Once served, carry your cup of soup (pink lentils and zucchini, leek and ginger, a chilled fresh herb velouté) to your table on the little tray, settle in on a cushy banquette, and savor the delightfully casual atmosphere. And if, after being so good and eating all your vegetables, you feel you deserve a treat, homespun desserts await: caramelized pear cake, mango and passion fruit soup, chestnut blancmange . . .

Lunch formules: 8.50 to 12€; everything can be purchased to go. In the evening, Zoé Bouillon turns into a regular restaurant—table service, real dinnerware, and a menu that includes a few plats du jour—but the prices remain very reasonable (three-course dinner formule: 21€; à la carte: 26.50€).

66 rue Rébeval, 19th. CROSS STREET: Rue Pradier. M° Pyrénées or Belleville. PHONE: 01 42 02 02 83. WEB: www.zoebouillon.fr. Mon–Sat 11:30am–4pm; Tue–Sat 6:30pm–10:30pm.

PRICELESS MENU

I adore gastronomic restaurants, really, I do: the plush atmosphere, the read-your-mind service, the low stool that is proffered for your purse or your poodle, the feeling that you've entered a time warp . . . But the one old-world tradition that makes me roll my eyes without fail is this: women are often handed the *menu sans prix*, a blind menu with no prices.

The reasoning behind this practice is that female diners, those precious creatures, should be free to order whatever they fancy without worrying about such mundane matters as prices and tabs.

When that happens, I try not to be irked by this anachronistic sexism—I may very well be the one footing the bill, and if I'm not, I want to make sure I don't force my generous companion into bankruptcy—and I just ask for a menu with prices instead.

20ème arrondissement and beyond!

Le Baratin
Bar à vin

This out-of-the-way wine bar has acquired enough of a glowing reputation to attract a clientele from across town, who's willing to schlep all the way to the top of the Belleville hill and fight the neighborhood regulars for a table.

The wine list is short but edgy, the fare hearty and high-spirited (tuna tartare, citrus-braised beef cheeks, tripe with Spanish paprika and chickpeas), and the rowdy atmosphere matches the slipshod décor perfectly. Le Baratin is open for lunch (15€ formule) and dinner (about 30€), but also welcomes customers who just want to stop in for a drink at the bar (wine by the glass starts at 3.50€).

3 rue Jouye-Rouve, 20th. CROSS STREET: Rue de Belleville. M° Pyrénées.
PHONE: 01 43 49 39 70. Tue–Fri noon–2pm; Tue–Sat 8pm–11pm.

Krung Thep
Thai, see page 136

Les Magnolias
Chic

If you know a little about the typical Parisian diner, you are surely aware of how difficult it is to lure him beyond the *périphérique* (the freeway that runs all around the city), and knowing this helps take the measure of Jean Chauvel's talents.

This young wizard of a chef trained in the most prestigious establishments (La Tour d'Argent, Taillevent, Le Crillon, and even a brief stint in the prime minister's kitchens) before setting out on his own just as he turned thirty, taking over a restaurant in a quiet suburb, a few miles east of Paris.

Les Magnolias could have remained a local's secret, but word got out that someone was shaking things up in Le Perreux-sur-Marne: the restaurant's reputation grew quickly, and with it, the number of insular Parisians ready to take the trip and see for themselves (see directions below).

Their reward is this: a cryptic-poetic menu, whimsical dishes that spring in every direction, abstract presentations, and at the root of it all, a joyful approach to haute cuisine, one that doesn't take itself too seriously, and strives to surprise and entertain.

The dining room is uneventfully bourgeois and the service very traditional, but this only serves to enhance the playfulness of the cuisine. Because of the transportation issue, I recommend Les Magnolias chiefly for lunch, when you can take advantage of the 37€ two-course menu. But if you don't mind taking a taxi home, dinner is a fine experience, too (three courses for 52€; 85€ tasting menu).

Directions: Take the RER (express train), line E from Saint-Lazare–Haussmann or Gare du Nord–Magenta in the direction of Villiers-sur-Marne or Tournan; check the board to make sure the train will stop at Nogent–Le Perreux. Trains leave every fifteen minutes. Get off at Nogent–Le Perreux; it is a twenty-minute ride. Take the Le Perreux exit (east of the railroad tracks) and walk down the boulevard de la Liberté until it ends in the avenue de Bry, about five minutes. The restaurant will be at the intersection, on your right-hand side.

48 avenue de Bry, Le Perreux-sur-Marne. CROSS STREET: Boulevard de la Liberté. RER: Nogent–Le Perreux. PHONE: 01 48 72 47 43.
WEB: www.lesmagnolias.com. Tue–Fri 12:15pm–1:15pm; Tue–Sat 8pm–9:30pm.

Les Symples de l'Os à Moelle
Bar à vin, see page 120

LOCAL PRESS: KEEP YOURSELF UPDATED

For the latest on restaurant openings and trends, and reliable reviews, check the following publications (in French):

À Nous Paris is a free weekly paper that's distributed inside métro stations on Mondays or Tuesdays; it includes one page of restaurant reviews. Watch for piles on metal racks by the turnstiles.

Le Figaroscope is the art and entertainment section of the daily paper *Le Figaro*. It is sold with the Wednesday edition and has several pages on restaurants. It is the most respected source for reviews.

L'Express is a news magazine published on Thursdays. The Saveurs section includes two pages of restaurant reviews.

shops

Dining out plugs you right into the city's gastronomic scene, but you'd be missing out on an extraordinary chunk of Parisian life if you skipped the food shopping dimension. Greenmarkets, bakeries, and specialty foods shops beckon at every street corner, and if you're anything like me, you may find yourself sacrificing a museum or two to make the most of the edible experience. That's okay. Enjoy your almond croissant while you can; Degas will always be there.

marchés / greenmarkets

Paris offers no fewer than eighty greenmarkets: the vast majority of them are open-air markets (*marchés volants*, or roving markets) that operate two or three half-days a week, most often in the morning. The remaining handful are indoor markets (*marchés couverts*) that open every day.

Whether or not you need to buy anything, few activities are more refreshing—and appetite whetting—than walking through one of these markets, negotiating your way from stall to stall, dodging the little old ladies' carts, and stopping to smell the strawberries.

A few things to note:

- There are no greenmarkets on Mondays, ever.

Nous vous conseillons

* Le Bleu de chèvre

* Le reblochon fermier

* Le grand murols

* Le machecoulais

- Weekend days are far busier than weekdays: there are more customers and more food vendors then.
- At most markets, you will find one or two stalls that sell snacks to go—crêpes, prepared foods, pastries—so you can plan a visit around lunchtime if you'd like.
- If you are planning on making purchases, go through the entire market first, to see what's available and make sure you get the best quality and price.
- Few produce vendors are actually growers, except at organic markets: they are most often retailers, who buy their goods from the Rungis wholesale market (see page 239).
- Although the fruits and vegetables are within reach of patrons, you should assume that the stall keeper will choose and bag them for you. If it's okay to help yourself, he will gesture for you to do so.
- Most vendors let you taste small fruits (strawberries, cherries, grapes), but it's best to ask first ("*Je peux goûter?*").
- Haggling isn't customarily done, except when the vendors are wrapping up; they may then agree to cut you a deal on what's left of their goods.

Wherever you are staying, there is a good chance that you have a market near you. A full list of locations and days can be found at **http://chocolate andzucchini.com/parismarkets/**; below is a list of the most noteworthy in terms of charm, size, and vendors.

Le Marché des Enfants Rouges (3rd)   VEG-FRIENDLY/OUTDOOR SEATING
A covered market with many prepared foods options and picnic tables (see page 33).

39 rue de Bretagne. Mº Filles du Calvaire. Tue–Sat 8:30am–1pm and 4pm–7:30pm; Sun 8:30am–2pm.

Marché Baudoyer (4th)

One of the few open-air markets to be open in the afternoon.

Place Baudoyer. M° Hôtel de Ville. Wed 12:30pm–8:30pm; Sat 7am–3pm.

Marché Monge (5th)

On a pleasant square just outside the métro station.

Place Monge. M° Place Monge. Wed, Fri, Sun 7am–2:30pm.

Marché Raspail (6th)

All-organic farmers' market on Sundays; posh clientele and the occasional celebrity sighting.

Boulevard Raspail, between rue du Cherche Midi and rue de Rennes. M° Rennes. Tue, Fri 7am–2:30pm; Sun 9am–3pm.

Marché Saxe Breteuil (7th)

Unobstructed view of the Eiffel Tower.

Avenue de Saxe, between avenue de Ségur and place de Breteuil. M° Sèvres-Lecourbe. Thu, Sat 7am–2:30pm.

Marché Bastille (11th)

One of the city's largest open-air markets.

Boulevard Richard Lenoir, between rue Amelot and rue Saint-Sabin. M° Bastille. Thu, Sun 7am–2:30pm.

Marché d'Aligre and Marché Beauvau (12th)

A daily open-air market and an indoor market, side by side. The latter is more upscale than the former.

Rue d'Aligre and place d'Aligre. M° Ledru-Rollin.
Open-air market: Tue–Sun 9am–12:30pm.
Indoor market: Tue–Fri 9am–1pm and 4pm–7:30pm; Sat 9am–1pm and 3:30pm to 7:30pm; Sun 9am–1:30pm.

Marché Brancusi (14th)
A small all-organic farmers' market.

Place Constantin Brancusi. M° Gaîté. Sat 9am–3pm.

Marché Convention (15th)

Rue de la Convention, between rue Chartier and rue de l'Abbé Groult.
M° Convention Tue, Thu, Sun 7am–2:30pm.

Marché de Grenelle (15th)
A large market under the elevated métro tracks—a convenient feature on a rainy day.

Boulevard de Grenelle, between rue de Lourmel and rue du Commerce.
M° La Motte-Picquet Grenelle. Wed, Sun 7am–2:30pm.

Marché du Président Wilson (16th)
Home to Joël Thiébault's produce stall (see page 215).

Avenue du Président Wilson, between rue Debrousse and rue d'Iéna.
M° Alma-Marceau, Iéna. Wed, Sat 7am–2:30pm.

Marché des Batignolles (17th)
All-organic and friendly farmers' market.

Boulevard des Batignolles, between rue Boursault and rue des Batignolles.
M° Rome. Sat 9am–2pm.

~ Aside from greenmarkets (see page 000), the most pleasant food shopping destinations in Paris are the *rue commerçantes*, market streets that offer a high concentration of food shops—bakeries, butcher shops, fish markets, cheese shops, Mediterranean delis, wine shops, charcuteries, tea and spice shops—as well as cafés with terraces, where you can sit and relax before or after running your errands.

Avoid Mondays, Sunday afternoons, and holidays; most shops are closed then. Once you've walked up and down the central market street, do explore the side streets that shoot off from it, too; they often lead to thrilling discoveries. At produce shops, it is wise to favor fruits and vegetables from the sidewalk display: this is where the best deals and special prices *(promotions)* are kept, to attract customers.

I've outlined a few of my favorite shopping streets below; some of them are closed to traffic, either permanently or on Sunday mornings, and the shopkeepers then set up stalls that spill out onto the street, giving it even more of a bustling market feel.

Rue Montorgueil (1st and 2nd)

In the former *ventre* (belly) of Paris. Closed to traffic.

M° Les Halles.

Rue des Rosiers (4th)

In the old Jewish neighborhood: kosher delis, pastry shops, restaurants.

M° Saint-Paul.

Rue Cler (7th)

Closed to traffic; the clientele is a mix of posh locals and foreigners.

M° École Militaire.

Rue des Martyrs (9th)

Start from the intersection of avenue Trudaine and Rue des Martyrs and work your way down toward the Notre-Dame de Lorette church.

M° Anvers.

Rue du Faubourg Saint-Denis (10th)

A tad scruffier than the other streets in this list, the Faubourg Saint-Denis offers an excellent mix of ethnic shops: Eastern European, Turkish, African, Indian, Caribbean . . .

M° Château d'Eau.

Rue Daguerre (14th)

Closed to traffic.

M° Denfert-Rochereau.

Rue de Lévis (17th)
Closed to traffic.
ᴹ° Villiers.

Rue Poncelet (17th)
Closed to traffic.
ᴹ° Ternes.

Rue des Abbesses and **rue Lepic (18th)**
Closed to traffic on Sundays and holidays. Start from place des Abbesses, and turn left into the lower part of rue Lepic.
ᴹ° Abbesses.

boulangeries / bakeries

Among the many romantic fantasies that people entertain about Parisians' food habits, this one is true: most of us do need fresh bread like we need fresh air, we do benchmark our neighborhood *boulangers* to determine who bakes the best loaf, and once that private prize has been awarded, we are willing to wait in the snaking line outside the shop for our fix, ready to negotiate hard with the customer just ahead of us if he's about to snatch—oh, the horror!—the last baguette.

You may think good bread is a given in France, but it hasn't always been the case. After World War II, people favored white bread, which had been scarce during wartime, so that is what bakers focused on over any other kind. The industrialization of the bread-baking process in the fifties and sixties kept the prices low, but the overall quality, too, and the competition of cheap supermarket bread drove many independent bakeries out of business.

In the eighties and nineties, a number of bread bakers and flour mills started to look for ways to make bread flavorsome again, and thus up their sales. They reinstated artisanal methods, developed new production processes around them, and worked to educate the consumer. It is around that time that brands of baguettes (Banette, Campaillette, Baguépi) appeared, created by flour mills and licensed to bakeries, who received the technical instructions to bake them, and the marketing tools to help sell them.

Their efforts paid off: it is now easier than ever to find good bread—though I hasten to add that the exact notion is subject to one's personal preferences—and walking into a random bakery in Paris should turn up an acceptable loaf. But if *outstanding* is what you're after, the following bakeries will make you bread-happy.

Eric Kayser
Bakery

Superstar bread baker Eric Kayser has built a naturally leavened empire of two dozen bakeries, half of them in Paris, half of them abroad. The most recently created branches lack the authenticity of his flagship shop on rue Monge, but the bread is of equal quality: made with high-grade flours and Kayser's signature starter, it has crunch, body, and flavor.

The rustic Tourte Monge (stone-ground wheat flour, liquid *levain,* and salt from Guérande) is a much acclaimed classic, the specialty loaves (hazelnut and turmeric, fresh fig, olives, walnuts, comté . . .) are delicious if you don't mind their tendency to verge on the brioche, and the bread of the month (saffron, cocoa, rose, *saucisson*) is always fun to try.

The *viennoiseries* and pastries are up to par, especially the bite-size *finan-*

VIENNOISERIES AND BAKERS' PASTRIES

In addition to bread, bakeries sell a variety of cakes, pastries, and *viennois-eries*. This generic term refers to baked goods made with leavened and often layered dough, sweetened with sugar, and sometimes enriched with milk and eggs.

Viennoiseries are traditionally served for breakfast: croissant, *croissant aux amandes* (croissants filled with almond cream, topped with sliced almonds, and sprinkled with confectioners' sugar), *pain au chocolat* (croissant dough rolled into a rectangular shape around one or two bars of chocolate), brioche, *kouglof* (an Alsatian brioche with raisins and almonds, also spelled *kugelhopf*), *pain aux raisins* (brioche dough studded with raisins, garnished

with pastry cream, and shaped into a spiral), *palmier* (a double swirl of crisp, caramelized puff pastry), and *chausson aux pommes* (a puff pastry apple turnover).

The rest of the display case features **cakes and pastries,** simpler than those found at pastry shops, and intended as afternoon snacks rather than dessert: *quatre-quart* (the French pound cake), *cake* (a loaf-shaped fruitcake), flan, *financiers* (almond cakes shaped like gold ingots), *kouign amann* (a thick disk of flaky yeast dough, caramelized and buttery), *sablés* (butter cookies), *beignets* (doughnuts, usually filled with raspberry jam, apple compote, or chocolate), madeleines, *canelés* (see page 173), and *chouquettes* (sugar puffs; see recipe on page 134).

Quiches, sandwiches, and basic salads round out the selection, and many Parisians turn to the *boulangerie* for a quick lunch to go.

ciers and the *canelés*. Kayser has a stand at Lafayette Gourmet (see page 250). His second boutique on rue Monge specializes in organic bread, while the boulevard Malesherbes location has a sitting area where you can have lunch (salads, *tartines*, plat du jour) or tea.

8 rue Monge, 5th. CROSS STREET: Rue des Bernardins. M° Maubert-Mutualité. PHONE: 01 44 07 01 42. WEB: www.maison-kayser.com. Wed–Mon 6:30am–8:30pm; Closed on Tuesday.

Alternate locations:

14 rue Monge, 5th. CROSS STREET: Rue des Bernardins. M° Maubert-Mutualité. PHONE: 01 44 07 17 81. Tue–Sun 8am–8:15pm.

85 boulevard Malesherbes, 8th. CROSS STREET: Rue de Lisbonne. M° Miromesnil. PHONE: 01 45 22 70 30. Mon–Sat 7am–8:15pm.

Bread & Roses
Bakery / Salon de thé / Lunch / Breakfast / Brunch VEG-FRIENDLY/OUTDOOR SEATING

Bread & Roses is equal parts bakery, pastry shop, and deli, but the star of the show is undoubtedly the bread: a dozen varieties, made with organic flours and baked in the downstairs *fournil*. Not your run-of-the-mill loaves, these show a real commitment to quality and taste, from the Puissance 10 bread (made with a blend of ten flours) to the sunny *fougasse* (the Provençal focaccia; see recipe on page 161) and the dried fruit loaf, which works equally well with butter for breakfast, or with foie gras for dinner.

The sweets selection includes an old-fashioned brioche made with fresh butter and fresh eggs (a rarer feature than one might think), seasonal fruit tarts, and gorgeous loaf cakes.

The sunny room also functions as a restaurant open for breakfast, lunch, and tea. Menu options are designed to flatter the bread that will be served with them, rather than the other way around. There are sadly no formules and the à la carte prices climb fast, but the freshness of the fare is correspondingly high. (Breakfast costs around 10€, lunch 20€, tea and a pastry 12€.)

Bread & Roses is but a block from a little-used entryway into the Luxembourg Garden, so you may opt to buy a sandwich and a slice of marble cake, and go find the perfect bench to eat them on.

7 rue Fleurus, 6th. CROSS STREET: Rue Madame. M° Rennes or Saint-Placide. PHONE: 01 42 22 06 06. WEB: www.breadandroses.fr. Mon–Sat 8am–8pm.

Poilâne
Bakery

Poilâne is the Mona Lisa of bread: you can't quite come to Paris without dropping by to say hello. Founded in 1932 on the chic rue du Cherche Midi, this bakery produces the most famous starter bread in the world, simply called *pain Poilâne* or *miche Poilâne*. The traditional manufacturing process uses stone-milled gray flour and Guérande salt, a slow natural fermentation, and wood-burning ovens.

The giant wheels, of which you can buy a half or a quarter, boast a thick crust slashed with the signature "P" at the top and slightly charred at the bottom, and a moist, fragrant crumb that begs for a dab of butter or some gooey cheese.

Aside from this star item, the bakery also sells specialty breads (with rye flour, raisins, or Périgord walnuts), croissants, flans, apple tartlets, and *punitions,* pale blond butter cookies worth selling your soul for. These can be sampled from a basket at the register; I challenge you to resist buying a sachet afterward.

The line of Poilâne-endorsed accessories will make nice gifts for the bread lover: embroidered aprons, bread bags, bread knives, bread boxes . . . A short behind-the-scenes tour of the shop can be arranged, by appointment only; call 01 69 33 23 00.

The charismatic Lionel Poilâne, who had inherited the bakery from his father, Pierre, was among the most vocal proponents of artisanal bread in the eighties. He died tragically in a helicopter crash in 2002; his young daughter, Apollonia, now holds the reins of the business.

8 rue du Cherche Midi, 6th. CROSS STREET: Rue de Sèvres. Mᵒ Saint-Sulpice or Sèvres-Babylone. PHONE: 01 45 48 42 59. WEB: www.poilane.fr. Mon–Sat 7:15am–8:15pm.

Alternate location:

49 boulevard de Grenelle, 15th. CROSS STREET: Rue Clodion. Mᵒ Dupleix. PHONE: 01 45 79 11 49. Tue–Sun 7:15am–8:15pm.

Boulangépicier
Bakery / Lunch, see page 65

Arnaud Delmontel
Bakery / Pastry shop, see page 170

Du Pain et des Idées
Bakery

This beautiful 1889 bakery—the windows! the counters! the ceiling!—was taken over a few years ago by Christophe Vasseur, a former sales manager who woke up one morning to realize that bread-making was his true calling.

The corporate world's loss is the bread lover's gain, as praiseworthy loaves and *viennoiseries* emerge from Vasseur's brick ovens. His is a narrow range, as was the case in traditional bakeries forty years ago, and Vasseur explains it is the only way anyone can guarantee the constant quality and freshness of each item.

His slowly fermented Pain Pagnol and Pain des Amis come highly recommended, as do the organic multigrain *boules* and the *mini-pavés,* bread rolls stuffed with all manner of goodies (goat cheese and figs, tomatoes and olives, banana and chocolate, apples and almonds). The sweet ones are ideal as a snack, and the savory ones complement a bowl of salad or soup beautifully.

In the pastry department, try the *escargot chocolat pistache* (a swirl of brioche dough filled with pistachio cream and chocolate), the fresh fruit turnovers (apple, apricot, fig), the delectable *tendresse aux pommes* (see recipe on page 177), or, in early January, the outstanding *galette des rois*.

34 rue Yves Toudic, 10th. CROSS STREET: Rue de Marseille. M° Jacques Bonsergent. PHONE: 01 42 40 44 52. Mon–Fri 6:45am–8pm.

L'Autre Boulange
Bakery

This bakery is operated by Michel Cousin, a very kind, very mustachioed man who is deservedly famous for his organic breads, baked in a wood-burning oven. I very much enjoy the *pain de campagne* that comes in giant loaves (you can buy just a section), the *ocarina* (a dense little loaf chock-full of dried fruits), and the flaxseed bread, and I will confess a weakness for the daily selection of regional pastries (madeleines, *canelés*, flans, tartlets), which are just the sort of humble-looking, grandmotherly confections I find the most appetizing.

The *sablés* (butter cookies) are particularly remarkable, and if I have to play favorites, I shall name the *spéculoos*, a subtly spiced gingersnap coated with crunchy sugar crystals.

43 rue de Montreuil, 11th. CROSS STREET: Rue Roubo. M° Faidherbe-Chaligny. PHONE: 01 43 72 86 04. WEB: lautreboulange.com. Tue–Fri 7:30am–1:30pm and 3:30pm–7:30pm; Sat 7:30am–1:30pm.

Vandermeersch
Bakery

Once you've taken a look at your métro map and figured out where this bakery is, you may have second thoughts about going. Yes, it is all the way out in the 12th arrondissement, and no, the neighborhood doesn't offer much in the way of distractions, but when a baker chooses such an off-center location and still draws in crowds from the other side of the city, he's probably doing something right.

And indeed, Stéphane Vandermeersch, who trained at Pierre Hermé's side, puts out a range of simple, flawless breads (baguette, sourdough, multigrain) and *viennoiseries,* including delicious madeleines and *chouquettes,* a perfect croissant, a wonderful *galette des rois,* and a spectacular *kouglof,* specialty of the house and available on weekends only.

278 avenue Daumesnil, 12th. CROSS STREET: Rue du Colonel Oudot. M° Porte Dorée. PHONE: 01 43 47 21 66. Wed–Sun 7am–8pm.

Des Gâteaux et du Pain
Bakery / Pastry shop, see page 174

Le Quartier du Pain
Bakery

After distinguishing himself as the youngest baker to earn the Meilleur Ouvrier de France title (see page 156) at age twenty-six, Frédéric Lalos went on to open three bakeries in Paris (see page 156 for alternative locations), where bread enthusiasts get in line for his expertly crafted loaves.

The range includes a naturally leavened *boule* made with stone-ground flour, a rustic dense-crumbed *pain auvergnat,* a fantastic *pain de seigle* (80 percent rye, 20 percent wheat), and golden baguettes in different outfits (plain, sesame, poppy seed). A limited-time "bread of the month" is also available on Saturdays.

The baked goods (cakes, tartlets, etc.) are hit or miss, but the service is uncommonly friendly—the saleswoman once saw me peering at the *chouquettes* next to the register and just handed me one, something that hadn't happened to me since I was five.

74 rue Saint-Charles, 15th. CROSS STREET: Rue Beaugrenelle. M° Charles Michel. PHONE: 01 45 78 87 23. Mon–Fri 7am–8pm; Sat 7am–7:30pm.

MEILLEUR OUVRIER DE FRANCE

The Meilleur Ouvrier de France title is the ultimate medal of honor for the craftsman. Created in 1924, this highly selective competition is held every three years in two hundred métiers, ten of which are food related—chef, pastry chef, butcher, charcutier, maître d', sommelier, bread baker, ice cream maker, chocolatier, and cheese refiner.

The applicants go through several rounds of examinations, as a jury of seasoned peers assesses their work. The competition is fierce, and it takes years of intensive training to even entertain the hope of receiving the title. But for the handful of candidates who make it past the final selection, it is a prestigious recognition of their talent, skills, and dedication that will help their business tremendously. MOFs also earn the right to wear a blue, white, and red ribbon around their collar.

(Note: Laureates are commonly referred to as Meilleur Ouvrier de France, but the exact title is Un des Meilleurs Ouvriers de France, one of the best craftsmen in France.)

Le Quartier du Pain alternate locations:

270 rue de Vaugirard, 15th. CROSS STREET: Rue Maublanc. M° Vaugirard. PHONE: 01 48 28 78 42. Mon–Sat 6:30am–8pm.

116 rue de Tocqueville, 17th. CROSS STREET: Boulevard Pereire. M° Wagram. PHONE: 01 47 63 16 28. Mon–Fri 7am–8pm.

Boulangerie Toro
Bakery

This corner bakery isn't the sort that tries to woo you with enough varieties of bread to make your head spin and your palms sweat with indecision: the Toro bread family has few members, but each of them has panache and character. Of particular merit among them are two different baguettes: a sumptuously flavorful multigrain *baguette des prés* and a single-slashed *flûte Gana,* which follows the formula invented by Bernard Ganachaud.

The pastry case follows suit, offering simple but delightful baked goods. I must draw your attention to the *palmier,* a giant double swirl of crunchy caramelized puff pastry; the *chausson aux pommes à l'ancienne,* a fresh apple turnover dotted with crystals of sugar; and the *gâteau au chocolat* in large wedges, which hides a dense, melt-in-your-mouth interior under a crisp outer crust.

And as a bonus with your purchases, you get to watch the ballet of bread bakers at work through the large window at the back of the shop.

59 rue d'Orsel, 18th. CROSS STREET: Rue des Martyrs. M° Abbesses. PHONE: 01 42 23 62 81. WEB: gana.fr. Tue–Sat 7am–8pm; Sun 7:30am–1:30pm.

Coquelicot
Bakery / Lunch / Breakfast / Brunch   VEG-FRIENDLY/OUTDOOR SEATING

Once settled in Montmartre, it didn't take me long to elect this bakery as my favorite, and I make an alarming consumption of their Piccola baguette (free form, lightly dusted with flour, and astoundingly flavorful), their naturally leavened Paume, and their seasonal specialty breads: violet and pineapple, goat cheese and hazelnuts, buckwheat and cherry . . .

The line often snakes out onto the sidewalk, but it moves briskly, and the wait gives you an opportunity to weigh your options and decide whether to get a bag of first-rate *chouquettes*, a slice of *quatre-quart au citron* (lemon pound cake), or a thin chocolate baguette twist.

Coquelicot offers indoor and outdoor seating to enjoy a breakfast of café au lait and buttered *tartines*, or a light lunch of salads and omelets.

24 rue des Abbesses, 18th. CROSS STREET: Place des Abbesses. M° Abbesses. PHONE: 01 46 06 18 77. WEB: www.coquelicot-montmartre.com. Tue–Sun 7:30am–8pm; SALON DE THÉ: Tue–Sun 9:30am–4pm.

Alternate locations:

Le Grenier de Félix. 64 avenue Félix Faure, 15th. CROSS STREET: Rue Duranton. M° Boucicaut. PHONE: 01 45 54 57 48. Mon–Sat 7am–8pm.

La Prairie de Coquelicot. 50 bis rue de Douai, 9th. CROSS STREET: Rue de Bruxelles. M° Blanche or Place de Clichy. PHONE: 01 48 74 41 52. Mon–Fri 7:30am–2pm and 3:30pm–8pm; Sat 7:30am–3pm.

DEMI-BAGUETTE ET PAIN TRANCHÉ

Even though it is rarely advertised, bakeries will sell you a half-baguette (*une demi-baguette*) for half the price of a regular one. For other varieties of bread, it is sometimes possible to buy half, or a quarter of the loaf, especially if it's a large one, but you will have to ask. ("*C'est possible d'en prendre juste la moitié?*" for half, and "*C'est possible d'en prendre juste un quart?*" for a quarter.)

When you buy a loaf of bread, the attendant will offer to run it through the slicing machine by asking, "*Je vous le tranche?*" or simply "*Tranché?*" I prefer to slice my own bread—it goes stale faster when pre-sliced, and I find the machine-cut slices too thin—but if you don't have access to a bread knife or a cutting board, it can be convenient.

LA MEILLEURE BAGUETTE DE PARIS

Every year in March, the mayor's office organizes a competition to elect the city's best baguette: a jury of experts—bread bakers, chefs, restaurant owners, food writers—gathers to examine, weigh, smell, squeeze, taste, and grade the baguettes that have been submitted.

The winner receives a prize of a few thousand euros, and the exclusive right to provide the Palais de l'Élysée—the French White House—with its daily dose of baguettes, which, disappointingly, is only twenty-five a day. But beyond the cash and the honor, it is a unique way for the baker to receive media attention, and attract a larger clientele than just the neighborhood regulars.

A similar competition is held in early January to name Paris's best *galette des rois.*

La Boulangerie par Véronique Mauclerc
Bakery / Salon de thé / Breakfast / Brunch   VEG-FRIENDLY

Formerly named Au Vieux Four, this historic bakery is home to one of the few wood-burning bread ovens that remain in operation in France, a century-old construction of brick and cast iron in which the young Véronique Mauclerc bakes her artisan loaves.

In plain view in the middle of the shop, and not hidden behind a counter as they usually are, the bread shelves display a dozen different kinds on any given day (country bread, multigrain, rye, quinoa, spelt, chestnut, with nuts or cheese . . .), all of them organic and naturally leavened, their crust kissed by the intense heat of the venerable oven.

The selection of savory tarts and pastries—plump little brioches, sugar-dusted almond croissants, pistachio swirls, *kouign amann*, a stupendous pear and chocolate cake-tart (see recipe on page 192)—is no less tempting.

The little room at the back operates as a *salon de thé* where you can sample the shop's offerings for breakfast, brunch, or lunch. But if the weather is mild, I suggest you take your purchases to the nearby Parc des Buttes Chaumont, the largest, steepest, and most beautiful park in Paris.

83 rue de Crimée, 19th. CROSS STREET: Rue Manin. Mᵒ Laumière. PHONE: 01 42 40 64 55. Thu–Mon 8am–8pm; SALON DE THÉ: until 6pm; Closed Tuesday and Wednesday.

Fougasse au Romarin
Rosemary Fougasse

~

Fougasse, sometimes spelled *fouace,* is a Provençal cousin to the Italian focaccia—a flat loaf flavored with olive oil and Mediterranean-inspired ingredients. It can be found in Parisian bakeries in various shapes and incarnations, and may be made with either puff pastry, as is sometimes done in the Languedoc region, or bread dough. I find the latter kind lighter and more versatile, and this is the recipe I use when I want to bake my own, to serve with roasted summer vegetables, dry-cured ham, and goat cheese for a simple dinner spread.

$4^{1}/_{4}$ cups (18 ounces; 500 g) all-purpose flour, plus extra for sprinkling

$1^{1}/_{3}$ cups (320 ml) lukewarm water

1 teaspoon granulated instant yeast

1 to 2 teaspoons fleur de sel or kosher salt, plus extra for sprinkling
    (see Note 1)

2 tablespoons fresh rosemary, roughly chopped, plus extra for sprinkling
    (substitute 1 tablespoon dried rosemary)

2 tablespoons extra virgin olive oil, plus extra for brushing

Makes 2 loaves
Resting time: 30 minutes for proofing, 1½ hours for the first rise,
20 minutes for the second rise

1. Put the flour in a large bowl and form a deep well in the center. Pour the water into the well, sprinkle with the yeast, and leave to soften for 5 minutes.

2. Using the fingers of one hand and without going all the way to the bottom of the bowl, stir gently to combine part of the flour with the water to

form a soupy paste. Cover the bowl with a kitchen towel and let rest at room temperature for 25 minutes, until bubbles form at the surface.

3. Add the salt, rosemary, and oil, and, still working with one hand, stir the entire contents of the bowl to incorporate the rest of the flour, until the dough forms a shaggy ball. Turn out onto a lightly floured surface and knead until smooth and springy, 12 to 15 minutes; you can also use a stand mixer fitted with the dough hook. The dough will be rather sticky, but this is the key to a light-textured fougasse, so try to resist adding extra flour. Clean the bowl and grease it lightly. Return the dough to the bowl, cover with the towel, and let rise at room temperature until doubled in size, about $1^1/2$ hours.

4. Preheat the oven to 400°F (200°C) and sprinkle flour lightly on a baking sheet.

5. Punch down the dough and divide it into two balls. Shape each ball into a flattened leaf-shaped oval, about 5 by 9 inches (13 by 23 cm), and place side by side on the prepared baking sheet. Use the dull side of a knife to cut five or six deep slits in each fougasse, cutting all the way across the dough. Pull gently on the edges of each loaf to widen the slits, and use your fingers to open each slit widely enough that it won't close during the baking. Cover with the towel and let rise for 20 minutes as the oven preheats.

6. Bake for 30 to 40 minutes, until crusty and golden. Brush with olive oil, sprinkle with a little more fleur de sel and rosemary, and transfer to a rack to cool completely. The second loaf can be frozen for up to a month (pop the thawed loaf in the oven for 5 minutes at 400°F [200°C] to revive its texture), and any leftovers can be used to make bruschetta the next day (see Note 2).

VARIATIONS: The fougasses can also be flavored with chopped olives, green or black, with finely chopped sun-dried tomatoes, with lardons sautéed until crisp, with caramelized onions . . . Fold these ingredients in during the final stages of the kneading.

NOTE 1: Use just 1 teaspoon salt if you intend to serve the fougasse with rather salty ingredients, such as cured ham, aged cheese, or olives; use 2 teaspoons if you want to enjoy it on its own, or with a salad of greens.

NOTE 2: Day-old fougasse may be used to make bruschetta. Slice the loaf in two horizontally. Rub the inside of each half with a split garlic clove, top with diced tomatoes and chopped onions, drizzle with olive oil, and sprinkle with salt, pepper, and freshly grated Parmesan. Bake for 8 to 10 minutes in a 400°F (200°C) oven, until the fougasse is crisp and the cheese melted. Cut in two-bite pieces with a serrated knife, top with shredded basil, and serve as an appetizer.

pâtisseries / pastry shops

In Paris, the tip of the pastry iceberg is made up of big names—Dalloyau, Fauchon, Ladurée, Lenôtre, Pierre Hermé—that invest in marketing and public relations, and thus get the most press coverage. Those houses tend to spearhead the trends—Pierre Hermé was the first to present his pastry creations like a fashion collection—and they provide a good illustration of the zeitgeist, but there are plenty more talents to discover if you're willing to look deeper.

In fact, the most humble *pâtisserie de quartier* (neighborhood pastry shop) may very well provide a good rendition of the classics (see below), these absolute delights that avant-garde pastry chefs tend to disregard, in search of more scintillating challenges.

Jean-Paul Hévin
Pastry shop / Chocolate shop / Salon de thé, see page 181

Stohrer
Pastry shop

Nicolas Stohrer worked for a few years in Versailles as pastry chef to King Louis XV, and he is credited for being the first to introduce the French to the *baba au rhum,* a rum-soaked yeast cake that went on to become one of the greatest classics of French pastry. His eighteenth-century pastry shop on Rue Montorgueil is still standing in all its glory: the façade and murals are well preserved, and the successive owners have kept the spirit alive with a lavishly appetizing line of old-school pastries.

The *baba* is prominently featured, sharing the limelight with the enchanting house specialty called *puits d'amour* (literally, well of love), a pillow-shaped, caramelized custard tart named after a late-nineteenth-century operetta. The original is sized for six (25€); the miniature version

(3.40€) makes for easier sampling. The mille-feuille, *religieuses,* and éclairs are exemplary.

51 rue Montorgueil, 2nd. CROSS STREET: Rue Marie Stuart. M° Sentier or Étienne Marcel. PHONE: 01 42 33 38 20. WEB: www.stohrer.fr. Mon–Sun 7:30am–8:30pm.

Pain de Sucre
Pastry shop / Bakery

Didier Mathray and Nathalie Robert had been working for famous chef Pierre Gagnaire for years when they decided to open their own pastry shop behind the Centre Georges Pompidou, in an area that didn't seem particularly suited to the sort of high-flying pastries they planned to produce.

But the gamble was a winning one, and their reputation quickly extended past the borders of the arrondissement, as one gourmand after another was tipped off on their sublime tartlets (fig and thyme, ricotta and wild strawberries), their revamped classics (orange flower *calisson,* mango éclair), and their shimmering *verrines* (multilayered desserts in a glass). Pastries cost around 4€.

Also available at Pain de Sucre (literally, sugarloaf) are *viennoiseries,* fresh butter brioches, chocolate-coated marshmallows, and a range of breads.

14 rue Rambuteau, 3rd. CROSS STREET: Rue du Temple. M° Rambuteau. PHONE: 01 45 74 68 92. Thu–Mon 9am–8pm; Closed Tuesday and Wednesday.

Sadaharu Aoki
Pastry shop / Chocolate shop

Because he was trained in the art of pastry making in both Japan and France, Sadaharu Aoki had the genius idea to combine the two sensibilities, slipping Japanese ingredients into French confections, and applying the Japanese eye for detail to the presentation and packaging.

CLASSICS OF FRENCH PASTRY

Baba au rhum: a spongy yeast cake soaked with rum syrup, often served with whipped cream.

Chou à la crème: cream puff.

Éclair: an oblong shell of *pâte à choux* (choux pastry) filled with pastry cream and topped with a layer of fondant. Éclairs are classically flavored with chocolate (*éclair au chocolat*) or coffee (*éclair au café*).

Fraisier: two layers of *génoise* (sponge cake) filled with fresh strawberries

and kirsch-flavored pastry cream, and topped thinly with marzipan.

Macaron: two rounds of smooth almond meringue, sandwiched together by a jam, ganache, or cream filling. (This is the best-known type of macaron, also called *macaron parisien,* but the name is also given to many regional confections made with ground almonds, sugar, and egg whites.)

Mille-feuille: a napoleon, i.e., a rectangular pastry made of alternating layers of puff pastry and vanilla pastry cream, iced with white fondant or sprinkled with confectioners' sugar.

Mont Blanc: a round meringue topped with vanilla whipped cream and thinly piped chestnut purée, sprinkled with confectioners' sugar. It is named after the highest mountain in the Alps.

Opéra: a rectangular pastry made of thin, alternating layers of chocolate sponge cake, ganache, and buttercream.

Paris-Brest: a ring of choux pastry filled with praline-flavored pastry cream and sprinkled with sliced almonds and confectioners' sugar. It is named after a bygone bicycle race.

Religieuse: a large choux pastry puff topped with a smaller one to form a sort of snowman figure; both puffs are filled with pastry cream and iced with fondant. Similar to éclairs but constructed differently, *religieuses* also come in chocolate and coffee incarnations (*religieuse au chocolat* and *religieuse au café*).

Saint-Honoré: caramelized cream puffs placed in a circle on a tart crust and garnished with *crème Chiboust* (a blend of pastry cream and whipped cream). It is named after the patron saint of pastry makers.

Salambo: an oval cream puff filled with kirsch-flavored pastry cream, topped with green fondant on one half and chocolate sprinkles on the other; a favorite of mine when I was little.

Tartelette aux fruits de saison: a tartlet garnished with seasonal fruit, which may be arranged on a bed of pastry cream and thinly topped with a translucent glaze.

His pastries offer polished looks, balanced flavors, and successful texture combinations: try his green tea opéra, his black sesame éclair (the choux pastry casing filled with a nutty and lightly smoky pastry cream), his acidulated yuzu tartlet, or his *dôme* of green tea mousse, hiding a heart of red bean paste and crisp *feuillantine*. Aoki is just as good with unadulterated classics, a point well made by the vanilla mille-feuille (napoleon) and the *chou à la crème* (cream puff). Pastries cost about 5€.

His bite-size green tea *financiers,* his flavored truffles (matcha, sesame, yuzu), his chocolate-dipped orange slices, or his red bean and milk jam make for lovely food gifts.

35 rue de Vaugirard, 6th. CROSS STREET: Rue Cassette. M° Rennes or Saint-Sulpice. PHONE: 01 45 44 48 90. WEB: www.sadaharuaoki.com. Tue–Sun 11am–7pm.

Alternate locations:

56 boulevard de Port Royal, 5th. CROSS STREET: Rue Bertholet. M° Les Gobelins. PHONE: 01 45 35 36 80. Tue–Sun 8am–7pm. Small salon de thé area.

Lafayette Gourmet, 40 boulevard Haussmann, 9th. CROSS STREET: Rue de Mogador. M° Auber or Chaussée d'Antin. Mon–Wed and Fri–Sat 9:30am–8:30pm; Thu 9:30am–9pm.

Christian Constant
Pastry shop / Chocolate shop / Ice cream / Salon de thé, see page 48

Pierre Hermé
Pastry shop / Chocolate shop

A relentless alchemist of flavors, Pierre Hermé has worked his way up since his apprenticeship at Lenôtre at age fourteen, sharpening his style at Fauchon and Ladurée before he opened stores under his own name in Tokyo, then Paris. His luxurious and whimsical creations are a feast for the eye, the taste buds, and the intellect, as one reads the catalog description and tries to connect the sensory dots.

Hermé was the first to introduce fashion concepts into the stiff world of French pâtisserie, and his pastry collections are organized around flavor combinations (strawberry, rhubarb, and passion fruit; chocolate, yuzu, and grapefruit; cherry and pistachio; fig and raspberry) that appear in several incarnations: cakes, tarts, verrines, jams, fruit pastes, and filled chocolates. Pastries cost around 6€.

I like my macarons to have substance and personality, and Hermé is my provider of choice. Fleshy and delicate, these two-bite numbers boast unusual flavors that fill me with delight—milk chocolate and passion fruit, wild rose and chestnut, olive oil and vanilla, white truffle and hazelnut—and, more often than not, a surprise morsel hidden in the center of the filling—a crushed hazelnut, a halved sour cherry, a cube of pistachio praline. (7.40€ for 100 g, about five petit-four-size macarons.)

The original Ispahan (a large raspberry macaron filled with rose cream and litchi, and topped with fresh raspberries) is the unchallenged best seller. Each new line is an opportunity to sample avant-garde pastries, but don't ignore Hermé's take on traditional confections, such as the *2000 feuilles* (a caramel and praline napoleon) or the outstanding croissant.

The sleek Rue de Bonaparte boutique can be intimidating, but the staff is, in fact, quite helpful. Just around the corner, at 8 place Saint-Sulpice, Le Café de la Mairie serves as the unofficial *salon de thé* for Pierre Hermé addicts: order drinks, keep your table tidy, and the waiters will look the other way as you dig into your pastries. The second Pierre Hermé location, in the 15th arrondissement, is more colorful and less crowded.

72 rue Bonaparte, 6th. CROSS STREET: Rue du Vieux Colombier. M° Saint-Sulpice or Mabillon. PHONE: 01 43 54 47 77. WEB: pierreherme.com. Mon–Fri and Sun 10am–7pm; Sat 10am–7:30pm.

Alternate location:

185 rue de Vaugirard, 15th. CROSS STREET: Boulevard Pasteur. M° Pasteur. PHONE: 01 47 83 89 96. Tue–Wed 10am–7pm; Thu–Sat 10am–7:30pm; Sun 10am–1:30pm.

La Maison du Chocolat
Pastry shop / Chocolate shop, see page 189

Aurore-Capucine
Pastry shop

With its dark wood counters, dim lighting, and lacy drapes, Aurore-Capucine seems like a cross between an apothecary and an antiques shop. It

is neither, but rather a little-known pastry shop, where the confections offer singular flavor combinations, and a profoundly handcrafted, flamboyant look, as if assembled from velvet, silk, and fake pearls by an eccentric duchess.

So temptingly baroque is the selection that you may find it difficult to make up your mind: a pear, pistachio, and grapefruit tartlet, or a rose and papaya cookie? An assortment of dried herb cookies, or a violet and chocolate crackled macaron? A coconut and geranium *dôme*, or a puffy raspberry turnover? The loopy-lettered signs and the kind

staff will help you make an informed decision, but you may find it imperative to plan a return visit.

3 rue de Rochechouart, 9th. CROSS STREET: Rue Lamartine. M° Cadet.
PHONE: 01 48 78 16 20. Tue–Sat 11:30am–8pm.

Arnaud Delmontel
Pastry shop / Bakery / Breakfast

Although Delmontel's bread loaves are honorable—his Renaissance baguette was voted Meilleure Baguette de Paris in 2007—what draws me back to his shop is his talent for pastries and *viennoiseries*. His fleshy croissants would brighten any breakfast table and they are no less delicious in their almond version (*croissant aux amandes*), but if you'd like to try something unusual, get the *feuilleté de seigle au miel*, a flaky roll made with rye flour and lightly sweetened with honey.

The pastries range from reliable classics (*financiers*, seasonal fruit tarts, mille-feuille) to brilliantly simple inventions (a lemon turnover called *bichon*, an almond and orange flower tartlet called *mirliton*, a walnut streusel cake called *croustinoix*) and glossy edible sculptures—I like the Dôme, a chocolate caramel mousse with a heart of meringue on a chocolate cookie, as well as the Choco Miss and the Marquise, two whimsical creations shaped like toys.

39 rue des Martyrs, 9th. CROSS STREET: Rue de Navarin. M° Notre-Dame de Lorette. PHONE: 01 48 78 29 33. WEB: arnaud-delmontel.com. Wed–Mon 7am–8:30pm; Closed on Tuesday.

Alternate location:

57 rue Damrémont, 18th. CROSS STREET: Rue Lamarck. M° Lamarck-Caulaincourt. PHONE: 01 42 64 59 63. Tue–Sat 7am–8:30pm; Sun 7am–2pm.

Le Valentin
Pastry shop / Salon de thé, see page 89

La Bague de Kenza
Pastry shop / Salon de thé

If the line that extends outside the shop doesn't catch your eye as you walk by, the luxurious display of pastel confections certainly will: La Bague de Kenza is the ideal place to get acquainted with Algerine-style pastries, aromatic delights filled with nuts, figs, or dates, and flavored with honey, rose water, orange blossom, mint, citrus, or vanilla.

While they couldn't be considered diet-friendly by any stretch of the imagination, these bite-size treats show a balance of flavors that sets them apart from the cloying, oily specimens one ordinarily comes across. And since La Bague de Kenza is highly popular, their turnover is high and their selection correspondingly fresh.

Don't worry if you don't know any of the names: the staff often caters to novices, so you can simply smile and point, or ask for an assortment. But just to get you started, I can recommend the *cornes de gazelle*, the *skandriates*, the *doigts de Kenza*, the *cornets aux amandes*, and, of course, the *baqlavas*.

Most of the boutique is devoted to sweets, but don't overlook the savory section close to the register: the *coca* and *bourek* (flaky or crisp turnovers filled with meat or vegetables), *m'hajeb* (bell pepper and tomato crêpe), and semolina breads deserve just as much of your palate's consideration.

The Rue Saint-Maur location is attached to a *salon de thé*, where one can sample some of the pastries with a glass of piping hot mint tea. The owners have issued a beautiful and poetic cookbook called *Les douceurs de Kenza*, and all the ingredients you need to make these recipes can be found at their baking supplies shop.

106 rue Saint-Maur, 11th. CROSS STREET: Rue Oberkampf. Mº Parmentier. PHONE: 01 43 14 93 15. Mon–Thu and Sat–Sun 9am–10pm; Fri 2:30pm–10pm.

Alternate locations:

Le Faubourg de Kenza. 173 rue du Faubourg Saint-Antoine, 11th. CROSS STREET: Rue de la Forge Royale. Mº Faidherbe-Chaligny. PHONE: 01 43 41 47 02. Mon–Thu and Sat–Sun 9am–8pm; Fri 2:30pm–9:30pm.

Les Secrets de Kenza. 84 rue Jean-Pierre Timbaud, 11th. CROSS STREET: Rue Saint-Maur. Mº Parmentier. NO TELEPHONE. Tue–Sun 2pm–12am.

For more North African pastries, visit **La Ruche à Miel**, a restaurant and salon de thé close to the Marché d'Aligre, or **Les Doigts de Fée**, a deli and pastry shop at the top of the Belleville hill.

La Ruche à Miel. 19 rue d'Aligre, 12th. CROSS STREET: Rue Crozatier. Mº Ledru-Rollin. PHONE: 01 43 41 27 10. Tue–Thu and Sun 9am–7:30pm; Fri–Sat 9am–10:30pm.

Les Doigts de Fée. 356 rue des Pyrénées, 20th. CROSS STREET: Rue Levert. Mº Jourdain. PHONE: 01 43 49 12 34. Mon–Sun 9am–9pm.

Blé Sucré
Pastry shop

Fabrice Le Bourdat used to be a pastry sous-chef at Le Bristol (see page 66), and this is where he met his wife, the charming Céline. But after years of serving a *palace* hotel clientele, they decided they would rather fly on their own wings, and they purchased a bakery on the pretty Square Trousseau, not far from the Marché d'Aligre (see page 145).

With their pedigree, they could have shot for the stars and made a killing with sophisticated and overpriced pastries. Instead, they opted for a more democratic approach, selling perfectly done classics (*baba au rhum*, strawberry or lemon tartlet, glazed madeleines, flan, coffee éclair, Mont Blanc, *tarte au sucre* . . .) and a handful of creations (a rice pudding with apricots; a *dôme* of almonds, flaked praline, and chocolate; a caramel *religieuse*) for accessible prices. (Pastries run from 2.50 to 5€.)

Blé Sucré also sells good chocolates—I have fallen head over heels for the chocolate bar with crunchy specks of salted caramel—and sandwiches (5.50€ formule for a sandwich, a drink, and a dessert).

7 rue Antoine Vollon, 12th. CROSS STREET: Rue du Faubourg Saint-Antoine. Mº Ledru-Rollin. PHONE: 01 43 40 77 73. Tue–Sat 7am–7:30pm; Sun 7am–2pm.

Pâtisserie de Choisy
Pastry shop, see page 111

Pâtisserie de Saison
Pastry shop, see page 111

Baillardran
Pastry shop

It might not feel right to look for a pastry shop in a train station, yet you will have to dive into the depths of Gare Montparnasse to find the Parisian branch of Baillardran, the famous *canelé* maker from Bordeaux.

The canelé is a small pastry that looks like a section of a Roman tower, short and squat with vertical ridges. If you've never had one before, you're in for a sweet discovery: flavored with rum and vanilla, it is crusty and deeply caramelized on the outside, moist and chewy on the inside.

This emblematic specialty from Bordeaux has been around since the eighteenth century, but it has gained national popularity over the past decade. Canelés can now be found in many Parisian bakeries, but Baillardran remains the best source: their canelés are still baked in copper molds the old-fashioned way, and they let you choose how you want them done—from light gold to dark brown, the darker the crustier. (The shop sells copper canelé molds, but E. Dehillerin has better prices; see page 273.)

Gare Montparnasse, Level C, facing platform 13, plus two burgundy-and-gold carts, 14th. Mᵒ Montparnasse. PHONE: 01 40 47 99 24. WEB: www.baillardran.com. Mon–Sun 9am–7:30pm.

Des Gâteaux et du Pain
Pastry shop / Bakery

It is still unusual to find a woman at the head of a Paris restaurant, and female pastry chefs are even more of a rarity, but it would be silly to reduce the talk on Claire Damon's pastry shop to a gender discussion. Yes, she is a fresh-faced, bright-smiling woman in her early thirties, but what's more important is that she spent time training with the best (including Pierre Hermé) before opening her own boutique to sell, as the name plainly indicates, cakes and bread.

While I don't approve of the extra sleek design and dramatic lighting (with such a deliciously candid name, why not stick to a deliciously candid décor?), Damon's goods demonstrate haute-pastry skills and cleverly injected doses of creativity, capturing the spirit of classics, and casting a contemporary light on them.

The pastry case—inexplicably hidden at the back of the shop—reveals an eye-catching procession that passes taste tests with flying colors: a salted butter caramel *religieuse,* a raspberry rhubarb tartlet, a violet Saint-Honoré, a milk chocolate and hazelnut éclair, an apricot blancmange, a verbena and berry mille-feuille . . . (Pastries around 4€.)

Equally impressive is the bakery side of the boutique, presenting a line of artisanal bread, *viennoiseries,* cakes and cookies; try the pistachio and cherry mini-cakes and the tubs of *spéculoos.*

63 boulevard Pasteur, 15th. CROSS STREET: Rue Mizon. M° Pasteur. PHONE: 01 45 38 94 16. Wed–Mon 7:30am–8:30pm; Closed on Tuesday.

Lecureuil
Pastry shop

Laurence Edeler spent her childhood in her parents' chocolate boutique and she married a pastry chef, so when she saw that this pastry shop on rue de Lévis was going out of business, she rose to the challenge.

She renovated the place to give it a fresh look, classy yet joyful, and with her husband's help, she created a range of pastries in the same spirit as the new décor: contemporary, colorful, and thoroughly appealing.

The fruit-based creations are particularly successful—the caramelized pear tart, the raspberry *dôme* flavored with violet and pistachio, the mango and passion fruit mousse in a white chocolate casing—and the smaller confections make for adorable snacks or food gifts—moist little cakes shaped like corks, whirligig cookies, and petits fours that seem right out of a children's book.

The display case includes a savory section, too, with fresh salads, sandwiches, and quiches that can be packed for a picnic.

96 rue de Lévis, 17th. CROSS STREET: Rue Cardinet. M° Malesherbes or Villiers. PHONE: 01 42 27 28 27. WEB: www.lecureuil.fr. Tue–Fri 9am–7pm; Sat 9am–8pm; Sun 10am–1pm.

Arnaud Larher
Pastry shop / Chocolate shop

At age twenty-five, after working with Pierre Hermé at Fauchon for a few years, Arnaud Larher left to open his own pastry and chocolate shop in the back of the Montmartre hill. At such a young age and in such a residential area, that was one leap of faith, but more than a decade later, his customers still prove him right.

Whether from the neighborhood or from all the way across the city, they come for his line of refurbished classics (*baba au rhum* with chocolate liqueur, orange mille-feuille, chocolate tartlet with cacao nib *nougatine*), his chocolates (I am very fond of his filled *tablettes*), his ice creams and sorbets, or his pastry creations: most of them involve chocolate in flattering pairings, such as the Suprême, a delicate construction of chocolate cake, blackberry and tea crème brûlée, and blackberry chocolate mousse.

Of particular note is his talent for slipping just the right amount of salt in his confections, as illustrated by his jarred caramel spread, his sweet and savory nut mix (addictive stuff, that), his milk chocolate *tablette* filled with crunchy *praliné,* or his crisp chocolate cookies.

53 rue Caulaincourt, 18th. CROSS STREET: Rue Juste Métivier. Mᵒ Lamarck-Caulaincourt. PHONE: 01 42 57 68 08. WEB: www.arnaud-larher.com. Tue–Sat 9am–7:30pm.

La Petite Rose
Salon de thé / Pastry shop, see page 128

Le Stübli
Salon de thé / Lunch / Pastry shop, see page 129

Tendresse aux Pommes
Alsatian Bread Pudding with Apples

Adapted from a recipe by Christophe Vasseur, bread baker at Du Pain et des Idées (see page 153).

~

One of the most striking characteristics of Christophe Vasseur's bakery is the limited number of goods on offer each day. Not only does this ensure their irreproachable freshness—yesterday's pastries have all been sold out, so you won't find them on today's shelves—but it also casts a brighter light on each item: had it been squished somewhere in the middle of a crowded pastry case, I'm not sure I'd have noticed the *tendresse aux pommes,* and what a loss that would have been.

Inspired by a treat that Vasseur's nanny used to bake for him, this guileless confection can be described as the Alsatian bread pudding, a poor man's cake designed to use up leftover bread—its original name, *bettelman,* means "beggar" in the dialect of Alsace. Warmly sweet and softly spiced, Vasseur's rendition offers a lightly crusty top and a moist, tender heart; I find it the ideal snack on a gray afternoon.

$1^1/_3$ to $1^2/_3$ cups (320 to 400 ml) milk, depending on the dryness of the brioche

$^1/_2$ cup (100 g) sugar, plus extra for sprinkling

1 vanilla bean, split lengthwise (substitute 1 teaspoon pure vanilla extract)

1 teaspoon ground cinnamon

2 tablespoons dark rum

A pinch fine sea salt

$^1/_4$ cup (25 g) dark raisins

2 crisp and juicy apples, about 10 ounces (280 g) each, such as Golden
   Delicious, Granny Smith, Gala, or Jonagold, peeled and diced
12 ounces (340 g) stale brioche, challah bread, or croissants, cut in bite-
   size cubes
Unsalted butter for greasing
2 large eggs, lightly beaten

Serves 6
Resting time: 8 to 24 hours

1. Combine 1⅓ cups (320 ml) of the milk with the sugar and the vanilla bean
in a medium saucepan. Cover and bring to a simmer over medium heat.
Remove from the heat and let cool, uncovered, for 5 minutes.

2. In a large bowl, combine the milk mixture, cinnamon, rum, salt, raisins, and
apples. Add the brioche and stir well to combine. If the brioche is quite dry
and seems to soak up all the milk, add the remaining ⅓ cup (80 ml) milk.
Cover with plastic wrap and refrigerate for at least 8 hours, and preferably
an entire day, stirring the mixture again once or twice in the intervening
time.

3. When ready to bake the bettelman, preheat the oven to 350°F (180°C).
Grease a glass or ceramic medium baking dish (such as a 10-inch [25-cm] oval
dish or an 8-by-8-inch [20-by-20-cm] square dish) with butter, sprinkle with
sugar, and shake the dish to coat.

4. If you used a whole vanilla bean, fish it out of the brioche mixture, scrape
the seeds with the tip of a knife, return the seeds to the bowl, and discard
the bean (or: rinse, let dry completely, and slip in a jar of sugar or a bottle
of olive oil to flavor it). Add the eggs and stir well to combine. Pour into the
prepared dish, level the surface with a spatula, sprinkle lightly with sugar,

and put in the oven to bake for 35 to 45 minutes, until the top is set and golden brown.

5. Let cool and serve, slightly warm or at room temperature, on its own for breakfast or tea, with vanilla ice cream or *crème anglaise* (vanilla custard sauce) for dessert.

VARIATIONS: Bettelman can also be made with cherries and kirsch, instead of apples and rum. You can also add ½ cup (80 g) chocolate chips (add them along with the eggs), or use chopped dates, figs, or prunes in place of the raisins. You can also substitute leftover baguette or country-style bread for part of the brioche. The bettelman can be baked in muffin molds; reduce the baking time to 25 minutes.

chocolatiers / chocolate shops

The many chocolate shops of Paris—almost three hundred at last count—were not all created equal, and the quality of their goods varies greatly. I've chosen to highlight the work of artisans who make chocolate bonbons by hand, using high-quality, fresh, natural ingredients, and chocolate that is made with cocoa butter only (see page 185). This approach has a price, but I believe in eating a smaller amount of the good stuff rather than gorging on the mediocre.

Because they position themselves as luxury goods stores, the best chocolate shops in the city tend to go for the jewelry store ambiance, complete with snooty shopkeepers. Don't be intimidated: step in, say *bonjour,* and take all the time you need to study the goods (with your eyes rather than your hands).

The chocolate bars and packaged assortments are placed on self-service shelves, while the chocolate bonbons and confections are presented on a glass-cased display that is off-limits to customers: a gloved attendant will take your order and slip the items in a cellophane bag, if you're just buying a few, or in a box. In some shops, each chocolate bonbon is clearly labeled with its name and flavoring; in others, you will need to have them described to you as you make your selection.

The price of chocolate bonbons is most often indicated by weight; depending on their size, 100 grams (3$^{1}/_{2}$ ounces) will get you nine to twelve pieces.

Croissant au beurre from Vandermeersch (page 154)

Pear and chocolate cake-tart from
La Boulangerie par Véronique Mauclerc (page 159)

Caramel religieuse from Des Gâteaux
et du Pain (page 174)

Canistrelli
Châtaigne Miel

KG 14€90

Corsican cookies from
U Spuntinu (page 212)

Chocolate bark from
L'Étoile d'Or (page 195)

Burgundy snails from La Maison de l'Escargot (page 214)

Jean-Paul Hévin
Chocolate shop / Salon de thé

A Meilleur Ouvrier de France circa 1986, Jean-Paul Hévin adopts the purist's approach in his chocolate creations: he uses nothing but the best quality of ingredients, and sticks to flavor combinations that exalt the chocolate, rather than reduce it to a mere covering. The resulting bites display a balance and a smoothness seldom found elsewhere.

Although his cheese-flavored *chocolats apéritifs* provide an atypical taste experience, to say the least, it is for the classics that I turn to Hévin: the plain ganaches and pralines (9.10€/100 g), the truffles and chocolate *tablettes*, the *orangettes* and the *mendiants*.

The rue Saint-Honoré boutique has a *salon de thé* upstairs, where you can update your blog (astonishingly enough, it offers a WiFi Internet access) as you enjoy a cup of hot chocolate (the mix is for sale at the shop), a pastry, or a trio of chocolate macarons. The chocolate éclairs (3.40€) are textbook perfect, but they are available on Saturdays only and they sell out at lightning speed.

231 rue Saint-Honoré, 1st. CROSS STREET: Rue de Castiglione. M° Tuileries.
PHONE: 01 55 35 35 96. WEB: www.jphevin.com. Mon–Sat 10am–7:30pm; SALON
DE THÉ: Mon–Sat noon–7pm; LUNCH SERVICE: noon–2:30pm.
Alternate locations:
3 rue Vavin, 6th. CROSS STREET: Rue d'Assas. M° Notre-Dame des Champs.
PHONE: 01 43 54 09 85. Tue–Sat 10am–7pm.
23 bis avenue de la Motte-Picquet, 7th. CROSS STREET: Rue Bougainville.
M° École Militaire. PHONE: 01 45 51 77 48. Tue–Sat 10am–7:30pm.

Sadaharu Aoki
Chocolate shop / Pastry shop, see page 165

Christian Constant
Chocolate shop / Pastry shop / Ice cream / Salon de thé, see page 48

CHOCOLATES AND CONFECTIONS

Ballotin: a boxed assortment of chocolate bonbons. Chocolate shops stock pre-made assortments, but you can also have a salesperson fill one to your specifications.

Bonbon de chocolat: a bite-size chocolate filled with ganache, *praliné,* or marzipan; it is also referred to, more simply, as *un chocolat.* A quality bonbon should be chocolate-dipped rather than molded, and the chocolate casing should be thin.

Bouchée de chocolat: an oversize *bonbon de chocolat,* large enough to fill your hand (and your mouth).

Calisson: an almond-shaped confection of marzipan flavored with candied melon, topped with a crisp sugar coating. It is a specialty from Aix-en-Provence.

Chocolat de couverture: chocolate that has been tempered so it will melt evenly and have a shiny finish when it sets. This is the chocolatier's raw material.

Éclats de fève de cacao or **grué de cacao:** cacao nibs, i.e., flecks of roasted cacao beans, not sweetened or processed any further, and added for crunch to chocolate bars and bonbons.

Florentin: a small disk of caramelized almonds and candied fruits dipped in chocolate.

Ganache: a smooth mixture of chocolate and cream or butter, which may be infused with other flavors. Ganache can be dipped in chocolate to form bonbons that are also referred to as ganaches.

Guimauve: the French marshmallow.

Marron glacé: a chestnut that is cooked in several baths of sugar syrup until meltingly tender.

Mendiant: a disk of chocolate topped with dried fruit and nuts.

Nougatine: grilled, chopped almonds cooked in a light caramel. As it hardens, the mixture can be molded to form crunchy cups or sheets.

Orangette: a chocolate-dipped strip of candied orange peel.

Pâte à tartiner: a sweet, spreadable paste.

Pâte d'amande: marzipan, i.e., blanched almonds ground with sugar. *Pâte d'amande* is used as a filling for bonbons and *calissons,* or to sculpt little figures.

Pâte de fruit: fruit paste, i.e., sweetened fruit purée reduced to a firm and chewy consistency, cut into cubes, and rolled in sugar.

Pâte de pistache: similar to *pâte d'amande,* but made with pistachios.

Pralin or **praliné:** a mixture of almonds and hazelnuts that are grilled, ground with caramelized sugar, and combined with chocolate. If the texture is coarse, it is referred to as *praliné à l'ancienne* (old-fashioned). *Pralin* can be used as a filling for chocolate bonbons and in pastries.

Praline: a chocolate bonbon filled with *praliné.* Also: a whole almond that's been cooked in sugar so it develops a caramelized coating when it cools.

Rocher: a chocolate bonbon filled with *praliné* and specked with chopped almonds.

Tablette de chocolat: a chocolate bar, i.e., a thin and flat rectangle of chocolate, usually divided into squares, and sometimes flavored, stuffed, or studded with other ingredients.

Pierre Hermé
Chocolate shop / Pastry shop, see page 168

Pierre Marcolini
Chocolate shop

Belgium's most acclaimed chocolate artisan has made a name for himself on the Parisian scene. This is no small feat when you consider how chocolate-chauvinistic the French can be, the common perception being that Belgian chocolates are too rich, too sweet, and, well, a bit pedestrian.

But Marcolini is a different story, and the finesse of his chocolates makes him an undisputed member of the chocolatiers' pantheon. His chocolate bonbons are made from carefully sourced ingredients, and the sobriety of their looks belies the vividness of their flavor: try the Violette (violet-infused ganache), the Cendrillon (orange-flavored ganache topped with *nougatine*), the Quatre Épices (spiced caramel), and the Palets Fins (super-thin ganache-filled bites). Limited edition flavors join the classics at every season, such as red currant, rose, or mango (9.30€/100 g).

His square chocolate bars are outstanding (try the smooth Fleur de Cacao, 85 percent cacao solids without a trace of bitterness), as are his *pâtes de fruits* and his chocolate-covered *guimauves*. Marcolini also sells tins of chocolate chips to be melted into a hot chocolate, and an enormous chocolate bar aptly named Le Familial; both make good gifts.

89 rue de Seine, 6th. CROSS STREET: Rue Clément. M° Odéon.
PHONE: 01 44 07 39 07. Mon 2pm–6pm; Tue–Sat 10:30am–7pm.

Jean-Charles Rochoux
Chocolate shop

After working as Chaudun's right-hand man for many years (see page 187), Jean-Charles Rochoux set up his own shop on rue d'Assas, a modern but inviting boutique, in which the young and bespectacled artisan can often be seen on his way in or out of the downstairs lab.

COCOA BUTTER

In order to make chocolate, cacao beans first need to be fermented, roasted, and ground. The resulting substance is then separated into the two basic ingredients of chocolate: cocoa solids (*pâte de cacao*) and cocoa butter (*beurre de cacao*).

Dark chocolate is made by adding cocoa butter and sugar to cocoa solids, and the ratio of cocoa solids in the finished product is indicated as a percentage on chocolate *tablettes*. Milk chocolate is made by combining cocoa solids with cocoa butter, powdered milk, and sugar; white chocolate by combining cocoa butter with powdered milk and sugar.

Since 2000, a European regulation has allowed chocolate makers to replace the pricey cocoa butter with other kinds of vegetable fat, including hydrogenated palm oil. This regulation was voted at the instigation of industrial chocolate makers and to the outrage of chocolate artisans, who are adamant that their chocolate be made with cocoa butter only.

This means that cheap chocolate has become cheaper, and that the gap that sets it apart from quality artisanal chocolate has become wider. If you buy chocolate from the supermarket or an untrusted source, pay attention to the ingredients list, and insist that only *pur beurre de cacao* chocolate pass your lips.

Just like his former master, Rochoux assembles his own *chocolat de couverture* from different origins, and his thinly coated chocolate bonbons (starting at 8.40€/100 g) shine with the freshness and quality of the ingredients he uses. I am particularly fond of the *rocher,* the pistachio paste bonbon, the fresh basil ganache, the salted caramel bonbon (Rochoux adds *fleur de sel* at the last possible moment so the flecks won't have time to melt), and the pepper ganache, made with five varieties of peppercorn.

The chocolate *tablettes,* made of dark or milk chocolate, are generously crowned with caramelized hazelnuts or pistachios, *nougatine,* candied apricots or orange rind, or flavored with spices. Jean-Charles Rochoux also concocts a tablette stuffed with a different seasonal fruit every Saturday: caramelized apples or clementine segments in the winter, fresh cherries or peaches in the summer (7.20€).

16 rue d'Assas, 6th. CROSS STREET: Rue de Rennes. M° Rennes or Saint-Sulpice. PHONE: 01 42 84 29 45. Mon 2:30pm–7:30pm; Tue–Sat 10:30am–7:30pm.

Patrick Roger
Chocolate shop

Patrick Roger has a knack for making his window displays spring to life like so many scenes from a multicolored fantasia: life-size chocolate penguins cohabit with cartoon-like cows, giant bubble fish, and adorably expressive marzipan creatures. The thirty-something chocolatier, who earned the MOF title (see page 156) in 2000, is as much an artist as he is an artisan—a wildly creative one at that, who just chooses to work with chocolate where others might opt for clay.

Beyond his extravagant sculptures and whimsical ideas, Roger's principal focus remains the taste experience, and his chocolates and confections are flawless. Favorites include the semiliquid caramel bites, the lime and passion fruit ganache, the brightly colored *cabochons* (half-globes of crisp chocolate filled with ganache and caramel), and the clusters of chocolate-coated, caramelized almond slivers. (Chocolate bonbons: 9€/100 g.)

108 boulevard Saint-Germain, 6th. CROSS STREET: Rue Hautefeuille. M° Odéon. PHONE: 01 43 29 38 42. WEB: www.patrickroger.com. Mon–Sat 10:30am–7:30pm.

Alternate location:

45 avenue Victor Hugo, 16th. CROSS STREET: Rue Paul Valéry. M° Victor Hugo or Kléber. PHONE: 01 45 01 66 71. Tue–Sat 11am–7:30pm.

Patrice Chapon
Chocolate shop

After working as a pastry chef at Le Crillon (see page 64) and as an ice cream maker at Buckingham Palace, Patrice Chapon finally settled on chocolate as his medium of expression, and his line of chocolate bonbons treads a tasteful line between the classic and the inventive.

The plain, single-origin ganaches are exquisite, as is the pear and almond milk ganache, the *dôme* (a lightly salted praline in a *nougatine* shell), the cashew praline, the litchee and violet caramels, or the *palet,* a thin disk of chocolate filled with Xeres- or Sauternes-flavored ganache that you're instructed to place on your tongue, where it will slowly melt. And because Chapon is not the most renowned of chocolatiers (yet), his prices are still reasonable, at 7.50€/10 0g.

Both boutiques are charming, but I have a preference for the rue du Bac location: the shopkeeper is particularly kind, and antique chocolate molds line an entire wall. Chapon is one of the artisans who team up with fashion designers to create dresses made of chocolate for the Salon du Chocolat every year (see page 280).

69 rue du Bac, 7th. CROSS STREET: Rue de Grenelle. M° Rue du Bac. PHONE: 01 42 22 95 98. WEB: www.chocolat-chapon.com. Tue–Sat 10am–12:45pm and 3pm–7pm.

Alternate location:

52 avenue Mozart, 16th. CROSS STREET: Rue du Ranelagh. M° Ranelagh. PHONE: 01 42 24 05 05. Tue–Sat 10am–12:45pm and 3pm–7pm.

Michel Chaudun
Chocolate shop

Entering Michel Chaudun's chocolate shop feels like stepping inside a chocolate truffle—the atmosphere warm, the décor all rich shades of brown, the air heavy with voluptuous scents.

A true chocolate artisan, Chaudun creates his own blends of chocolate out of nine different origins that he assembles to reach the gustatory profiles he's looking for. His chocolate bites, which remain within the realm of classics, show superb balance and a subtle dosage of flavoring ingredients. Favorites include the cacao nib ganache, the roasted sesame and peanut praline, and the bittersweet truffle flavored with *fine de Champagne* brandy. (Chocolate bonbons: 9.40€/100 g.) Another of Chaudun's not-to-be-missed specialties is the *pavé* (paving stone), a diminutive cube of cocoa-dusted

ganache that turns to silk on your tongue and begs for all of its siblings to be eaten, too.

As seriously talented as he is, Michel Chaudun is not without a sense of humor, as demonstrated by his Dadaist display of chocolate sculptures: soccer balls, baby bottles, *saucissons,* a horseshoe, a sphinx, and even an electric drill.

149 rue de l'Université, 7th. CROSS STREET: Rue Malar. M° Invalides. PHONE: 01 47 53 74 40. Mon–Wed and Fri–Sat 9:15am–7pm; Thu 9:15am–noon and 1pm–7pm.

Debauve & Gallais
Chocolate shop

The good Monsieur Sulpice Debauve was a pharmacist who believed in the health benefits of chocolate. His "remedies," which he supplied to four successive kings of France, made him wildly famous in the early nineteenth century and led him to open some sixty retail shops all over the country. Only two remain in France today, both of them in Paris: the rue des Saints-Pères boutique dates back to 1818, while the rue Vivienne location was built in the late nineteenth century.

Two centuries of chocolate history have resulted in a range of classic ganaches and old-fashioned pralines (11€/100 g) that display clear-spoken flavors, and a moderate use of sugar. Les Pistoles de Marie-Antoinette (thin disks of chocolate from different origins) make for a fun chocolate tasting party, and the glazed chestnuts are remarkable.

The packaging is old-fashioned but not overstatedly so, and this will please those who want to bring home a taste of the *ancien régime*.

30 rue des Saint-Pères, 7th. CROSS STREET: Rue Perronet. M° Saint-Germain des Prés or Rue du Bac. PHONE: 01 45 48 54 67. WEB: www.debauve-et-gallais.com. Mon–Sat 9:30am–7pm.

Alternate location:

33 rue Vivienne, 2nd. CROSS STREET: Rue Feydeau. M° Bourse or Richelieu-Drouot. PHONE: 01 40 39 05 50. Mon–Sat 9:30am–6:30pm.

La Maison du Chocolat
Chocolate shop / Pastry shop

Because La Maison du Chocolat has boutiques all over the world now—Paris, London, New York City, Tokyo—and because artisanal producers often spread themselves thin when they overexpand, I tend to approach their goods with a touch of suspicion, bracing myself for a possible decline in quality. But the freshness and zing of these chocolates never disappoint, even as the charismatic and perfectionist founder, Robert Linxe, gradually hands the reins over to his successors.

The chocolate lover should also appreciate them in light of the pioneering role Linxe has played over the past three decades in the history of haute couture chocolate. He was the first to open an all-chocolate boutique in

1977 and, in so doing, he cleared the path and set his exacting standards for the young guard, from Hévin to Roger and Marcolini (see pages 181, 186, and 184).

Among the chocolate bonbons (9.50€/100 g), I favor the Caracas (plain ganache), the Arneguy (citrus zest ganache), and the Jolika (pistachio paste with a hint of kirsch), but the seasonal additions to the range (vine peach, mirabelle plum) are always worth a taste. I also like the caramel truffles and the Lingots Arriba, super thin squares of robust ganache covered in chocolate. The line of pastries includes faultless chocolate tartlets and éclairs.

All confections are handcrafted by a staff of fifty in a laboratory just outside of Paris, before they are delivered to the Paris boutiques or shipped abroad. This means that the chocolates sold in Tokyo or New York are the same as the ones sold in Paris, but they've come a much longer way.

225 rue du Faubourg Saint-Honoré, 8th. CROSS STREET: Rue de la Néva. Mº Ternes. PHONE: 01 42 27 39 44. WEB: www.lamaisonduchocolat.com. Mon–Sat 10:30am–7pm; Sun 10am–1pm.

Alternate locations:

19 rue de Sèvres, 6th. CROSS STREET: Boulevard Raspail. Mº Sèvres-Babylone. PHONE: 01 45 44 20 40. Mon–Sat 9:30am–7:30pm; Sun 10am–2pm.

8 boulevard de la Madeleine, 9th. CROSS STREET: Rue Godot de Mauroy. Mº Madeleine. PHONE: 01 47 42 86 52. Mon–Sat 10am–7:30pm.

L'Étoile d'Or
Chocolate shop / Candy shop, see page 195

Jacques Genin
Chocolate shop

This gifted chocolatier has chosen to remain undercover. He exercises his magic in an anonymous lab in the 15th arrondissement, and sells the fruits of his labor to upscale hotels and restaurants in the city (who rarely rush to tell you their chocolates aren't made in-house), to companies who give them away as corporate gifts, and to individuals who are willing to accept the two conditions: one, call ahead to set up an appointment, and two, place a minimum order of one kilogram (a little over two pounds).

The simplest option is to ask for a one-kilo assortment of everything he'll be making on the day you come: this should result in a combination of ganaches (plain or flavored), pralines, nougats, fruit pastes, light-as-air *guimauves,* and some of the best caramels you'll sample in your entire life, especially if you get the mango and passion fruit ones.

You do need to find a few friends to split the bounty with while it's fresh, but somehow I doubt that will be a problem. And at 60€ a kilo, this is, hands down, the best chocolate bang you'll get for your buck.

A limited selection of Jacques Genin's chocolates and caramels are for sale at the pastry shop Pain de Sucre (see page 165) in the fall and winter, and Yves Camdeborde (see page 49) serves them with coffee at Le Comptoir—and credits him on the menu.

18 rue Saint-Charles, 15th. CROSS STREET: Rue du Docteur Finlay. M° Dupleix.
PHONE: 01 45 77 29 01. By appointment only.

Arnaud Larher
Chocolate shop / Pastry shop, see page 176

Tarte-Gâteau Poire Chocolat
Pear and Chocolate Cake-Tart

The first time I visited Véronique Mauclerc's bakery (see page 159), I bought one of her pear and chocolate tartlets, and trotted on to the nearby Parc des Buttes-Chaumont. Once I'd climbed up a hill and found the ideal bench—in the semi-shade, amid the twitter of birds, with a faraway view of the Sacré-Cœur—I unwrapped my rustic-looking tartlet, took a bite, and beamed to myself.

I have eaten a fair amount of chocolate tarts in my life, but this one was a ravishing novelty: its brittle, not-too-sweet crust held a fudgy and slightly leavened chocolate filling—rather than the classic layer of ganache—as if it couldn't quite decide whether to be a tart or a cake. The following recipe is a re-creation of what I've come to think of as, quite simply, a *tarte-gâteau*.

FOR THE PÂTE BRISÉE
1 large egg yolk (save the white for the filling below)
3 tablespoons plus 1 teaspoon (50 ml) ice-cold water
A pinch fine sea salt
2 tablespoons (25 g) sugar
2 cups (250 g) all-purpose flour, sifted, plus extra for sprinkling
8 tablespoons (1 stick) plus 1 tablespoon (125 g total) unsalted butter, diced, plus a pat for greasing

FOR THE PEARS
2 tablespoons (25 g) sugar
3 tablespoons (45 ml) dark rum (optional)
2 pears, ripe but still firm, about 1 pound (450 g) total (choose a variety that will keep its shape when poached, such as Anjou, Bartlett, Bosc, or Winter Nellis)

   3 tablespoons (25 g) all-purpose flour
   $1/4$ teaspoon baking powder
   A pinch fine sea salt
   $4^1/2$ ounces (125 g) good-quality bittersweet chocolate
   7 tablespoons (75 g) unsalted butter, diced
   $1/2$ cup (100 g) sugar
   1 large egg
   1 large egg white (saved from the crust recipe above)

Serves 12
Resting time: 1 hour

1. Prepare the crust. In a small bowl, beat together the egg yolk, water, salt, and sugar, and set aside. Combine the flour and butter in the bowl of a food processor, and process at low speed for 10 seconds, until the mixture forms coarse crumbs. Pour in the egg yolk mixture all at once and process for a few more seconds, just until the dough comes together. If it is too dry, add a little more ice-cold water, 1 teaspoon at a time, until it reaches the right consistency. Turn out on a lightly floured work surface and gather into a ball without kneading. Flatten the ball slightly, wrap in plastic, and refrigerate for 30 minutes, or up to a day (if you refrigerate it for more than an hour, let stand at room temperature for 10 minutes before using).

2. While the dough chills, poach the pears. Combine 1 cup water, the sugar, and the rum in a medium saucepan, and bring to a simmer over medium heat. Peel and core the pears. Cut each of them lengthwise into sixths, rather than quarters, in order to get twelve pieces total. Add the pears to the saucepan, bring back to a simmer, and cook for 4 minutes, until tender and slightly translucent. Lift the pears from the syrup cautiously with a slotted spoon, and set aside in a colander to drain. *(continued)*

3. Remove the dough from the refrigerator. Grease an 11- to 12-inch (28- to 30-cm) tart pan with a pat of butter (see Note). Working on a lightly floured work surface with a lightly floured rolling pin, roll the dough out into a 13- to 14-inch (33- to 35-cm) circle and line the pan with it, trimming off the excess dough. Cover loosely with plastic wrap and refrigerate for 30 minutes; this will prevent the dough from shrinking as it bakes. Preheat the oven to 350°F (180°C) and put the tart pan in the oven for 10 minutes.

4. While the crust blind-bakes, prepare the chocolate filling. Combine the flour, baking powder, and salt in a small bowl, and set aside. Melt the chocolate and butter in a double boiler, or in a heatproof bowl set over a pan of simmering water, stirring regularly to combine. Transfer to a medium bowl, add the sugar, and stir with a wooden spoon. Add the egg and egg white, stirring well between each addition. Add the flour mixture and stir again until just combined.

5. Remove the pan from the oven, but leave the heat on. Pour the chocolate filling into the tart shell and even out the surface with a spatula. Arrange the pear pieces over the filling in a sun-ray pattern, the small ends pointing toward the center of the tart. Return to the oven and bake for 20 minutes, until the filling is just set at the center—it will continue to cook as it cools— and the crust is golden. Transfer to a rack and let cool completely before serving, on its own, with a scoop of yogurt gelato, or with a dollop of whipped cream.

NOTE: The recipe can be made in eight 4-inch (12-cm) tartlet molds, rather than one large tart. You should then cut each pear into fourths, rather than sixths, and reduce the baking time of the chocolate filling to 15 minutes.

confiseries / candy shops

France has a rich candy culture, and the smallest town one visits is likely to boast some sort of quirky confection, based on regional ingredients: Negus de Nevers, Babelutte de Lille, Rigolette de Nantes, Bergamote de Nancy, Prasline de Montargis . . .

Old-fashioned in name, flavor, and looks, they often come with a quaint story of how the baker's son accidentally dropped the blueberries in the sugar syrup, or how the pharmacist was, in fact, looking to invent a cure for migraine, or how the candy maker named his creation after his cat.

L'Étoile d'Or
Candy shop / Chocolate shop

Denise Acabo, the pigtailed chatelaine of L'Étoile d'Or, is one of the most novel-worthy vendors I know. Opinionated and exacting, she holds her providers to high standards and stocks nothing but the best. From a customer's perspective, you are not so much visiting a shop as you are let into Denise's gilded boudoir: it is an experience that must be approached with the manners and docility of a guest, and it is best to come when you are not pressed for time.

And as soon as Denise feels that your interest is sincere, that you understand that this shop is her life's work, she will show you around fondly, twirling her tartan skirt around the shop to tell you all about the regional candies she stocks, before she moves on to the most prized items of her collection: Le Roux's salted butter caramels from Quiberon, and the artisanal chocolates Bernachon and his disciple Bernard Dufoux make in Lyon (11.80€/100 g).

Denise's goods are not cheap—such is the price of quality—but if you tell her your budget, however small, she will create an assortment you can afford.

30 rue Pierre Fontaine, 9th. CROSS STREET: Rue de Douai. M° Blanche.
PHONE: 01 48 74 59 55. Mon 3pm–7:30pm; Tue–Sat 11am–7:30pm.

À la Mère de Famille
Candy shop

As its eye-catching façade attests, this candy shop has been in business since 1761, and this makes it the oldest *confiserie* in the city. A veritable temple devoted to all things sweet, its antique shelves and counters are loaded with traditional confections from all over France: crystallized violets, candied fruits, marzipan figures, *pâtes de fruit, calissons,* nougats, pralines, *pains d'épice,* cookies, madeleines . . . Artisanal jams and house-made chocolates complete the selection, and a range of ice creams, available by the tub or on a cone, blooms in the spring and summer.

35 rue du Faubourg Montmartre, 9th. CROSS STREET: Rue de Provence. Mº Cadet or Grands Boulevards. PHONE: 01 47 70 83 69. WEB: www.lameredefamille.com. Mon–Sat 9:30am–8pm; Sun 10am–1pm.

Alternate locations:

39 rue du Cherche-Midi, 6th. CROSS STREET: Rue du Regard. Mº Sèvres-Babylone or Saint-Placide. PHONE: 01 42 22 49 99. Mon 1pm–7:30pm; Tue–Sat 10am–7:30pm.

107 rue Jouffroy d'Abbans, 17th. CROSS STREET: Avenue de Wagram. Mº Courcelles or Wagram. PHONE: 01 47 63 15 15. Mon 1:30pm–7:30pm; Tue–Sat 10am–7:30pm.

glaciers / ice cream shops

As well kept a secret as the Eiffel Tower, Berthillon remains the quintessential destination for the ice cream lover in Paris, but it would be a shame to limit yourself to theirs, for the city offers other sources for artisanal ice creams and sorbets—the winning strategy being to have one a day, from a different provider each time.

Berthillon

Ice cream shop / Salon de thé

Founded over fifty years ago, Berthillon is still in the hands of the original owners, who pride themselves on using the highest grade of ingredients and zero additives. Their artisanal ice creams and sorbets attract crowds of tourists and Parisians alike, who get in line—the sunnier the day, the longer the wait—for a taste of the legendary flavors: vanilla, salted butter caramel, *marron glacé*, praline and pine nut, chocolate (ice cream or sorbet), *fraise des bois*, peach, black currant, pear, blood orange . . .

The scoops are smallish, and I would wish for less sugar in their composition, but the quality is otherwise evident in the fullness of the flavors and the smoothness of the textures. Besides, never has an ice cream parlor benefited from such a splendid location: a *cornet* (3€ for two scoops) adds an extra layer of felicity to a stroll along the banks of Île Saint-Louis.

The Berthillon family has recently opened a *salon de thé* next door, where you can sit down for a cup of ice cream or a pastry. If you find the original location is closed (on Mondays and Tuesdays, and, believe it or not, for six weeks between mid-July and late August), or too crowded, you may turn to the numerous retailers that can be found throughout the island and the city.

29–31 rue Saint Louis en l'Île, 4th. CROSS STREET: Rue des Deux Ponts. M° Pont Marie. PHONE: 01 43 54 31 61. WEB: www.berthillon-glacier.fr. Wed–Sun 10am–8pm.

Pozzetto

Ice cream shop

If Milan-style ice cream is your thing, Pozzetto is bound to sate your hunger for the subtly sweet and the lusciously smooth. Their gelato is made fresh daily from carefully sourced ingredients, with no artificial colorings or flavorings, and it is protected from the heat and light in lidded buckets (*pozzetti* in Italian)—proof that this ice cream maker doesn't let visual seduction compete with taste and texture.

A dozen seasonal choices are available each day, among which you may find Sicilian pistachio, *gianduja* (chocolate and hazelnut), lemon, peach, pear, coconut, or fig, each of them capturing the essence of the flavor to perfection. My favorite, however, is yogurt: they were out of it once, and I looked so crushed that the owner was moved to whip up a fresh batch for me.

There is no limit to the number of flavors one can sample. Buy your ice cream to go, in a cup or a cone (starting from 3€), or take a seat inside, by the window, for a robust cup of Italian coffee and a healthy session of people-watching.

39 rue du Roi de Sicile, 4th. CROSS STREET: Rue du Bourg Tibourg. M° Saint-Paul. PHONE: 01 42 77 08 64. WEB: pozzetto.biz. Mon–Sun 10am–midnight.

Alternate location:

21 rue de Lévis, 17th. CROSS STREET: Rue des Dames. M° Villiers. NO TELEPHONE. Mon–Sun 10am–midnight.

Le Bac à Glaces
Ice cream shop

If you need a refreshing pause after a run through Le Bon Marché, treat yourself to a scoop or two from Le Bac à Glaces, just a block away. Their ice creams and sorbets are made on the premises, and you can either buy a cone to go (4€ for two scoops) or sit down to eat it (6€ for two scoops), preferably at one of the tables on the narrow sidewalk.

The sixteen flavors available for sampling are mostly classics—I recommend the chocolate sorbet, paired with the black currant sorbet or the salted butter caramel ice cream—but their freezer chest hides more creative ones—chocolate and bitter orange, peach and rosemary, coffee and macarons—that may be purchased by the half-liter tub (7 to 10€) or the individual cup (3.40€).

109 rue du Bac, 7th. CROSS STREET: Rue de Babylone. M° Sèvres-Babylone. PHONE: 01 45 48 87 65. WEB: www.bacaglaces.com. Mon–Sun 11am–7pm.

Martine Lambert

Ice cream shop

This is the Parisian outpost of Martine Lambert, a Deauville-based artisan who makes her ice creams and sorbets with top-quality ingredients, milk from Normandy, and the most perfectly ripe fruit. Until you've tasted hers, you haven't really experienced the smooth intensity of a chocolate sorbet, the aromatic richness of a vanilla ice cream, or the wild zing of a mango sorbet.

Her all-natural concoctions (unpasteurized, preservative free, and without colorings) come in over forty flavors, from time-proven classics (strawberry, coconut, pistachio, salted butter caramel) to successful creations (cherry and black currant; grapefruit and ginger; honey with toasted almonds; guava, lime, and strawberry).

About twenty flavors are for sale on any given day, and a rotating selection of fourteen can be sampled in a cup or cone (3.80€ for two scoops). There is nowhere to sit inside the shop, but the nearby rue Cler makes for a pleasant scenery in which to enjoy your ice cream.

192 rue de Grenelle, 7th. CROSS STREET: Rue Valadon. M° École Militaire.

PHONE: 01 45 51 25 30. Wed–Fri 10am–1pm and 3pm–8pm; Sat–Sun 10am–8pm.

La Marquisette

Ice cream shop

La Marquisette isn't in the most attractive of neighborhoods, I'll grant you that, but if you find yourself in Montmartre and in dire need of an ice cream—it happens to the best of us—I suggest you eschew the seventh circle of touristy hell around the place du Tertre and head farther west, beyond the Montmartre cemetery, to where local kids rush after school, brandishing their coins and shrieking with excitement.

La Marquisette has been a local institution for over sixty years, and the range of artisanal ice creams and sorbets includes everyone's favorites (seasonal or exotic fruit sorbets, vanilla, chocolate, coffee, yogurt) as well as unusual flavors (peanut, lemon and lavender, date and walnut, rose, licorice), which you can buy to go (two scoops for 3.50€) or eat inside the little shop.

31 avenue de Saint-Ouen, 17th. CROSS STREET: Rue Fauvet. M° La Fourche.
PHONE: 01 45 22 91 65. Wed–Fri 10am–1pm and 3pm–8pm; Sat–Sun 10am–8pm.

bons produits / specialty shops

When hunting for a particular gourmet item, the Parisian shopper can either turn to the food emporiums listed on page 248, or head directly for the specialist: whether it is honey, truffles, mustard, caviar, snails, or any other delicacy, you can be reasonably confident that there is a shop, somewhere in the city, that has made a specialty of it.

G. Detou
Cooking and baking supplies in bulk

Although it is primarily geared toward professionals, this shop is also open to the public, and it was a favorite destination of my thrifty grandmother's when she had four sweet-toothed sons to feed.

The complete list of goods would fill a phonebook, but on past shopping trips I have walked away with brick-size hunks of *chocolat de couverture,* ganache drops and caramel chips, nuts of all kinds, *praliné* paste and pistachio paste, candied violets, vanilla beans, flower extracts, candied orange peel, pearls of sugar to sprinkle on *chouquettes* (see page 134), thin bars of chocolate to slip into *pains au chocolat,* chestnut flour, and a variety of vinegars, nut oils (pistachio, peanut, hazelnut, hemp, argan), dried mushrooms, and flavored *fleur de sel.*

G. Detou also has great prices on specialty items in regular size—purple mustard from Brives, vegetable confits, canned sardines from Belle-Île, Espelette pepper jelly, verjuice, fish soups, dried Tarbais beans, spreadable *calisson* paste, honey (chestnut, rosemary, orange flower), salted butter caramels, chocolate (Valrhona, Cluizel, or Bonnat)—that travel well and make great food gifts.

And if you like foie gras, you will love Robert Dupérier's: this producer from Les Landes is the purveyor of top chefs across the country, and G. Detou is one of his few Parisian outlets.

58 rue Tiquetonne, 2nd. CROSS STREET: Rue Étienne Marcel. M° Étienne Marcel or Sentier. PHONE: 01 42 36 54 67. Mon–Sat 8:30am–6:30pm.

Mavrommatis
Greek specialties, see page 39

Da Rosa
Luxury goods / Lunch   OUTDOOR SEATING

José Da Rosa's job is to forage across Europe for the cream of the crop in luxury goods. He supplies his finds to gastronomic restaurants and hotels in Paris, and makes them available to the public in his rue de Seine boutique: foie gras, caviar, truffles, aged cheeses and cured hams (including a thirty-month DOP Parmigiano-Reggiano and a thirty-six-month Iberico Bellota Unico), tuna belly, rare oils and chocolate, artisanal butter by Jean-Yves Bordier, spice mixes by Cancale chef Olivier Roellinger . . . Sampler plates can be ordered and eaten in the tasting room upstairs, or out on the streetside terrace (lunch formule: 21€).

62 rue de Seine, 6th. CROSS STREET: Rue de Buci. M° Mabillon. PHONE: 01 40 51 00 09. Mon–Sun 10am–midnight; TASTING ROOM: noon-midnight.

Maison Giraudet
Quenelle dumplings, see page 101

FOOD GIFTS

There are restrictions to what you can bring back into the United States, and all food items should be declared to the customs authorities when you land. (Keep the receipts handy to prove the country of purchase.)

In general, fresh produce is prohibited, as are meat-derived products, and cheeses that have been aged for less than sixty days. Some canned or cured meat preparations (pâtés, duck confit, foie gras . . .) and hard cheeses are sometimes allowed in, but the line is fuzzy, and the decision remains in the hands of the customs agent. Regulations change often, so it's best to check the U.S. Customs and Border Protection Web site (cbp.gov) before you leave, and print the list of approved items.

On this list you will be relieved to find: bottled condiments, herbs, and spices; baked goods, breads, and candy; canned fruits and sauces; fruit jams and vegetable confits; tea and coffee; seeds for planting and consumption (see page 210); and alcohol, in reasonable amounts.

Below are a few suggestions of edible souvenirs that travel well; put any liquid or jelled goods in your checked luggage.

- Olive oil and alternative oils (hazelnut, walnut, pistachio, argan, truffle . . .)
- Mustard (including *moutarde violette de Brives*)
- Jarred *aïoli* (garlic mayonnaise) and *rouille* (a spicy mayonnaise-like sauce traditionally served with fish soups)
- Harissa (Moroccan chili paste)
- Dried white beans (*coco*, Tarbais, *flageolet*)
- Dried mushrooms (*cèpes, morilles, girolles*)
- Dried *fumet de poisson* (fish stock)
- Dried fruits, including quality prunes from Agen or Burgundy

- Jarred *cornichons*
- French farmed caviar
- Soft wheat berries (the Ebly brand, in grocery stores)
- Rice from Camargue
- Chocolate (chocolate bars especially; filled chocolates are fresh goods that should travel in a soft cooler)
- *Pâtes de fruit*
- Salted butter caramels
- Candied flower petals
- Artisanal jams (Christine Ferber's in particular) and vegetable confits
- *Confiture de lait*
- Flavored sugar
- A fresh loaf of bread, whole and unsliced so it will keep longer
- *Pain d'épice*
- Cookies and *sablés*
- Honey
- Chestnut goods: canned chestnut purée, *crème de marron* (sweet chestnut paste), candied chestnuts, chestnut flour, and jarred chestnuts
- Tea and herbal tea
- Roasted coffee beans
- Eau de vie, liqueurs, and apéritifs
- Brandy (Armagnac, Cognac, etc.)
- Spices and *piment d'Espelette*
- Herb blends and *bouquets garnis* (tiny bundles of dried herbs to flavor soups and stews)
- Dried lavender buds (check that it is unsprayed and suitable for cooking)
- *Fleur de sel* and *sel gris* (gray sea salt)

Bellota-Bellota
Spanish specialties / Lunch

This boutique specializes in premium goods imported from Spain: canned and jarred products (tuna belly, smoked anchovies, *piquillo* peppers, gazpacho), cheese, wines, and charcuterie (*lomo, chorizo,* and *pata negra,* the Rolls-Royce of Iberico hams), of the highest quality and well worth the splurge.

Owner Philippe Poulachon is so serious about his ham that he has put his head together with porcelain manufacturer Bernardaud to design a special volcano-shaped plate that brings the slices to the optimal tasting temperature. Take a moment to admire the luxurious selection, and don't miss the *torta de la Serena,* a sheep's milk cheese from Extremadura whose creamy, moussy heart is scooped out fondue-like from the rind, or the chestnut honey madeleines from the French Cévennes.

The shop also functions as a restaurant, where you can enjoy well-assembled tasting plates, but the prices are a bit steep for everyday consumption (20 to 30€) and I prefer to order a *bocadillo* to go—a divine sandwich of *pata negra,* manchego, and tomato confit assembled to order on organic bread (6.50€).

18 rue Jean Nicot, 7th. CROSS STREET: Rue Saint-Dominique. M° Invalides. PHONE: 01 53 59 96 96. Tue–Thu 11am–10:30pm; Fri 11am–11:30pm; Sat 10am–11:30pm.

Alternate location:

Jabugo Iberico & Co. 11 rue Clément Marot, 8th. CROSS STREET: Rue de la Trémoille. M° Alma-Marceau. PHONE: 01 47 20 03 13. Mon–Sat 10am–9pm.

↜ If you're looking for Spanish goods on the Right Bank, head over to **Donostia**, in the 10th arrondissement.

20 rue de la Grange aux Belles, 10th. CROSS STREET: Rue Juliette Dodu. M° Colonel Fabien. PHONE: 01 42 08 30 44. Tue–Sat 11am–8:30pm; Sun 11am–5pm.

Petrossian

Caviar

Since its establishment in 1920, Petrossian, under family management, has devoted its energies to finding and importing über-luxurious goods for the Parisian happy few.

Caviar is the glorious spearhead of that selection; the founding brothers were the first to introduce the French to it. Nowadays the shop carries the classic trio of beluga (large, black grains), osetra (medium, golden brown grains), and sevruga (small, dark gray grains), but also stocks farmed caviar such as the Transmontanus from California (medium, mild-flavored grains) or the French Baeri from the Gironde region (small, intensely flavored grains).

Petrossian also sells smoked fish (wild salmon, eel, trout, white tuna, halibut), fish roe, tarama, and *poutargue* (dried and cured fish roe) from Mauritania or Greece, as well as foie gras, black or white truffles, and a range of vodkas.

Tiptoe around the beautifully kept boutique, and gape in awe at the large tins bulging with the Other Black Gold, as the white-gloved attendants weigh it out for their posh clientele. And if you don't quite have the means to buy some for yourself—an ounce of caviar ranges from 62 to 219€—you can still get a cute mother-of-pearl spoon: it is the traditional caviar tasting instrument and, at 6€, a much more affordable souvenir.

18 boulevard de Latour-Maubourg, 7th. CROSS STREET: Rue de l'Université. M° Invalides. PHONE: 01 44 11 32 22. WEB: petrossian.fr. Mon–Sat 9:30am–8pm.

Maille

Mustard

Enter the temple of Dijon mustard on place de la Madeleine and bow to the might of mustard on tap, poured to order in an earthenware crock. You have a choice between three kinds, made with either dry white wine, Chablis, or

SHOPKEEPERS AND ATTITUDE

If you're accustomed to the cheerful American style of customer service—
"And how may I help you today?"—you may be taken aback by the attitude
of some shopkeepers in Paris, who behave in a less than charming way.

The most important thing to realize is that this attitude has very little to
do with you, where you're from, or what you look like; born-and-raised
Parisians complain about it, too. Once that's established, feelings of annoy-
ance or frustration can be avoided by a better understanding of cultural dif-
ferences.

In general, the French like to be *of service* to their customers, but not *at
their service,* and they are particularly sensitive to situations that make them
feel like nameless servants, reduced to their role as shop attendants.

A snooty or brusque attitude can be the mark of those who feel their job
puts them on an inferior social level; acting in this manner is a way for them
to reassert their position of power. This is particularly common in luxury
goods stores, where the attendants are regularly treated with little consideration by the most pompous of their customers, and where, additionally,
they may feel protective of their goods, guarding them against rank amateurs who might not appreciate their value.

You can't change much about this, but what you can do is be respectful
and polite, and show your appreciation for the help or service they provide,
in the hope that they will loosen up. Smiles go a long way, too.

It is also important to keep in mind that, in France, the act of shopping
is not merely an exchange of money for goods; it is also a social interaction

between the customer and the shopkeeper—and, occasionally, everyone else present in the shop. Just like restaurants (see page 5), shops are not really perceived as public spaces, and the customer is expected to show the same kind of consideration as if he were visiting someone's home and the shopkeeper were his host; this is especially true of small businesses.

When you step inside a shop, you should always greet the attendant by saying *"Bonjour,"* but be reasonably patient if he's in the middle of something and doesn't immediately spring to attention. The smaller the space, the faster you will be asked what it is you're looking for. Feel free to say that you're just looking (*"Je regarde simplement, merci!"*), then move around the shop discreetly.

Take as much time as you need to decide what you'd like to buy. Once the salesperson has started to serve you, you are expected to place your order swiftly and decisively, but don't hesitate to ask for advice if you need it. And if you're not buying anything, just say *"Merci, au revoir!"* before you step out.

I state all this in an effort to make your shopping experience as smooth as possible, but at the end of the day, it is the customer's prerogative to choose whom he's giving his euros to: if you feel you're not treated with the consideration *you* deserve, turn on your heel and walk away. It's happened to me more times than I care to count.

And every once in a while, you'll meet a shop attendant who goes out of his way to help and inform, and who will demonstrate such kindness and such dedication that, teary-eyed with gratitude, you may feel like hugging him (don't).

Chardonnay, and at the first taste you will realize that the real deal, freshly made and tailored to the French palate, is fuller-flavored and hotter than what is shipped abroad. A 100-gram pot (about 3 ounces) will set you back 8€; once it is empty you may bring it back for a cheaper refill.

Beyond the classic range of jarred mustards—plain, *à l'ancienne* (with whole mustard seeds), or flavored (tarragon, shallot, honey)—the shop carries exclusive seasonal variations (fig and coriander, hazelnut and nutmeg, olive and lemongrass) that come in tiny jars and make lovely, affordable gifts. As for the line of country-kitsch mustard pots and accessories, you will enjoy it if you're into that sort of thing.

6 place de la Madeleine, 8th. CROSS STREET: Rue Royale. Mᵒ Madeleine. PHONE: 01 40 15 06 00. WEB: www.maille.com. Mon–Sat 10am–7pm.

La Maison de la Truffe
Truffles / Lunch   VEG-FRIENDLY/OUTDOOR SEATING

La Maison de la Truffe is a tiny shrine erected to the world's most prized fungus. From September until December it honors the *truffe blanche d'Alba,* the white truffle from Piedmont, and from November until March it sings the glories of the true black truffle, a.k.a. *tuber melanosporum* or *truffe du Périgord,* at its peak in January. The price tag is subject to market fluctuations, but you can expect to pay around 65€ for a one-ounce black truffle, and 140€ for a one-ounce white truffle.

When the season of fresh truffles is over, you can still fall back on the high-quality jarred truffles—whole, in pieces, or in shavings—as well as by-products and accessories (truffle juice, truffle purée, truffle sauce, truffle oil, truffle vinegar, truffle slicer), and a range of charcuteries, terrines, and foie gras, some truffled, some not.

CHOOSING A FRESH TRUFFLE

If you're going to trade a wad of bills for a black diamond, you might as well get a first-class specimen: a good truffle should be firm, it should give off a suave (not dank) smell, and its skin should be dry, with no trace of water or furry growth.

If a fragment of the truffle has been cut off (this is how the truffle buyer checks the inside, a process called *le canifage*), it should reveal a chocolate brown flesh with a dense network of white veins. Finally, for the same weight, it is best to buy two small truffles rather than a single large one.

The shop also operates as a restaurant with a small terrace that looks out on place de la Madeleine, and there you can enjoy a few truffle-based dishes: a salad of *mâche*, truffle, and foie gras (35€), a truffle omelet (30€), a white truffle risotto (75€), a truffled Brie (15€) . . .

Remarkably enough, considering the nature of its specialty and its prestigious location, La Maison de la Truffe seems immune to the ambient snobbery; the atmosphere is unpretentious and the staff very kind.

19 place de la Madeleine, 8th. CROSS STREET: Rue Chauveau-Lagarde. M° Madeleine. PHONE: 01 42 65 53 22. WEB: www.maison-de-la-truffe.fr. Mon–Sat 9:30am–9pm; RESTAURANT SERVICE: Mon–Sat noon–8pm.

Olsen
Danish specialties / Lunch

In this boutique you will find Danish goods made by Olsen, an artisanal producer of smoked fish based on the island of Bornholm, in the Baltic Sea. The pale-fleshed wild salmon, salted and smoked over an alderwood fire right off the fishing boats, is remarkably delicate, but smoked fish fans will be tickled by the breadth of the other offerings: sustainably fished wild trout, eel, halibut (*flétan*), codfish (*morue*), and shrimp, as well as farmed tuna, swordfish, and sturgeon (from 4.50 to 7€ for 100 g).

In addition to the range of beers and aquavits—the beverages of choice to pair with smoked fish—Scandinavian delicacies abound: treasures from the sea, mostly (white tarama, fish roe, marinated herring), but also cheese, mustard, and chocolate from Denmark, cold-smoked reindeer from Lapland, flatbread from Sweden, and berry jams from Finland.

The deli case displays *smørrebrød* (open sandwiches), salads (crab and potato; shrimp, cucumber, and apple), and prepared dishes (dill-marinated salmon, *frikadeller* meatballs) that can be purchased to go, or eaten at one of the high tables at the back of the shop. Lunch formules: 15€ and 26€.

6 rue du Commandant Rivière, 8th. CROSS STREET: Place Chassaigne-Goyon. M° Saint-Philippe du Roule. PHONE: 01 45 62 62 28. WEB: www.olsen.fr. Mon–Wed 9am–7:30pm; Tue–Fri 9am–10pm; Sat 10am–7pm.

Pousse-Pousse

Lunch / Seeds and sprouts   VEG-FRIENDLY

Culinary trends come and go, but considerations of nutrition and flavor remain: sprouted seeds are packed with minerals and vitamins, and they make piquant additions to salads, sandwiches, soups, and dips.

To buy some or grow your own, you can turn to Pousse-Pousse, which stocks an unrivaled array of sproutable seeds, grains, and legumes (sunflower, clover, radish, broccoli, lentil, mustard, chickpea), and sets of germinating trays, although a simple colander would suffice.

The entire shop is devoted to live food (*alimentation vivante*), an eating philosophy that promotes the consumption of uncooked, unprocessed, organic foods, the better to benefit from their micronutrients. As such, it also sells different varieties of seaweed, fresh herbs, and fresh pollen, as well as electric dehydrators, juice extractors, and blenders.

Flamboyantly decorated, and much more flattering to one's complexion

THE GOOD SEED

Packaged plant seeds make for great souvenirs to bring home: they're practically weightless, and they allow you to grow French varieties of herbs, fruits, or vegetables in your garden, or on your windowsill.

In particular, keep an eye out for seeds to grow *cornichons, patissons* (a white winter squash), shallots, green beans, pink radishes, salad greens, *mâche* and *mesclun, crapaudine* beetroot, *charentais* melon, and strawberries, including the elusive *fraise des bois* (wild strawberry).

Envelopes of seeds are for sale at hardware stores, at **Établissements Lion** (see page 216), at the gardening store **Truffaut,** and in any of the gardening shops on quai de la Mégisserie, in the 1st arrondissement.

Truffaut. 85 quai de la Gare, 13th. CROSS STREET: Rue Georges Balanchine. M° Quai de la Gare. PHONE: 01 53 60 84 50. WEB: www.truffaut.com. Mon–Sun 10am–8pm.

(Note: The U.S. Customs and Border Protection allows you to bring in seeds for planting and consumption, but you should declare them for inspection. Keep the receipts handy to prove the country of purchase.)

than the average natural foods store, the room offers a single table and a bar, where you can lunch on an assortment of crudités, legumes, and sprouted seeds, and a glass of made-to-order fruit, vegetable, or herb juice (17€ formule). Cooking classes are held monthly; call for details. (The name is a pun on *pousse*, sprout, and *pousse-pousse*, rickshaw.)

7 rue Notre-Dame de Lorette, 9th. CROSS STREET: Rue Saint-Lazare. M° Notre-Dame de Lorette. PHONE: 01 53 16 10 81. Mon–Fri 11am–3:30pm and 4:30pm–7:30pm.

U Spuntinu
Corsican specialties

Henri Ceccaldi is the unofficial ambassador of fine foods from the Island of Beauty. The front of the stage is occupied by cheeses (including a farmhouse *brocciu*) and artisanal charcuterie—*coppa* and *lonzo* (two kinds of smoked cured pork), *figatelli* (a fresh sausage of pork and garlic), donkey or boar *saucissons*, hams, jarred pâtés—but the rest of the shelf space holds treasures, too: chestnut flour and chestnut honey, jams, olive oil, wines, liqueurs, beers (try the Colomba), and even the local Corsica Cola.

The local office crowd flocks in at lunchtime to buy baguette sandwiches assembled from these specialties and, for dessert, the sweet-toothed throw in a single-serving *fiadone* (the Corsican cheesecake) or a handful of *canistrelli* and *cuciole* (cube-shaped cookies, crisp and aromatic; see recipe on page 218).

21 rue des Mathurins, 9th. CROSS STREET: Rue Tronchet. M° Havre-Caumartin or Auber. PHONE: 01 47 42 66 52. Mon–Fri 9am–7pm.

Ronalba
Central European specialties

At the heart of a multicultural neighborhood enriched by successive waves of immigration, Ronalba specializes in Central European gastronomy. Spices and condiments, oils and vinegars, cured meats and sausages, olives and marinated vegetables, fat pickles and grilled nuts, prepared dishes and fresh soups, poppy seed rolls and fresh cheese cakes, vodkas and brandies—this is your chance to taste the finest goods from Poland, Hungary, Romania, and the former Yugoslavia.

60 rue du Faubourg Saint-Denis, 10th. CROSS STREET: Rue du Château d'Eau. M° Château d'Eau. PHONE: 01 47 70 98 38. Tue–Sat 9am–1pm and 4pm–7:30pm; Sun 9am–1pm.

Les Secrets de Kenza
Baking supplies for Algerine pastries, see page 172

Les Abeilles
Honey

Perched on top of the Butte-aux-Cailles hill, Les Abeilles is a shop that specializes in beekeeping gear and beehive-derived goods: beeswax soap, throat-soothing *bonbons au miel,* propolis, royal jelly, and an equally royal selection of honey.

There are dozens of varieties to choose from, produced by bees that feed on different sorts of flowers, trees, and shrubs. Most are available for tasting, and come in medium or small jars: it is thus easy to take an assortment home if you can't decide between the mild and creamy spring honey, the sappy chestnut honey from the Cévennes, the Greek pine honey, and the rare specimens, such as the crystallized heather honey named *callune* or the rhododendron honey from the Pyrénées.

Under no circumstances should you leave the shop without a good chunk of *pain d'épice,* a moist and profoundly aromatic honey spice cake. It will keep for weeks if well wrapped, but I doubt it will last that long.

The owner has been known to close shop and go for a stroll at unpredictable hours of the day; if that is the case when you visit, take this opportunity to explore the bucolic neighborhood while you wait for him to return.

21 rue de la Butte aux Cailles, 13th. CROSS STREET: Rue des Cinq Diamants.
Mº Corvisart. PHONE: 01 45 81 43 48. Tue–Sat 11am–7pm.

Boucherie Desnoyer
Butcher shop

The best breeds of beef (Limousine, Aubrac, Salers) milk-fed veal, lamb from Lozère, pork from Dordogne, Bresse chicken or Gauloise blanche (a white-crested chicken), duck from Challand . . . The spectacular quality of Hugo Desnoyer's meat is well illustrated by the mile-long list of prestigious customers he purveys to, from the Palais de l'Élysée to the best restaurants in the city—L'Astrance, Caïus, Le Sévéro, and Le Verre Volé in particular (see pages 121, 125, 114, and 94).

The thirty-something, passionate butcher works directly with the producers, holds them to the highest standards, and oversees the aging of the meat himself, to ensure optimal flavor. He also sells ready-made meat preparations—roasts studded with various flavorings, *paupiettes*, butterflied poultry—as well as terrines and cured meats.

45 rue Boulard, 14th. CROSS STREET: Rue Mouton-Duvernet. M° Mouton-Duvernet. PHONE: 01 45 40 76 67. WEB: www.regalez-vous.com. Tue–Fri 7am–1pm and 4pm–8pm; Sat 7am–5pm.

Beau et Bon
Miscellaneous

Valérie Gentil quit her job in advertising to open this dollhouse of a boutique, where she highlights the work of French artisans. Her never-ending quest for whimsical edibles sends her on a yearly Tour de France, during which she cherry-picks such gems as saffron meringues, Vin d'Hypocras (a medieval mulled wine), a geranium and green tea jelly, a potato jam, a merlot-flavored salt, or a pink garlic soup, all of them tasted and approved by herself and her family—it's a tough job, but somebody's got to do it.

81 rue Lecourbe, 15th. CROSS STREET: Rue des Volontaires. M° Volontaires or Sèvres-Lecourbe. PHONE: 01 43 06 06 53. WEB: beauetbon.free.fr. Tue–Sat 10:30am–1pm and 3pm–7:30pm; Sun 10:30am–1pm.

La Maison de l'Escargot
Snails

The pink and green neon snail winks at you from a distance, and you know you've come to the right place—an impression that is confirmed when you push the door open and a warm whiff of garlic and parsley greets you.

La Maison de l'Escargot, established in 1894, prides itself on the quality of its fresh wild snails—wild snails as opposed to farmed snails, the culture of which, you may be happy to learn, is called heliciculture. They are delivered live to the shop every week, to be cooked and prepared on the premises.

Two varieties are on offer: the gray-shelled *gris* (gray) from Provence, often hunted for (okay, picked up) at the foot of vines, and the beige-shelled *bourgognes,* which, despite their name, come from Poland or Hungary because wild *bourgogne* snails no longer roam the French countryside.

Each variety comes in several sizes, but the *calibre* you select is simply a matter of personal preference (I like the large ones best). All snails are sold by the dozen (from 6 to 12€), garnished with *beurre d'escargot* (the traditional stuffing made of fresh butter, garlic, and herbs), but you can also opt for *feuilletés d'escargots,* little nests of puff pastry garnished with a *bourgogne* snail.

All the equipment needed to serve snails is for sale here (snail prongs, snail picks, and snail plates, including disposable foil ones), as well as the perfect dry white wine to accompany them: a Bourgogne aligoté (10€). You can also buy canned snails *au naturel,* empty snail shells, and *beurre d'escargot* by the weight.

79 rue Fondary, 15th. CROSS STREET: Rue Frémicourt. M° Émile Zola or La Motte-Picquet Grenelle. PHONE: 01 45 75 31 09. WEB: www.maison-escargot.com. Tue–Sat 9:30am–7pm.

Joël Thiébault
Produce

The endless display of fish, meat, and flowers is a thing of beauty in any market, but at Président Wilson or Rue Gros, what causes most passersby to stop in their tracks is the veritable show of multicolored carrots, bizarrely shaped tomatoes, and eccentric herbs on Joël Thiébault's stall.

This modern-day farmer, who even has a Web site (joelthiebault.fr), specializes in rare and forgotten vegetables, of which he grows over 1,600 varieties. He hunts for them all over the globe (he says it's gotten much easier now, with the Internet), gives them a few seasons to prove themselves, and decides if they're worthy of his clientele's palate—quirky looks alone do not a good vegetable make.

Renowned Parisian chefs and home cooks alike call upon him to add sparkle to their vegetable rotation (I hear children eat cauliflower with much more enthusiasm if it's purple) or, in some extreme veggie-lover cases, to compose ornamental platters that will be used as centerpieces at fancy dinner parties.

It is fortunate that neither Thiébault's incredible popularity nor his publication of a coffee table book have gone to his head, and he is still very prompt to share tips and trivia about his botanical wonders.

Marché du Président Wilson. Avenue du Président Wilson, 16th. CROSS STREET: Rue Debrousse. M° Alma-Marceau. Wed, Sat 7am–2:30pm.

Marché Rue Gros. Rue Gros and rue La Fontaine, 16th. CROSS STREET: Avenue Théophile Gaultier. M° Église d'Auteuil. Tue, Fri 7am–2:30pm.

Établissements Lion
Miscellaneous

It is a picture-perfect corner shop that lets its potted plants burst out onto the sidewalk when the weather is nice. The anteroom is devoted to gardening—utensils and seeds to grow herbs, fruits, vegetables, or flowers—while the rest of the space holds myriads of gift-worthy artisanal specialties: *pain d'épice* from Dijon, exceptional prunes from Burgundy, olive oil from Nyons, vegetable confits from Languedoc, dried apples and strawberries from Provence, crackers and cookies . . .

7 rue des Abbesses, 18th. CROSS STREET: Rue Houdon. M° Abbesses.
PHONE: 01 46 06 64 71. Tue–Sat 10:30am–8pm; Sun 11am–7pm.

THE KING'S VEGETABLE GARDEN

Le Potager du Roi was built by Jean-Baptiste La Quintinie in the late seventeenth century. He had been appointed by Louis XIV as the Director of All Royal Fruit and Vegetable Gardens a few years before, and part of his mission was to build a vegetable garden just south of the Château de Versailles, to fill the court's needs for fresh produce.

He was allotted some twenty acres of swamps: he dried them out, structured them into gardens, and proceeded to plant a wide variety of fruits and vegetables, experimenting and inventing a few horticultural techniques along the way.

More than three centuries later, his potager would still do him proud: although smaller—some elements have disappeared or been replaced—it is still rife with three hundred varieties, cared for by the school of horticulture next door. It yields over seventy tons of produce each year, and some can be purchased at the gift shop on Tuesdays, Thursdays, and Saturdays, along with jams, juices, and gardening books.

Le Potager du Roi is open to visitors year-round, but on a more restrictive basis during the colder months. Guided tours of the gardens (free, in French) are organized on weekends and holidays from April to October; you can also walk around on your own using the mini-guide (available in English). Admission: 3 to 6.50€. Check the Website for opening days and hours, and guided tour schedules.

10 rue du Maréchal Joffre, Versailles. CROSS STREET: Rue des Bourdonnais. RER Versailles-Rive Gauche. PHONE: 01 39 24 62 62.
WEB: www.potager-du-roi.fr.

Canistrelli

Corsican Cookies

Walking down rue des Mathurins is a true exercise in self-control for anyone with a sweet tooth: as you draw near the Corsican goods shop at number 21 (see page 212), you must cross the street or, at the very least, avert your eyes, so as not to look at the heaps of *canistrelli* in the window. If you accidentally do, and however flashing the glance, these fat little cookies will hold you in their hypnotizing power, and you will have no choice but to step in and buy as many as you can carry.

Canistrelli are the most emblematic cookies of Corsica. Aromatic and crunchy, with a heart that shatters into flaky crumbs, they draw their subtle flavors from the use of olive oil, white wine, and, if available, chestnut flour. They are remarkably easy to make, and can be served with tea, coffee, or a glass of Corsican white.

1^{1}/3 cups (160 g) all-purpose flour
^{2}/3 cup (90 g) whole wheat or chestnut flour
1^{1}/2 teaspoons baking powder
7 tablespoons (85 g) sugar
Zest from 1 organic lemon, finely grated
^{1}/3 cup (80 ml) extra virgin olive oil
^{1}/3 cup (80 ml) dry white wine

Makes about 25 cookies

1. Preheat the oven to 350°F (180°C) and line a baking sheet with parchment paper.

2. In a medium bowl, combine the flours, baking powder, sugar, and lemon zest. Form a well in the center and pour in the olive oil and wine. Stir the liquids into the solids, working gently with a fork, until the dough comes together and forms a ball. Knead quickly until smooth, without overworking the dough. The dough will be moist, but it shouldn't be sticky; add a little more flour if it is.

3. Transfer the dough to a lightly floured work surface and use the palm of your hand to pat it into a disk about $3/4$ inch (2 cm) in thickness. Slice the dough into 1-inch (2.5-cm) squares or diamonds with a sharp knife, and transfer the pieces one by one to the prepared baking sheet, leaving a little space between them.

4. Bake for 15 minutes, lower the heat to 325°F (160°C), and bake for another 15 minutes, until the canistrelli are set and just starting to turn golden. Transfer to a rack to cool completely. Keep in an airtight container for up to a week.

VARIATIONS: Instead of lemon zest, use 1 tablespoon orange flower water, or 1 tablespoon whole fennel seeds or aniseed. You can also substitute honey for part of the sugar, or add $1/2$ cup (40 g) sliced almonds to the dough along with the dry ingredients. Canistrelli may be brushed with milk and sprinkled with sugar just before baking.

épiceries / spice shops

If your spice rack is anything like mine, it is a jumble of jars and tubs and grinders and plastic bags filled with all manner of seasonings, whose sole purpose in life is to impart their vivid flavors to my dishes.

Every once in a while, I roll up my sleeves, take the phone off the hook, and spend an afternoon repackaging, labeling, and alphabetizing my collection. But this fragile order is soon shattered by my impatient cooking hands, which can't be bothered to return the jars to their rightful place after use, or by the arrival of a fresh bounty of spices. I blame the providers below.

Goumanyat
Spice shop

The long-established Thiercelin family specializes in the trade of top-grade spices and condiments, which they hunt for, import, and process themselves. They sell the bulk of their goods to food manufacturers and restaurateurs, but this shop is the home cook's chance to lay his hands on the cream of the crop at gentle prices—a benefit of buying straight from the importer.

The neat and welcoming shop is stocked with a thousand objects of wonder, and a short session at the "sniff bar" is enough to knock your socks off, as you smell your way through the range of rare spices, peppercorns, and seasoning blends, of a quality and freshness that will make you swear off grocery store spices forever.

Gift-worthy condiments and spice- or flower-derived goods (caramels, oils, salts, mustards . . .) complete the selection, and if you've always wanted to cook with saffron but always recoiled at the price, you will be overjoyed to see that theirs, Iran-grown and intensely flavored, costs a mere 4.95€ per gram—enough to make twenty dishes glow.

3 rue Charles François Dupuis, 3rd. CROSS STREET: Rue Béranger.
M° République. PHONE: 01 44 78 96 74. WEB: www.goumanyat.fr. Tue–Fri 2pm–7pm; Sat 11am–7pm.

Izraël
Spice shop

Grains, flours, spices, nuts, dried fruits, condiments, syrups, and sauces: it would be physically impossible to cram even one more item in this tiny spice shop—and I'm sure the owners have tried. Whatever quirky ingredient you've been looking for all over, you stand a good chance of finding it here. And if you don't, it's probably just playing hide-and-seek in this glorious hodgepodge, but the knowledgeable, though sometimes overwhelmed, attendants will help you locate it.

30 rue François Miron, 4th. CROSS STREET: Rue du Pont Louis-Philippe.
M° Saint-Paul or Pont Marie. PHONE: 01 42 72 66 23. Tue–Sat 9:30am–1pm
and 2:30pm–7pm.

Heratchian
Spice shop

Founded in 1925 by two Armenian brothers, this old-fashioned shop stands at the crossroads between the Balkans and the Near East: dried fruits and nuts in wooden racks, legumes and grains in bulging bags, multicolored olives, fat pickles, and real feta cheese in giant buckets, flaky pastries under a snowfall of confectioners' sugar, golden *beureks* (crisp turnovers filled with meat, spinach, or cheese) lined up like soldiers on a tray, shelves laden with spices and condiments (zaatar, pomegranate molasses, honey from Kalymnos), clanky clouds of Turkish coffeepots hanging from the ceiling . . .

Everywhere you look, something exotic and tempting clamors for your attention, but don't miss the deli case: this is where they keep the homemade tarama, the *pastourma* (Greek spiced cured beef), and the stuffed eggplant.

6 rue Lamartine, 9th. CROSS STREET: Rue Cadet. M° Cadet.

PHONE: 01 48 78 43 19. Mon–Sat 8:30am–7:15pm.

~ If Heratchian doesn't carry what you're looking for, a two-block walk will take you to a similar shop called **Massis Bleue.**

27 rue Bleue, 9th. CROSS STREET: Rue Lafayette. M° Cadet.

PHONE: 01 48 24 93 86. Tue–Sat 7:30am–7pm.

Le Comptoir Colonial
Spice shop

This Montmartre shop is my favorite ticket to the spice route. The range of peppercorns from evocative origins (Sarawak, Pondicherry, Lampong, Penja, Malabar . . .) is superb, and many of the spices and spice mixes (over two hundred different kinds) are sold in bulk, allowing you to sample just a small amount.

The selection of condiments and exotic goods includes oils (argan, grapeseed), vinegars (raspberry, truffle), flavored mustards (pink peppercorn, nettle, black currant), exotic ingredients and sauces (Thai, Indian, Creole), candied fruits (ginger, apricots), dried flowers (rosebuds, lavender), jams (passion fruit, vine peach), and bars of chocolate (white chocolate and fennel, bittersweet chocolate and poppy seeds). The lady who runs the shop is patient enough to let you browse the shelves to your heart's content.

22 rue Lepic, 18th. CROSS STREET: Rue Cauchois. M° Blanche.

PHONE: 01 42 58 44 84. WEB: www.lecomptoircolonial.com. Tue–Wed and Fri–Sat 8:45am–1pm and 4pm–7:30pm; Thu 4pm–7:30pm; Sun 10:30am–1:30pm.

FINE FOODS FROM THE MONASTERY

Some of the best artisanal products in France come from abbeys and monasteries, whose members fund their communities this way, using traditional techniques and age-old recipes: soaps and candles, elixirs and remedies, linen and tableware, but also honey and jams, oils and condiments, candy and baked goods, liqueurs and tisanes . . . The most picturesque way to discover them would no doubt be a drive around the country but, short of that, these Paris shops act as tiny showrooms.

Monastica. 11 rue du Pont Louis-Philippe, 4th. CROSS STREET: Rue de l'Hôtel de Ville. M° Pont-Marie or Saint-Paul. PHONE: 01 48 87 85 13. Tue–Sat 10am–noon and 1pm–7pm.

Produits des Monastères. 10 rue des Barres, 4th. CROSS STREET: Rue de l'Hôtel de Ville. M° Pont-Marie or Saint-Paul. PHONE: 01 48 04 98 98. Tue–Sat 9:30am–noon and 2pm–6:30pm.

Aide au Travail des Cloîtres. 68 bis avenue Denfert-Rochereau, 14th. CROSS STREET: Rue Cassini. M° Denfert-Rochereau or Port-Royal. PHONE: 01 43 35 15 76. Mon–Fri noon–6:30pm; Sat 2pm–7pm.

fromageries / cheese shops

Cheese enthusiasts will take immense pleasure in visiting the most basic neighborhood *fromagerie* in Paris, but a few of them merit particular praise for the originality of their selection, and the care with which they age their cheeses—in their own cellars, and at the temperature and humidity levels that each variety requires. This is the difference between a *fromager*, a simple retailer of cheese, and a *fromager-affineur*, who buys young specimens and oversees their maturation.

Cheese is a seasonal item, so the availability and flavor of each variety vary from month to month; a good cheese vendor will tell you which ones are at their best when you visit. You can also ask for advice as to which specimens will travel well without too much suffering (on their part or yours),

and many cheese shops offer to vacuum-pack your purchases, usually for free.

The price of cheese is indicated either by weight or per item. Small cheeses, such as goat cheese *crottins* or Saint-Marcellin, are sold whole. Medium-size cheeses, such as Camembert or Reblochon, can be purchased halved or, occasionally, quartered. Larger cheeses, such as Roquefort or Comté, are sold *à la coupe*, which means that the vendor cuts a piece for you: he puts the cheese on a cutting board, positions the knife as if to cut a slice, and waits for you to tell him if the size is right. If you want a larger piece, say, *"un peu plus, s'il vous plaît"*; if you want a smaller piece, *"un peu moins, s'il vous plaît."*

Cheese shops are also the best source for anything dairy—butter *à la motte* (large golden mounds from which the vendor slices off a piece with a special wire), *crème fraîche crue* (unpasteurized thick cream), farm-fresh milk, and *œufs coque* (eggs that have been laid less than nine days before).

Pascal Trotté
Cheese shop

This minute Marais shop stocks an excellent selection of goat cheeses (the Saint-Nicolas is produced by monks in an orthodox monastery near

Montpellier) and Comtés, aged for up to forty months in stone cellars, as well as a few British specimens (Stilton, Montgomery's Cheddar, Shropshire Blue) provided by Neal's Yard Dairy in London.

97 rue Saint-Antoine, 4th. CROSS STREET: Rue de Sévigné. M° Saint-Paul. PHONE: 01 48 87 17 10. Tue–Fri 8am–1pm and 4pm–7:45pm; Sat 8am–7:45pm; Sun 8am–1pm.

Barthélémy
Cheese shop

Nicole Barthélémy's most notable specialty is Camembert, and she sells a variety of masterfully aged, raw milk specimens of different provenances, each with a different flavor profile. These should not, however, overshadow the display of more than two hundred cheeses, among which you can try the Aisy Cendré, the aged Salers, the Persillé des Aravis, or the homemade Fontainebleau. The posh location of this cute shop has earned it a following of assorted celebrities, and the prices have been adjusted accordingly.

51 rue de Grenelle, 7th. CROSS STREET: Boulevard Raspail. M° Rue du Bac. PHONE: 01 42 22 82 24. Tue–Sat 8am–1pm and 4pm–7:15pm.

Quatrehomme
Cheese shop

At any time of the year, this shop offers two hundred seasonal cheeses, most of them farm-made from raw milk, and aged partially or entirely by Marie and Alain Quatrehomme.

Pont l'Évêque, Fourme d'Ambert blended with Côteaux du Layon, homemade Cancoillotte, double-cream Brie de Meaux: the selection hails from France for the most part, but a few foreign cheeses (Shropshire Blue, Stilton, farm-produced Cheddar, Manchego, Parmigiano-Reggiano) demonstrate the owners' interest in the production of other European countries.

Testament to the quality of their work is the list of prestigious chefs they supply—Jean-François Piège (see page 64) serves their cheeses, and Pierre Marcolini (see page 184) uses their crème fraîche in his ganaches.

Marie Quatrehomme was the first woman to be named Meilleur Ouvrier de France in a food category (see page 156).

62 rue de Sèvres, 7th. CROSS STREET: Rue Pierre Leroux. M° Vaneau or Duroc. PHONE: 01 47 34 33 45. Tue–Thu 8:45am–1pm and 4pm–7:45pm; Fri–Sat 8:45am–7:45pm.

Coop. Latte Cisternino
Cheese shop

These shops are the Parisian outlets of a dairy cooperative based in Italy, a few miles to the south of Rome. Their milk, butter, cheese, fresh pasta, and charcuteries are delivered fresh twice a week, either from the cooperative itself or from nearby artisanal producers.

The mozzarella alone is worth the trip: it comes in several different kinds, among them an extraordinary buffalo mozzarella, but also a few unusual specialties such as the *burrata* (mozzarella layered with cream) or the *sfoglia* (mozzarella rolled with ham and arugula).

The shops also carry such life saving items as *pizza croquante* crackers (perfect with a pre-dinner drink), almond *cantuccini,* organic olive oil, legumes, grains, and flour, as well as sauces and pestos.

37 rue Godot de Mauroy, 9th. CROSS STREET: Rue des Mathurins. M° Havre-Caumartin or Madeleine. PHONE: 06 74 91 66 58. WEB: www.cooplatte cisternino.it. Mon–Sat 10am–1:30pm and 4:30pm–8pm.

Alternate locations:

46 rue du Faubourg Poissonnière, 10th. CROSS STREET: Rue des Petites Écuries. M° Cadet or Bonne Nouvelle. PHONE: 01 47 70 30 36. Tue–Sat 10am–1:30pm and 4:30pm–8pm.

108 rue Saint-Maur, 11th. CROSS STREET: Rue Oberkampf. M° Parmentier. PHONE: 01 43 38 54 54. Tue–Sat 10am–1:30pm and 4:30pm–8pm.

SHOPPING FOR ORGANIC FOOD

Agriculture biologique is French for organic farming, and organic goods are referred to as *produits bio*. Organic produce, grains, dairy, and meat are becoming increasingly popular, but they still come at a higher price than conventionally grown goods.

Many shops and *supermarchés* (see page 248) include organic options in their selection; for all-organic shopping, you should turn to organic greenmarkets (see page 142) and organic grocery stores.

The most common chains are **Naturalia, La Vie Claire,** and **Biocoop,** but there are plenty of smaller, independently owned shops, such as **Markethic,** which also sells fair-trade goods, **L'Épicerie Verte,** which serves a light vegetarian fare at lunchtime, or **Les Nouveaux Robinson,** which operates as a co-op and has three locations outside of Paris, in Montreuil, Neuilly, and Boulogne, all of them accessible by métro.

Markethic. 44 rue de la Folie-Méricourt, 11th. CROSS STREET: Rue Ternaux. Mº Oberkampf or Parmentier. PHONE: 08 72 19 28 79. WEB: www.markethic.fr. Mon 3pm–9pm; Tue–Sun 10am–9pm.

L'Épicerie Verte. 5 rue Saussier Leroy, 17th. CROSS STREET: Rue Poncelet. Mº Ternes. PHONE: 01 47 64 19 68. Mon–Fri 10am–8pm; Sat 10am–7:30pm; RESTAURANT: noon–4pm (salads still served after 4pm and until 7:30pm).

Les Nouveaux Robinson. 49 rue Raspail, Montreuil-sous-Bois. CROSS STREET: Rue Robespierre. Mº Robespierre. PHONE: 01 49 88 70 44. WEB: www.nouveauxrobinson.fr. Mon–Sat 10am–8pm.

Fromagerie Boursault
Cheese shop

Jacques Vernier is credited for having saved the Bleu de Termignon from oblivion, a near-extinct cow's milk cheese produced on a smaller-than-small scale in his native Savoie. His Beaufort, Tome des Bauges, and farmhouse Reblochon are impeccable, but Vernier's talent extends beyond his birth region, as demonstrated by the Époisses, the Provençal goat cheeses, and the selection of Corsican cheeses, Venacco and Corsa Cabra in particular. La Fromagerie Boursault is Yves Camdeborde's provider of choice (see page 49).

71 avenue du Général Leclerc, 14th. CROSS STREET: Rue d'Alésia. M° Alésia.
PHONE: 01 43 27 93 30. Tue–Sat 8am–1pm and 4:15pm–7:30pm; Sun 8am–1pm.

Laurent Dubois
Cheese shop

Laurent Dubois, Meilleur Ouvrier de France and nephew of Martine Dubois (see page 229), works out of a 1927 shop in a residential part of the 15th arrondissement. In the downstairs cellars, he refines three hundred varieties of cheeses and brings up for sale the most perfectly ripe and seasonally fit.

He also prepares *spécialités fromagères*—Fourme d'Ambert doused with Gewürztraminer, Roquefort layered with quince paste, Brie stuffed with dried fruits—that can be served in lieu of a traditional cheese platter for a nice change of pace.

The selection also includes an uncommonly wide selection of foreign cheeses coming from Great Britain, Portugal, and Italy. Dubois provides the dairy for L'Astrance (see page 121).

2 rue de Lourmel, 15th. CROSS STREET: Boulevard de Grenelle. M° Dupleix.
PHONE: 01 45 78 70 58. Tue–Thu 9am–1pm and 4pm–7:45pm; Fri 9am–1:30pm and 3:30pm–7:45pm; Sat 9am–7:45pm.

Alternate location:
47ter boulevard Saint-Germain, 5th. CROSS STREET: Rue Monge. M° Maubert-Mutualité. PHONE: 01 43 54 50 93. Tue–Sat 8am–7:30pm.

Alléosse
Cheese shop

In the Alléosse aging cellars lives an army of twenty thousand cheeses, representing roughly two hundred varieties. This is where they bide their time,

playing cards in between visits of the master cheese refiner, who comes to flip, bathe, brush, or massage them until they're ripe and ready to go out into the world.

No stroll down the cheerful rue Poncelet would be complete without dropping by the shop for Reblochon, raw milk Cîteaux (from an abbey in Burgundy), artisanal Laguiole, beer-bathed Maroilles, or the Mystère d'Ambert, a house specialty of blue cheese layered with raisins and walnuts.

Philippe Alléosse's cheeses are served at Les Ormes and Le Pré Catelan (see pages 62 and 122).

13 rue Poncelet, 17th. CROSS STREET: Rue Saussier-Leroy. Mº Ternes.
PHONE: 01 46 22 50 45. Tue–Thu 9am–1pm and 4pm–7pm; Fri–Sat 9am–1pm
and 3:30pm–7pm; Sun 9am–1pm.

Dubois et Fils
Cheese shop

It is difficult to make specific recommendations among Martine Dubois's cheeses, for they are all impossibly tempting and skillfully aged. The seasonal suggestions on the chalkboard may help you reach a decision, drawing your attention to the assertive Époisse rubbed with *marc de Bourgogne* brandy, the Cotentin Camembert, the French Mimolette, or one of the many artisanal goat cheeses—perhaps a chestnut-leaf-wrapped Banon, a Carré fondant du Tarn, or a delicate Rove des Garrigues, pervaded with the flavors of the herbs the goats have grazed on.

The *préparations fromagères* (a terrine of Mimolette with pistachios, a Camembert with apples and Calvados, a Roquefort mousse), the flaky cheese turnovers, and the raw crème fraîche from Normandie are not to be missed, either.

80 rue de Tocqueville, 17th. CROSS STREET: Rue Jouffroy d'Abbans. M° Wagram or Villiers. PHONE: 01 42 27 11 38. Tue–Fri 8am–1pm and 4pm–7:45pm; Sat 8am–7:30pm; Sun 9am–1pm.

Chez Virginie
Cheese shop

Virginie Boularouah is a third-generation cheesemonger who strives to promote the best artisanal producers. In her cheese lover's paradise of a boutique, you will find excellent advice and a reasonably priced selection that includes a goat cheese Vacherin, a sage-flavored Coulommiers, and a Machecoulais rubbed with Fine de Bretagne (apple brandy from Brittany).

Also of note are her seasonal cheese preparations, such as a goat cheese layered with pesto and tapenade in the summer, or a Brie de Meaux in a mantle of fresh truffles in the winter. Freshly cut, pre-assembled cheese platters are available for the bashful and the hasty.

54 rue Damrémont, 18th. CROSS STREET: Rue Lamarck. M° Lamarck-Caulaincourt. PHONE: 01 46 06 76 54. Tue–Sat 9:30am–1pm and 4pm–8pm; Sun 10am–1pm.

charcuteries / cured meats and prepared foods

La charcuterie is the French answer to the delicatessen: a shop that sells pork products (ham, sausages, pâtés, rillettes), prepared dishes (salads, quiches, *choucroute garnie,* beef Bourguignon, stuffed tomatoes), and a selection of cheeses and desserts.

Charcuteries are unrelenting keepers of a certain style of old-school French cuisine, one that doesn't shy away from aspic, béchamel sauce, pig's feet, and frilly dollops of mayo; I find their quaint charm irresistible.

I drop by the charcuterie every week or so for ham, sliced to order (I ask for them to be *assez fines,* or rather thin: the *charcutière* will slice one and show it to me for approval before she slices the others), the occasional *saucisson,* a slice of terrine, or the eggs in aspic for which Maxence and I have an insatiable fondness.

I like to cook so I have little use for prepared dishes, but half the time the customer in front of me will be an old lady or a middle-aged man who buys a single serving of *pot-au-feu* (beef stew) or *blanquette de veau* (veal in cream sauce) with a few steamed potatoes, and oh, why don't you throw in a bit of celeriac *rémoulade,* too.

Any neighborhood charcuterie is worth a visit, but the ones below offer goods of exceptional quality, and they're practically one-stop shops if you're planning a picnic (see page 234).

Gilles Vérot
Charcuterie

Did you know there was such a thing as a headcheese championship? Well, there is, and Gilles Vérot has won enough trophies to stop updating the list on his storefront.

This fourth-generation charcutier is a devoted craftsman who, beyond his celebrated *fromage de tête,* produces a remarkable range of artisanal preparations: a preservative- and phosphate-free brine-cured ham, a daily selection of terrines (monkfish and chorizo, rabbit and herbs, beef cheeks and caramelized onions, veal sweetbreads and morels), breaded pig's feet, rillettes of goose, rabbit, or lamb meat, six kinds of andouille sausages . . . the list goes on and on as your mouth waters and your head spins.

The prepared dishes are the sort you can take home, reheat, and have your guests believe you're a marvelous cook, on the condition that you hide the plastic containers. The shop is constantly abuzz with activity, but the holiday season, when Vérot whips up his foie gras, his *boudin blanc,* and his *cervelas* sausage with truffles and pistachios, is sheer craziness.

3 rue Notre-Dame des Champs, 6th. CROSS STREET: Rue de Rennes. Mº Saint-Placide or Rennes. PHONE: 01 45 48 83 32. Tue–Sat 8:30am–8pm.

Alternate location:

7 rue Lecourbe, 15th. CROSS STREET: Boulevard Pasteur. Mº Sèvres-Lecourbe. PHONE: 01 47 34 01 03. Tue–Sat 8:30am–8pm.

Pierre Oteiza
Basque specialties

If you ever have the good fortune to visit the French Basque country, your steps (or, more likely, your rental car) may take you to a valley of striking beauty, where the village of Les Aldudes nestles. This is the setting in which a near-extinct breed of pig, pink and black and delectable all over, was saved by a group of local farmers, who decided to reinstate *le porc basque* using the traditional feeding, breeding, and curing methods.

Among them was Pierre Oteiza, who has a shop in Les Aldudes and another one in Paris. Having visited both, I must say that the former has the distinct advantage of being in an ocean of greenery, but the latter is just as well stocked with cured ham, pâté, and boudin made from Basque pork, as well as charcuterie (*saucissons,* rillettes, pork belly) made from the more common white breed.

The canned or jarred regional dishes are excellent—*cassoulet, piperade, garbure* (a vegetable soup with ham and duck meat)—and the shop also sells Basque cheese (try the sheep's milk Ossau-Iraty, traditionally served with black cherry jam), Espelette chile pepper, and wine from Irouléguy.

13 rue Vignon, 8th. CROSS STREET: Rue de Sèze. Mᵒ Madeleine.
PHONE: 01 47 42 23 03. WEB: www.pierreoteiza.com. Mon 1pm–7pm; Tue–Sat
10am–2pm and 3pm–7pm.

Joël Meurdesoif
Charcuterie

Joël Meurdesoif learned the art of charcuterie from his father, and he stayed true to these traditional techniques for forty years, in a small shop off place d'Italie. Anonymous though the location was, hidden at the end of a nondescript alleyway, the superior quality of his pork preparations—*jambon à l'os* (bone-in ham), *rillons* (chunky *rillettes*), *fromage de tête* (headcheese), *boudin noir* (blood sausage), *andouillette* (tripe sausage, the best I've ever eaten in my life), *caillettes* (a small pâté of meat and herbs from Ardèche)—earned him a solid reputation.

Having now reached the age of retirement, he has passed on the torch to a young successor, David Kubika, who has kept the name but moved the shop to a new location, in the 14th arrondissement. Meurdesoif supplies Aux Lyonnais (see page 22) and Le Verre Volé (see page 94).

70 avenue Jean Moulin, 14th. CROSS STREET: Boulevard Brune. Mᵒ Porte
d'Orléans. PHONE: 01 45 41 68 59. Tue–Sat 10am–2pm and 4pm–8pm; Sun
10am–2pm.

PICNIC SPOTS

Official city regulations state that you're only allowed to picnic in desig-
nated parts of Bois de Boulogne, Bois de Vincennes, or Parc Floral, and do-

ing so anywhere else can, technically, get
you fined. That said, at the first sign of
balmy weather, Paris becomes a giant picnic
area, and every bench, every bank of the
river, and every patch of grass receives its
happy crowd of sandwich munchers.

Experience shows that if you stay off the
forbidden lawns (a sign will read, "*pelouse in-
terdite*" or "*pelouse au repos*"), if you keep
things reasonably quiet and impeccably tidy,
you won't get in any trouble.

The makings of a no-cook picnic can be
purchased from produce stalls, charcuteries,
bakeries, and specialty foods stores, but for
an utterly effortless spread, you can order
picnic baskets from restaurants such as
Astier (page 99), Chez Michel (page 91), L'Ami
Jean (page 58), or La Cave de l'Os à Moelle (page 119), who offer this service
in the spring and summer.

Below is a selection of picnic spots that are particularly pleasant, in terms
of both environment and view. Gated gardens and parks close at nightfall:
the exact time is displayed at the entrance, and the *gardien* (garden keeper)
blows a whistle when it is time for you to pack up your things and go.

Gardens

- **Jardin du Palais Royal** (1st), a rectangular French garden behind the Palais Royal, shielded from the city bustle by arcaded buildings all around. Closes at 8pm. м° Palais Royal.
- **Square Vert Galant** (1st), a small park dedicated to Henri IV at the western tip of Île de la Cité. Access by the stairs from the Pont Neuf bridge. Closes at 9:30pm in the summer. м° Pont-Neuf.

Riverside

- **Square Tino Rossi** (5th), on the quai Saint-Bernard. The large grassy areas offer a bankside view of the Seine, and professionals and amateurs use the arenas to dance the summer nights away in a whirlwind of salsa, tango, and samba. м° Jussieu or Gare d'Austerlitz.
- A little further north along the river, on **Quai de la Tournelle** (5th), the view of Notre-Dame makes up for the lack of grass. м° Maubert-Mutualité.
- **Canal Saint-Martin** (10th) is a popular picnic spot. On warm days, swarms of people settle all along its banks and in the nearby **Jardin Villemin**, which closes at 9:30pm in the summer. м° Jacques Bonsergent or Goncourt.
- If you want a view of the Tour Eiffel as you eat, you can go to **Parc du Champ de Mars** (7th, open all night) and sit at the foot of the Iron Lady with everyone else, or you can opt for a bench on the lesser-known **Allée des Cygnes** (15th), a narrow, tree-lined artificial island that's also home to Paris's very own, but miniature, Statue of Liberty. Access by the stairs from Pont Bir Hakeim. м° Bir Hakeim.

(continued)

Parks

- At **Parc de Bercy** (12th), you can bookend your meal with a stroll through the vegetable patch, the vineyard, the orchard, and the rose garden. Closes at 9:30pm in the summer. M° Cour Saint-Emilion.

- **Parc Floral** (12th) is a beautiful botanical garden of Japanese inspiration on the verge of the Bois de Vincennes, across from Château de Vincennes. A jazz festival is hosted inside the park every summer, from early June to late July. Closes at 8pm in the summer; admission: 2.50 to 5€. M° Château de Vincennes.

- **Parc Montsouris** (14th) is a sloped English-style park with lots of trees and a little lake with benches, where I used to eat my lunch when I worked close by. Closes at 9:30pm in the summer. On the other side of boulevard Jourdan is the **Cité Universitaire,** a privately owned (but open to the public) park and housing facility for students, where each building is designed in the spirit of a different country. RER (express train): Cité Universitaire.

- **Parc de la Villette** (19th) was built in the eighties, over the land that used to be occupied by the city's slaughterhouses; it is the largest park in the city, featuring vast expanses of grass and themed gardens, as well as concert halls, theaters, and museums. In the summer, it is home to a free outdoor film festival (more information at www.villette.com). Closes at 1am. M° Porte de la Villette.

- **Parc des Buttes Chaumont** (19th) offers breathtaking landscapes and happens to be the steepest park in the city. Some argue that this makes picnicking a challenge, but such is the spice of life. Closes at 10:15pm in the summer. M° Buttes-Chaumont.

- **Parc de Belleville** (20th) is a bit too sparse for my taste, but it is the highest natural vantage point in Paris, higher even than Montmartre, and it offers a sweeping view on the city. Closes at 9:30pm in the summer. M° Pyrénées.

Les Papilles Gourmandes
Charcuterie

After running a restaurant for fifteen years, Françoise Le Carrer decided to try something new and open a fine foods shop instead. While most similar businesses focus on jarred or canned items—much easier to stock and handle—she decided to sell fresh charcuterie and cheese made by some of the best artisans in France.

She travels all over the country to hunt for these goods, conducts multiple tastings, and elects her favorites. Brittany, Auvergne, Savoie, Alsace, the Lyon region, and the French Basque country are all represented in the most mouthwatering of spreads, and some of the products can be slipped into sandwiches assembled to order on organic bread (3.80€).

26 rue des Martyrs, 9th. CROSS STREET: Rue Manuel. M° Notre-Dame de Lorette. PHONE: 01 45 26 42 89. Mon 9:30am–2pm and 5:30pm–7:45pm; Tue–Sat 9:30am–2pm and 4pm–7:45pm; Sun 9:30am–1:30pm.

Schmid
Charcuterie

This little patch of Alsace is quite fittingly located outside the Gare de l'Est, the station at which trains arrive from Strasbourg. It doesn't look like much from the street, but once inside, you are faced with large display cases filled with the most prized items of Alsatian gastronomy: everything you need for a *choucroute* party (sauerkraut, sausages, cured or smoked pork cuts), Munster cheese, *pâté en croûte* (meat terrine baked in pastry dough), *feuilletés* (puff pastry turnovers), *tartes flambées* (the Alsatian pizza), fresh *spaëtzle* (egg noodles), duck and goose foie gras, soft pretzels, strudels, plum tarts, *kugelhopf* (a brioche with raisins and almonds), fresh cheese cake . . . and to wash it all down: wines, beers, and artisanal liqueurs.

76 boulevard de Strasbourg, 10th. CROSS STREET: Rue du 8 Mai 1945. M° Gare de l'Est. PHONE: 01 46 07 89 74. WEB: www.schmid-traiteur.com. Mon–Fri 9am–8pm; Sat 8:30am–8pm.

THE WORLD'S LARGEST FRESH FOOD MARKET

Paris's main food market used to be located in Les Halles, in the center of the city, but when the induced traffic and pollution became too much of a nuisance, it was moved to the outskirts in the mid-sixties. **Rungis** is now the world's largest wholesale market for fresh goods: six hundred acres divided into pavilions (seafood, meat, produce, flowers, dairy) that swarm with activity in the wee hours of the morning. Access to the market is reserved to registered professionals.

Maison Pou
Charcuterie

The name of this shop used to send my sister and me into fits of laughter when we were little (*pou* means headlouse, and this hardly seemed good marketing for a food shop), but we tried to keep it quiet because the venerable *charcuterie-traiteur*, founded in 1830, was held in high esteem by our grandmother: she considered it the ultimate provider to turn to when one needed to assemble a spread that would make an impression on honorable guests.

Decades later, it still lives up to its reputation, and the display is a veritable parade of old-school specialties: fish or meat terrines (try the green pepper duck terrine or the fresh foie gras terrine), *jambon d'York* (slowly aged, cooked ham), *jambon de Bourgogne* (parsleyed ham in aspic), *bouchées à la reine* and *vol-au-vent*, miniature *pâté en croûte*, sausages from Lyon, Montbéliard, Morteau . . .

16 avenue des Ternes, 17th. CROSS STREET: Rue Poncelet. M° Ternes.
PHONE: 01 43 80 19 24. WEB: maisonpou.com. Mon–Sat 9:30am–7:15pm.

poissonneries / fish shops

Fish is such a fragile ingredient that I can't imagine buying it from any other source than a bona fide *poissonnerie*, where I can feel confident the goods are fresh and have been handled with care. Despite a reputation of costliness, fish and shellfish can be entirely affordable if you look among the more humble, but no less flavorful varieties, and fish shops often run specials— look for tags that read *"Promotion!"* or *"Promo!"*

When buying a whole fish rather than fillets, you will be asked if you want it scaled and gutted (*"Gratté et vidé?"* the attendant will ask), and whether or not you want to keep the head (*"Vous voulez garder la tête?"*). While you go to the register and pay, the apron-clad men in the back will trim the tail and fins, scrape off the scales, and clean out the insides of the fish. This service is provided for free, but you're welcome to slip a coin in the tip jar. The process is similar when you purchase oysters or scallops, which can be shucked for you (*"On vous les ouvre?"*) at no additional charge.

I am partial to my neighborhood fish shop, the family-run **Poissonnerie Bleue**, as it mixes the perfect cocktail of quality, variety, and smiling service.

La Poissonnerie Bleue. 5 rue des Martyrs, 9th. CROSS STREET: Rue Notre-Dame de Lorette. M° Notre-Dame de Lorette. PHONE: 01 48 78 05 05. Tue–Fri 8:30am–12:30pm and 4:15pm–7:15pm; Sat 8:30am–1pm and 4:15pm–7:15pm; Sun 8:30am–1pm.

Most market streets in Paris (see page 147) offer similar providers, but the following are special enough to warrant a visit.

La Poissonnerie du Dôme
Fish shop

If you're in love with all things fish and curious to know where top chefs get theirs, this is the place to go: La Poissonnerie du Dôme may not be very large, but it is a sparkling ode to freshness and quality. The goods come in every morning through the wholesale market of Rungis (see page 239), and only the best makes it past Jean-Pierre Lopez's expert scrutiny.

Your wallet may not like it quite as much, but you won't be charged for admiring the luxurious display of wild salmon, turbot, sole, monkfish, lobster, crawfish, scallops, sea urchins, and a number of rarities—*civelles* (eel larvae), *vive* (a poisonous fish used in *bouillabaisse*), *pouce-pied* (a shellfish that looks like the toe of a dinosaur), *omble chevalier* (a freshwater fish from Lake Léman), or *étrilles* (miniature crabs). Seasonality is of the essence for seafood, too, and La Poissonnerie du Dôme is a good place to learn about that.

4 rue Delambre, 14th. CROSS STREET: Boulevard du Montparnasse. M° Vavin. PHONE: 01 43 35 23 95. WEB: www.poissonneriedudome.com. Tue–Sat 8am–1pm and 4pm–7:30pm; Sun 8am–1pm.

OYSTER BARS

The French love their oysters, and Paris is filled with brasseries that serve a fine selection, which can be gauged and admired on the street-side shellfish stands. But for a more intimate ambiance, I recommend the oyster bar instead: the following offer pristine specimens and friendly service, in dining rooms not much larger than an oyster shell. All of them sell oysters to go, but it is best to call ahead and place your order.

L'Écume Saint-Honoré. A tasting counter at the back of a fish shop. Formules starting at 10€ (a half-dozen oysters and a glass of wine).

6 rue du Marché Saint-Honoré, 1st. CROSS STREET: Rue Saint-Honoré. M° Tuileries or Pyramides.

PHONE: 01 42 61 93 87. SHOP: Tue–Thu 9:30am–8pm and Fri–Sat 9:30am–10pm; TASTING BAR: Tue–Thu 11am–7pm and Fri–Sat 11am–10pm

Huîtrerie Régis. Oysters from Marenne. Formules starting at 22.50€ (a dozen oysters, a glass of wine, and coffee). Closed from mid-July to mid-September.

3 rue Montfaucon, 6th. CROSS STREET: Boulevard Saint-Germain. M° Mabillon. PHONE: 01 44 41 10 07. Tue–Thu noon–3pm and 6pm–midnight; Fri–Sun noon–midnight.

Pleine Mer. Oysters from Cancale. Formules starting at 11€ (a dozen oysters and a glass of wine). Closed from early June to mid-September.

22 rue Chabrol, 10th. CROSS STREET: Cité de Chabrol. M° Poissonnière or Gare de l'Est. PHONE: 01 53 34 64 47. Wed–Sat 10:30am–2pm and 4pm–9pm; Sun 10:30am–1pm.

L'Écailler du Bistrot. See page 104.

La Criée du Phare
Fish shop

La Criée du Phare gathers three fishmongers under one roof, and it is as close to a fish market as you're going to find in Paris. It is a bit out of the way, in a hangar that doesn't look terribly inviting despite the papier-mâché lighthouse that crowns it (the namesake *phare*), but the vendors are helpful, and the stalls offer a rare combination of irreproachable freshness and gentle prices.

69 rue Castagnary, 15th. CROSS STREET: Rue des Morillons. M° Plaisance or Convention. PHONE: 01 45 31 15 00. Tue–Thu 9am–1pm; Fri–Sat 9am–1pm and 3:30pm–7pm; Sun 9am–1pm.

Bar en Croûte d'Amandes et Câpres
Sea Bass in Almonds and Capers Crust

~

The first time I returned to Le Violon d'Ingres (see page 63) after its renovation was on one of those radiant November days that are so becoming to the city, when the rays of sun slice through the clean air and make the façades shine like pale gold, when you are tempted to bundle up and take whatever work you have to do to the nearest café terrace.

Le Violon seemed to have caught on to this uplifting atmosphere: the dish I ordered, a fillet of sea bass from Saint-Malo baked in a shell of crisp almonds, served with Sicilian caper berries and tiny potatoes, was a perfect match for the day's mood, wintry yet bright. This mix of delicate sweetness and briny tang inspired the recipe below, in which small capers are integrated into the crust; it is a quick and effortless way to flatter any variety of mild, lean fish.

2 tablespoons (30 g) chilled unsalted butter, diced, plus a pat for
  greasing
18 ounces (500 g) skinless sea bass fillets, cut into 4 serving pieces
  (substitute another variety of lean fish such as halibut, tilapia, or
  mahi-mahi)
2 rounded tablespoons capers packed in vinegar, rinsed, drained, and
  chopped
1/4 teaspoon freshly ground black pepper
A pinch fleur de sel or kosher salt
1 teaspoon fresh thyme leaves (substitute 1/2 teaspoon dried thyme)
2 tablespoons unseasoned dry bread crumbs (see Note)
1/4 cup (20 g) sliced almonds

Serves 4

1. Preheat the oven to 350°F (180°C) and lightly butter a glass or ceramic baking dish large enough to accommodate the fish in a single layer. Arrange the fish at the bottom of the dish, skin side down if they have any skin.

2. In a small bowl, combine the capers, pepper, salt, thyme, and bread crumbs. Add the butter and mash it into the other ingredients with a fork until well blended. Add the sliced almonds and fold them in gently.

3. Divide the almond topping among the four pieces of fish, and spread it over their surface with the back of a spoon.

4. Bake for 8 to 12 minutes, depending on the thickness of the fillets, then switch the oven to the broiler setting and leave the fish in for another 5 minutes, watching closely, until the almond crust turns golden. Serve immediately with steamed fingerling potatoes.

NOTE: You can make your own bread crumbs by leaving slices of leftover baguette on the counter until completely dry, then grinding the bread to coarse crumbs in a food processor or blender. Panko bread crumbs can also be used.

grands magasins / gourmet stores

If you wish to stay in the know about food shopping trends, the stores below are the best spots to conduct your research: since they are self-service and always crowded, you can spend as much time as you like browsing the

aisles, a basket in one hand and a notepad in the other, studying the labels, peering through the display cases, and gaping at the profusion of it all.

La Grande Épicerie de Paris

Gourmet store   **VEG-FRIENDLY**

La Grande Épicerie occupies the ground floor of Left Bank–posh Le Bon Marché, the oldest department store in Paris, and the inspiration for Zola's *Au Bonheur des Dames*. The goods they sell often make the food pages of fashion magazines, and this should give you an idea of the store's spirit: chic, inspiring, and inevitably pricey.

Condiments, jams, spices, salts, vinegars, oils, coffee, tea, cookies, bread, cheese, meat, fish . . . With over 30,000 square feet of display shelves, produce baskets, and refrigerated cases, you are likely to wander around for hours, picking things up and probably not putting them down.

On one end of the store you'll find a lunch counter and a deli section that can provide the fixings for a classy picnic, but if you get hungry you can also hop upstairs to Délicabar (see page 60).

38 rue de Sèvres, 7th. CROSS STREET: Rue du Bac. M° Sèvres-Babylone. PHONE: 01 44 39 81 00. WEB: lagrandeepicerie.fr. Mon–Sat 8:30am–9pm.

Fauchon
Gourmet store

Fauchon occupies three adjacent buildings on place de la Madeleine to house a luxury goods store (spices, condiments, jams, teas, coffees, wine), a pastry shop, a bakery, a deli counter, and a tea salon.

I recommend a visit to any food enthusiast who comes to Paris, for Fauchon is a legendary landmark that keeps itself abreast of trends, but it is not the gastronome's haven it once was: appearances remain über-chic—sophisticated edibles, swank décor, and snooty staff—but the taste tests aren't always convincing, and at that price level, one would expect more sparkle.

26 place de la Madeleine, 8th. CROSS STREET: Rue de Sèze. M° Madeleine. PHONE: 01 70 39 38 00. WEB: www.fauchon.com. PASTRY SHOP AND DELI: Mon–Sat 8am–9pm; BAKERY: Mon–Sat 8am–8pm; BOUTIQUE: Mon–Sat 9am–8pm.

Hédiard
Gourmet store

Founded by one Ferdinand Hédiard in 1854, this grande dame of Parisian gastronomy started out as a small shop that specialized in exotic goods—fruits, spices, teas, and coffees—imported from the colonies. The scope broadened over the decades to include regional specialties from all over France, oils and condiments, smoked salmon and caviar, jams and confections (*pâtes de fruit* and glazed chestnuts in particular), luxury wines, and a deli counter that sells ready-made dishes and pastries.

The quality of the goods is reliable, and the price range wide enough that you can easily find affordable food gifts to take home. Hédiard is famous for its beautiful gift baskets, and the staff takes great care in wrapping up even the smallest of assortments in a signature red box.

21 place de la Madeleine, 8th. CROSS STREET: Rue Chauveau-Lagarde. M° Madeleine. PHONE: 01 43 12 88 88. WEB: www.hediard.fr. Mon–Sat 9am–9pm.

GROCERY STORES

Grocery stores are a fascinating illustration of the way locals shop, cook, and eat. I love to visit them whenever I travel, browsing the shelves methodically and finding myriads of intriguing products to taste and/or bring home.

French supermarkets may surprise you with the size of the dairy department—the French are yogurt addicts—and you are likely to find tempting goods in the cookie, chocolate, condiment, jam, and grains aisles in particular. (Make sure you study the labels: French products are not necessarily exempt from additives and hydrogenated fats.)

In the produce aisle, you are expected to weigh your own fruits and vegetables using the electronic scales: once you've managed to locate and punch the button that corresponds to your apples—the customers waiting behind you may feel compelled to help with the search—the machine will spit out a price tag to stick on the bag.

To protect small businesses in city centers, a French law regulates the size of supermarkets within the limits of a town or city; this is why the average grocery store in Paris is no larger than 8,000 square feet. Here are the different kinds you will encounter:

Supérettes

These miniature supermarkets sell produce and a limited selection of convenience goods at a high price, but they are open late in the evening and on Sundays. The most common chains are **8 à Huit** and **Proxi**.

Supermarchés

These medium-size grocery stores sell food and household goods. The most common chains are **Franprix, Champion, G20, Shopi,** and **Atac,** the latter being gradually renamed **Simply Market**. The standard of each store (quality of produce, breadth of selection, price level, cleanliness) depends largely on the neighborhood; the nicer ones carry a good selection of gourmet or organic foods. A few are large enough to have cheese, meat, and fish counters.

Discounters

These grocery stores sell a limited range of goods, labeled in their own brand and presented directly from the cartons to limit handling costs. The stores themselves are often on the shabby side, but some of the items are surprisingly tasty, and the prices are very low. The most common chains are **Ed** and **Leader Price.**

Hypermarchés

There are just three of these very large grocery stores within the city limits—one **Carrefour** and two **Casino** stores—and all of them are located on the outer rim, for real estate reasons. They carry competitively priced food items and other types of consumer goods, and offer parking space.

Other

Initially created as a dollar store where everything was at the same price (hence the name), **Monoprix** evolved into a chain that sells food and a broad range of consumer goods, from clothing to beauty products and tableware, and this puts it somewhere between the supermarket and the department store. The stores are often spread on two floors, one of which is devoted to food, offering higher-quality products at slightly higher prices than the average *supermarché*. **Monop'** is an offshoot of Monoprix that sells food only.

Picard is a chain of supermarkets that specializes in high-quality frozen foods, from flash-frozen produce, meat, and fish, to prepared dishes, appetizers, breads, desserts, and ice creams—a range so broad and so popular that people have been known to throw Picard-only dinner parties.

Lafayette Gourmet
Gourmet store   VEG-FRIENDLY

Smaller in size than its competitor La Grande Épicerie de Paris (see page 246), the gourmet section of the Galeries Lafayette department store still manages to ravish the gourmand and inspire the cook.

Amid the shelves and islands stocked with fresh or dry goods, the store is organized in concession stands, allowing you to find in one place what would otherwise require multiple expeditions across the city: Eric Kayser's fresh bread (see page 149), Sadaharu Aoki's pastries (see page 165), Bellota-Bellota's Spanish products (see page 204), Mavrommatis's Greek foods (see page 39), Giraudet's soups and quenelles (see page 101), and many more.

Several of these stands have sitting areas and tasting bars where you can plan to have lunch if you don't mind cramped spaces. The wine department warrants a visit, too: it offers a comprehensive selection of natural wines (see page 262) that can be sampled by the glass at the wine bar, Le Bar Rouge.

50 boulevard Haussmann, 9th. CROSS STREET: Rue de Mogador. Mᵒ Auber or Chaussée d'Antin. PHONE: 01 42 82 34 56. WEB: www.lafayettegourmet.com. Mon-Wed and Fri-Sat 9:30am-8:30pm; Thu 9:30am-9pm.

thé, café et tisanes / tea, coffee, and herbal teas

The French don't have nearly as much of a tea culture as the British do, but they demonstrate an increasing interest and appreciation for it. Beginner tea drinkers often start with flavored blends, which are easy to like and fun to collect, but after a while, their palate is likely to yearn for more subtle leaves. Whatever your profile, the tea shops listed below will cater to your needs.

As for coffee, you can certainly make do with ground and packaged coffee from the grocery store, but once you've tasted coffee brewed from freshly roasted and freshly ground beans from a good *brûlerie*, it is very difficult to go back. Even the atmosphere of these shops, heavy with malty scents, is addictive.

Finally, if caffeine isn't your thing, or if you enjoy a cup of something warm and comforting after dinner to match the cat on your lap and the slippers on your feet, you may turn to those shops that specialize in herbal teas, which the French call *tisanes* or *infusions* and consume in vast amounts.

L'Herboristerie du Palais Royal
Herbal tea

A treasure trove for the herbal tea lover, this boutique sells over four hundred varieties of dried herbs, fruits, and flowers. The tisane blends boast various health benefits and a potent, fresh flavor. My two favorites are the *Tisane rose composée* (hibiscus, rosehip, rose buds, and peppermint) and the *Tisane du pacha* (ginger, cinnamon, summer savory, cardamom, mint)—7€ per bag of 3 to 3.5 ounces.

The shop has been in business for almost forty years, and it is one of the few true herbalists that still remain in France. It is also a good source for essential oils, flower essences, and natural cosmetics.

11 rue des Petits Champs, 1st. CROSS STREET: Rue Vivienne. M° Pyramides or Palais Royal Musée du Louvre. PHONE: 01 42 97 54 68. WEB: www.herbo sante.com. Mon–Sat 10am–7pm.

Verlet
Coffee

My parents, who brew a pot of extra-strong coffee every day after lunch, swear by Verlet. The century-old shop stocks over twenty varieties of single-origin beans (Sidamo Moka from Ethiopia, Simao from China, Matari from Yemen) and four house blends (Grand Pavois, Haute Mer, Romain, and Saison, starting at 16€/kg), freshly roasted and gloriously aromatic.

Although they recommend you grind the beans yourself and at the last minute—as my father does—they can also do it for you, adjusting the setting to the brewing method you intend to use.

Verlet also operates as a *salon de café*, where you can sample the coffee of your choice (starting at 2.70€) with a pastry from Le Stübli (see page 129). The window seats in the upstairs room are particularly enviable.

256 rue Saint-Honoré, 1st. CROSS STREET: Rue de l'Echelle.
Mᵒ Palais Royal Musée du Louvre or Pyramides. PHONE: 01 42 60 67 39.
WEB: www.cafesverlet.com. Mon–Sat 9:30am–6:30pm.

Le Palais des Thés
Tea

When François-Xavier Delmas founded Le Palais des Thés in the late eighties, his idea was to create an alternative to the traditional tea shop: instead of going for the stiff and intimidating ambiance, he created a colorful and inviting space in which the customer can come and go, take a whiff of the smelling samples, and pour himself a cup of tea.

The marketing concept is polished and highly successful—it has now been replicated in fifteen stores from Paris and Tokyo to Beverly Hills—but it wouldn't amount to much if the teas weren't so fresh and of such high quality. Delmas imports his leaves directly from producers all over the world and sends buyers to the field, quite literally, to taste and select the best crops. The 250 varieties include organic teas and a few rarities (Wu Yi Xiao Hong Pao from China, Gao Shan Cha from Taiwan)—from 3 to 60€ per 100 g.

The catalog also offers a wide range of tastefully assembled *mélanges parfumés*—Thé des Amants, Thé du Hammam, Forêt Noire, 4€/100 g—and if my experience is anything to go by, the tea assortments and handsome accessories (tins, teapots, cups) make much appreciated gifts.

64 rue Vieille du Temple, 3rd. CROSS STREET: Rue des Francs Bourgeois. Mᵒ Saint-Paul or Rambuteau. PHONE: 01 48 87 80 60. Mon–Sat 10am–8pm.

Alternate locations:

61 rue du Cherche Midi, 6th. CROSS STREET: Rue de l'Abbé Grégoire. Mᵒ Vaneau or Saint-Placide. PHONE: 01 42 22 03 98. Mon 10:30am–6pm; Tue–Sat 10am–7pm.

25 rue Raymond Losserand, 14th. CROSS STREET: Rue Édouard Jacques. Mᵒ Pernety. PHONE: 01 43 21 97 97. Tue–Sat 10:30am–6:30pm.

La Brûlerie des Gobelins
Coffee

Three tons of coffee beans pass through Jean-Paul Logereau's hands each month: raw and green when they arrive in their jute bags, they go through the imposing roasting machine that takes up half of the shop and emerge moments later, chocolate brown, puffed up, and powerfully fragrant.

Take your pick among the dozen of pure-origin beans (Ethiopia, Papua, Indonesia, Guadaloupe . . . starting at 5€ for 250 grams) and the handful of house blends, or choose one of the limited-time offerings listed to the left of the counter: these are rare coffees that Logereau receives in small quantities, such as Kopi Luwak, a coffee harvested in Sumatra with the help of monkeys that pick the best coffee cherries.

La Brûlerie des Gobelins provides the coffee that's served at Yves Camdeborde's and Stéphane Jégo's restaurants (see pages 49 and 58). If you visit in the morning, you may witness the daily roasting of the beans; if you come in later, you'll have to settle for the lingering smells.

2 avenue des Gobelins, 5th. CROSS STREET: Rue de Valence. Mᵒ Censier-Daubenton. PHONE: 01 43 31 90 13. Tue–Sat 10am–1:30pm and 2:30pm–7pm.

Betjeman and Barton
Tea

Betjeman and Barton was founded in 1919 by two Englishmen, but it has been run by a French family since the late seventies, and this places it right at the crossroads between the British tradition of tea and the French taste for it.

If you're looking for rare leaves, small crops, or first flush Darjeeling from the spring harvest, you'll find an expert to talk to: the tall red and green canisters all around the shop contain carefully selected teas from prestigious gardens all over the world, subtly flavored blends with fruits, flowers, or spices, and excellent tisanes.

The rest of the shelf space is devoted to British and French delicacies that no cup of tea should ever go without—shortbread, fruitcakes, *croquets* from Dijon—and a selection of pretty mugs and teapots. The boutiques are elegant in a pleasingly low-key way.

23 boulevard Malesherbes, 8th. CROSS STREET: Rue d'Anjou. M° Saint-Augustin. PHONE: 01 42 65 86 17. WEB: www.betjemanandbarton.com. Mon–Sat 10am–7pm.

Alternate location:

24 boulevard des Filles du Calvaire, 11th. CROSS STREET: Rue Oberkampf. M° Filles du Calvaire. PHONE: 01 40 21 35 52. Tue–Sat 10am–1pm and 2pm–7pm.

Le Carré des Simples
Herbal tea

Poetically named and artfully presented, the fifty tisanes sold at Le Carré des Simples are assembled from organic and natural plants. The range includes herbal classics sold on their own (verbena, orange blossom, chamomile) as well as house blends to be enjoyed warm or chilled (La Madeleine de Proust, La Botanique de George Sand, Souvenirs d'enfance).

The baby blue boutique also sells all the accessories you need to steep your drink with style, essential oils that can be used in your cooking, and a selection of candles, cosmetics, and massage oils that can't.

22 rue Tronchet, 8th. CROSS STREET: Rue Vignon. M° Madeleine or Havre-Caumartin. PHONE: 01 44 56 05 34. WEB: lecarredessimples.com. Mon–Fri 10:30am–7:30pm; Sat 11am–7pm.

Le Parti du Thé
Tea

Founded by a thirty-something who realized he was much more passionate about his tea than his corporate job, Le Parti du Thé is a welcome indie on the Parisian tea scene, as Pierre Lebrun selects and assembles his teas with a subtlety and taste that sets him apart from the rank and file.

Black teas and green, red teas from South Africa and smoked teas from China, blue, white, or yellow teas, familiar or rare, pure or blended with flowers, fruits, and spices . . . You may spend more time than anticipated in the stark yet beautiful boutique, picking up the samples in glass jars, concentrating on the smells, and trying to choose a blend that will really be *you,* as if you were choosing a fragrance or a piece of jewelry.

Personal favorites include Pousse-Pousse (a mix of semi-smoked teas), Sables Blancs (a Pai Mu Tan Imperial white tea with discreet notes of coconut and vanilla), and the Oolong Fleurs d'Oranger (a semi-fermented tea from Taiwan with orange blossoms).

Teas can be purchased in any quantity starting from 100 grams ($3^1/2$ ounces), or in gift-worthy sets of miniature boxes. Prices range from 4 or 5€ per 100 grams to 75€ for a Pu-Erh tea that has been aged for twenty-two years.

34 rue Faidherbe, 11th. CROSS STREET: Rue Chanzy. M° Charonne or Faidherbe-Chaligny. PHONE: 01 43 72 42 04. WEB: www.lepartiduthe.com. Tue–Sat 10:30am–7:30pm.

SEASONAL TREATS

Just a week of dining and shopping in Paris will reveal something about the zeitgeist: all chefs breathe the same air and shop at the same markets, so if you pay attention to the window displays, the plating methods, the star ingredients, and the types of preparation, you will notice the emergence of food trends that may or may not last for more than a few weeks.

But some edibles and drinkables come and go on a seasonal basis like clockwork, and depending on the time of year, here are a few that shouldn't be missed.

La Galette des Rois

This puff pastry pie, filled with almond cream or *frangipane* (almond cream mixed with pastry cream), is traditionally served to celebrate the Epiphany on January 6. It is sold at bakeries and pastry shops a few weeks before and after that date. A porcelain or metal trinket hides in the almond filling: whoever finds it in his slice is king for the day, and gets to wear the paper crown that comes with the *galette.*

New variations appear every year (with pineapple, rose, chocolate, coconut), but I prefer to stick to the plain version, so simple yet so good. This type of galette is a northern French specialty; the southern equivalent is a wheel-shaped brioche adorned with candied fruit.

Le Chocolat

Don't worry: chocolate is available year-round, but chocolatiers outdo themselves with seasonal displays and limited-edition creations in preparation for three occasions. On Valentine's Day, everything becomes red, heart-shaped, and smoochy; Easter is all about chocolate hens, bunnies, eggs, and *friture* (tiny fish and shellfish made of chocolate); and for Christmas, the traditional themes are pine trees, snowflakes, and little Pères Noël (Santa Clauses).

Le Beaujolais Nouveau

Beaujolais Nouveau is a *vin de primeur,* i.e., a wine that is ready for consumption just six weeks after the grapes—in this case, Gamay—are harvested. Beaujolais Nouveau is officially released on the third Thursday of November each year, as announced by signs that read "*Le Beaujolais Nouveau est arrivé!*"

The occasion is marked by tastings at wine stores and celebrations at wine bars. *Le beaujo* is typically a fresh and fruity wine, but its quality varies greatly from one producer to the next, so it is wise to seek the advice of a trusted wine seller (see page 258) if you wish to avoid a headache the next day.

Le Gibier

See page 45 for more on game.

Marron Grillé, Marron Glacé

From late fall through the end of winter, street vendors sell paper cones of *marrons grillés,* or roasted chestnuts, still in the shell, ready to be pried open and gobbled up. They often set up their rudimentary roasting stations outside department stores, which are particularly busy this time of year, but the easiest way to find them is to follow the telltale smell.

The other chestnut treat that's at its peak during the cold months is the *marron glacé,* a chestnut candied in several baths of sugar syrup and covered in a thin, crackly sugar glaze. Cheap *marrons glacés* can be found at the grocery store, but you should save yourself for the artisanal, gold-foil-wrapped version, purchased from a good chocolate or candy shop: they are pricey, but worth every penny, and they're so sweet that one is more than enough. (Note: *une châtaigne* is a small, wild chestnut; *un marron* is the cultivated variety, larger in size.)

Traditions de Noël

Christmas is the most important holiday in France, and people go all out for their Christmas Eve dinner. The star delicacies to serve then include black truffles, foie gras, oysters, and sea scallops, and these ingredients are also featured on many a restaurant menu around that time.

La Bûche de Noël

This log-shaped cake, optionally decorated with meringue mushrooms, marzipan holly, and miniature plastic dwarves, is the traditional dessert on Christmas Eve. Whether it's a *bûche glacée* (an ice cream cake) or a *bûche pâtissière* (a frosted cake), and whether it is flavored with chocolate or fruit, it usually appears on the table long after everyone has forgotten what it was like to feel hungry. Pastry chefs come up with new creations every year, some of which stretch the log theme to the point of abstraction.

cavistes / wine shops

Considering that Paris is the capital of such a wine-proud country, it is no surprise that its streets are peppered with *cavistes*, those independently owned wine shops, a little cramped and a little dusty, the dark glimmer of bottles on every wall, and stacks of boxes in every corner.

Threatened by the competition of supermarkets and chain stores (Nicolas and Le Repaire de Bacchus), who buy in large quantities and can afford to keep the prices low, independent wine sellers hold their ground by playing the card of singularity: they work with artisan vintners, hand-pick their wines, and are thus in a position to suggest, advise, and enlighten.

Food and wine trade shows (see page 280) are good wine-buying opportunities, too, and they allow you to meet the producers.

Legrand Filles et Fils
Bar à vin / Wine shop

This shop was founded in the late nineteenth century inside Galerie Vivienne, a covered passageway of striking beauty, and its original façade and décor have been kept intact. The original owner imported goods from the colonies, but the Legrand family took over after World War I and gradually turned to the business of selling wine.

Three successive generations—Pierre Legrand, his son Lucien, and his granddaughter Francine—have since devoted their lives to the trade, and although the wine shop no longer belongs to its namesake family, it remains a reliable source for upscale nectars, and a few more gently priced bottles.

A selection of wines can be tasted by the glass at the polished counter inside the shop or, most pleasantly, under the arcades of the *galerie*. Glasses cost from 5 to 20€, and you can pair them with a plate of charcuterie and/or cheese for an additional 10 to 25€. Tasting classes and meet-the-winemaker events are held weekly; check the Website for details.

1 rue de la Banque, 2nd. CROSS STREET: Rue des Petits Champs. Mᵒ Bourse or Pyramides. PHONE: 01 42 60 07 12. WEB: www.caves-legrand.com. Mon 11am–7pm; Tue–Fri 10am–7:30pm; Sat 11am–7pm; TASTING BAR: noon–6:30pm.

Julien, Caviste
Wine shop

This bright and orderly shop, a few steps from the Marché des Enfants Rouges (see page 144), is run by Julien Aujeau, a young sommelier who trained in France and the UK, and thus speaks good English. His selection includes around 250 French wines, with a slight preference for southern wines, and bottles starting at 5€.

Free tastings are organized twice a month on Saturdays; call to inquire or give your e-mail address to receive the events schedule. (And because Julien's other passion in life is techno music, you may be interested to know that he is the unofficial *caviste* to the Parisian electro-clique.)

50 rue Charlot, 3rd. CROSS STREET: Rue de Bretagne. M° Filles du Calvaire. PHONE: 01 42 72 00 94. Tue–Sat 9:30am–1:30pm and 3:30pm–8:30pm; Sun 10am–1:30pm.

La Cave à Bulles
Beer shop

The world of artisanal beer deserves as much consideration as that of fine wine, and Simon Thillou has taken it upon himself to taste, select, and promote the best of French microbrews. Unfiltered and unpasteurized, these beers hail from all over the country: from the north, from Brittany, and from Alsace, but also from Provence, Savoie, Auvergne, or Dordogne.

They come in all styles, colors, strength, bitterness, and flavors (including chestnut, hemp, lentil, or seaweed), and Thillou happily plays matchmaker between his beers and his customers' tastes. He is also very good at suggest-

FOIRE AUX VINS

A nationwide wine fair is held every year in September: it is a promotional event during which grocery stores all over the country advertise special rates on a large number of bottles. The offerings are so abundant that it can be difficult to know what to buy, but catalogs are available from each store before the sales begin, and magazines and newspapers publish their recommendations in early September.

ing food and beer pairings, and if you're a group of eight to ten, he can host a beer appreciation class; he speaks good English.

Aside from his 150 French beers, Thillou also stocks forty from Belgium, including the one that made him fall in love with beer when he was seventeen: the number 10 Trappist beer from Rochefort, with a blue cap.

45 rue Quincampoix, 4th. CROSS STREET: Rue de Venise. M° Rambuteau or Châtelet. PHONE: 01 40 29 03 69. Tue–Sat 10am–2pm and 4pm–8pm.

Caves Augé
Wine shop

This 1850 wine shop proved it was still very much ahead of the game when it embraced the natural wine movement (see page 262) at its earliest stage, under the impulse of the passionate and outspoken owner, Marc Sibard.

The shelves and display tables are stacked high with what he calls *vins sincères:* atypical wines produced by independent vintners who are respectful of their soil, and work on a small scale. The impressive selection includes over 3,500 labels at all prices, starting at 6€, and in the spring and fall, convivial tasting sessions are held on the sidewalk, during which you can try wines and meet their maker. Call or drop by to inquire about the schedule of events.

Because the store is jam-packed with bottles, it is difficult to navigate without risking disastrous breakage, so the staff prefers that you ask for help rather than help yourself.

116 boulevard Haussmann, 8th. CROSS STREET: Rue d'Astorg. M° Saint-Augustin. PHONE: 01 45 22 16 97. Tue–Sat 9pm–7:30pm.

La Cave de l'Insolite
Wine shop

It looks like someone's loft, complete with vintage furniture, collectible odds and ends, and a handsome spiraling staircase, and indeed the owner of this cellar welcomes his customers with the geniality of a good host. Michel

Moulherat is a certified sommelier with a keen interest in natural wines, and a strong desire to share it: he will happily advise you, point you to lesser known appellations—*insolite* means "quirky," "out of the ordinary"—or suggest food and wine pairings.

Free tastings are held every week, usually on Saturdays, and often with the vintners in attendance; call to inquire and leave your e-mail address to be notified of events.

30 rue de la Folie Méricourt, 11th. CROSS STREET: Rue Saint-Sébastien.
M° Saint-Ambroise or Parmentier. PHONE: 01 53 36 08 33. Mon–Thu
10:30am–8:30pm; Fri–Sat 10:30am–9pm.

NATURAL WINES

In reaction to the chemically manipulated, mass-produced wines that flood the market, independent vintners all around the world have decided to go back to the traditional methods of winemaking and focus on this truism: wine is nothing more, but nothing less, than fermented grape juice. Their ambition is to let grapes and soil speak for themselves, and to intervene as little as possible in their natural expression.

There is no official certification for these wines yet, but they are often referred to as *vins naturels* or *vins nature*: **natural** wines are made in small quantities from unsprayed, hand-harvested grapes, with little to no chemical manipulation afterward (no enzymes, yeasts, or sugar, but limited amounts of sulfur may be added as a stabilizer at the time of bottling) and no filtering. They often bear facetious names, and simple labels that look like they were block-printed in someone's garage.

Biodynamic wine producers take the approach a step further, following a

Rouge Blanc & Bulles
Wine shop

Champagne buffs should traipse over to this *caviste*, just behind the Marché d'Aligre (see page 145), which specializes in the prestigious sparkling wine. The impressive catalog features two hundred labels, from 15€ to much, much more: big names or independent producers, white or rosé, old vintages or new, single varietal (100 percent Chardonnay or 100 percent Pinot Noir) or blended. Free tastings of wine or Champagne are organized on Fridays and Saturdays.

12 bis rue Parrot, 12th. CROSS STREET: Rue Abel. M° Gare de Lyon.
PHONE: 01 46 28 55 62. Tue–Sat 10am–8:30pm.

theory developed in 1924 by Rudolf Steiner, an Austrian philosopher and scientist. The idea is that the vine and the soil are part of a greater system in which all elements are interdependent, and balance is, therefore, everything. Biodynamic vintners follow a set of rules to tend to the vineyard, using traditional techniques and natural remedies, according to a calendar dictated by the cycles of the moon and the movement of the planets. Some frown upon the esoteric aspects of the philosophy, but few contest the fact that it yields authentic wines with a real sense of personality.

There is no official certification for **organic** wines in the European Union, and vintners aren't allowed to print the expression on their labels. When someone uses the term "organic wine" or "*vin bio,*" he usually refers to wine that was made from organically grown grapes, but this doesn't guarantee the nature of the production process *after* the grapes were harvested.

It's difficult to find natural or biodynamic wines from foreign countries: yields are limited so the entire production goes to the local market, but Chapeau Melon (see page 265) stocks a few wines from Italy, Sicily, and Chile.

L'Avant-Goût Côté Cellier
Wine shop

Situated right across from L'Avant-Goût, Côté Cellier is the wine-selling annex to this neo bistro favorite (see page 108). Here you will find the bottles featured on the restaurant's wine list and dozens more, all selected along the same philosophy: artisanal vintners, minimally engineered wines, and one-of-a-kind flavor profiles, with a strong focus on the regions of the Loire, Rhône, and Languedoc-Roussillon.

Prices range from cheap (3.50€) to pricey, and the advice is free—favorites are indicated by a little tag with handwritten tasting notes. The shop also acts as a deli of sorts, from which you can buy dishes to go (around 20€ for a full three-course meal) from the kitchen of L'Avant-Goût.

Themed tasting sessions are organized once a month: the group is introduced to the selection of wines at the shop first, and then crosses the street to partake in a meal that was designed to enhance them. Attendance is limited to ten, reservations are mandatory, and the minimum fee, which varies depending on the wines you'll taste, is 55€ per person.

37 rue Bobillot, 13th. CROSS STREET: Rue du Moulin des Prés. M° Place d'Italie. PHONE: 01 45 81 14 06. Tue–Fri noon–8pm; Sat 10:30am–1:30pm and 3:30pm–8:30pm.

Le Vin en Tête
Wine shop, see page 128

La Cave de l'Os à Moelle
Bar à vin / Wine shop, see page 119

La Cave des Abbesses
Wine shop / Bar à vin   OUTDOOR SEATING

La Cave des Abbesses is the essence of the neighborhood wine shop, unpretentious in spirit and offering a selection of *petites bouteilles* (wines for everyday consumption) by small vintners at an excellent price point—a few coins are shaved off your bill if you buy by the case. Favorites bear a little tag that reads *"Coup de cœur maison,"* and the staff is happy to advise on food and wine pairings—they've never let me down.

A handful of sidewalk tables and the speakeasy-like room at the rear of the shop serve as a wine bar, where regulars drop in for a glass of wine and a plate of rillettes or cheese on their way to or from their errand runs.

43 rue des Abbesses, 18th.

CROSS STREET: Rue Audran.

M° Abbesses.

PHONE: 01 42 52 81 54. Tue–Fri 10am–2pm and 3:30pm–9:30pm; Sat–Sun 9:30am–9:30pm; BAR SERVICE: Tue–Fri 5pm–9:30pm and Sat–Sun noon–9:30pm.

Chapeau Melon
Wine shop / Bar à vin

On the increasingly popular rue Rébeval (see Zoé Bouillon, page 137) is a wine shop that specializes in natural wines, called Chapeau Melon—bowler hat. The owner, Olivier Camus, co-founded the nearby Baratin (see page 139) and was among the first proponents of natural winemaking in the mideighties. He remains one of the most ardent, and one of the most knowledgeable.

Camus features two hundred wines from all over France, including a few privately labeled bottles, starting from 5€. In the evening, you can sit down to sample the wines (add an 8.50€ corkage fee to the store price; glasses start around 4€) alongside a fixed menu (four small plates for 29€). The room seats no more than twenty-five, so reservations are a must.

Tasting sessions are organized on Saturday afternoons, often in the presence of the vintner; call or drop by to inquire about the themes and hours.

92 rue Rébeval, 19th. CROSS STREET: Rue de Belleville. M° Pyrénées.
PHONE: 01 42 02 68 60. SHOP: Tue–Sat 11am–1pm and 4pm–8pm;
WINE BAR: Wed–Sat 8:30pm–11pm.

THE WINE EMPORIUM

The only wine superstore in the city and the largest such venue in Europe, **Lavinia** houses a vast selection of bottles (six thousand wines and spirits from over forty countries) at all prices, stored horizontally and under controlled conditions of temperature, humidity, and light. Do visit the basement cellar, where rare and precious bottles are kept. Some of them look like they've been salvaged from an ancient shipwreck, and you may find yourself whispering as if in a museum.

The classy, modern cellar makes up in comprehensiveness what it lacks in charm: it includes a section devoted to books and accessories for the wine lover, a tasting bar, and a lunch-only restaurant, where you can drink the wine of your choice at store price, sans corkage fee (reservations at 01 42 97 20 27).

3 boulevard de la Madeleine, 1st. CROSS STREET: Rue Cambon. M° Madeleine.
PHONE: 01 42 97 20 20. WEB: www.lavinia.fr. STORE AND TASTING BAR: Mon–Fri 10am–8pm; Sat 9am–8pm; RESTAURANT: noon–3pm.

Jarret de Veau à la Cuiller
Spoon-Tender Veal (or Beef) Shank

Adapted from a recipe by Stéphane Molé, chef at Les Ormes (see page 62).

~

In the interest of transparency, I should first emphasize that this is a slow-cooking recipe, and I do mean slow: it takes about ten and a half hours from start to finish. But before you gasp and turn the page, I hasten to add that you are free to go about your business for most of that time, while the shanks braise quietly in the oven, their flavors deepening, and their meat softening to so meltingly tender a consistency it can be served with a spoon, as the name suggests.

Stéphane Molé uses veal shanks in his signature dish, but beef is a fine—and cheaper—alternative. He plates each portion of *jarret* over seasonal vegetables (carrots, parsnips, scallions, sugar snap peas, simply poached) and surrounds it with potato gnocchi, but a side of mashed potatoes is lovely, too, as is polenta, celeriac mash, and anything that revels in a dousing of caramelized cooking juices.

$3^{1}/_{2}$ pounds (1.5 kg) bone-in veal or beef shanks, trimmed and cut into
    2-inch slices by the butcher
Coarse sea salt
2 medium carrots
1 large or 2 small yellow onions, about 12 ounces (340 g)
6 garlic cloves
6 large white mushrooms
1 tablespoon extra virgin olive oil
2 tablespoons (30 g) butter
$^{1}/_{2}$ teaspoon fine sea salt
2 teaspoons black peppercorns
2 teaspoons whole coriander seeds

3 sprigs fresh thyme or $^3/_4$ teaspoon dried thyme

1 bay leaf

5 stems fresh parsley (reserve leaves for another use; see Note 1)

1 rounded tablespoon tomato paste

1 cup (240 ml) red cooking port, from California or Spain

2 cups (480 ml) veal stock or vegetable stock (see Note 2)

1 bottle full-bodied red wine, such as Corbières or blend of Shiraz and
Grenache

Serves 6 as a main course

1. Start the recipe at least 10^1/2 hours before you intend to serve it. Place the meat on a platter large enough to accommodate it in a single layer (or use two plates) and sprinkle it with coarse salt; this will help draw out excess moisture. Set aside as you prepare the vegetables.

2. Peel the carrots and cube them roughly. Peel the onions and cube them roughly. Peel the garlic cloves, slice them in two lengthwise, and remove the germ. Slice off the stems of the mushrooms, discard them, and cube the caps roughly. Set the vegetables aside in a bowl. Rinse the meat and pat it dry with paper towels. (The meat and vegetables can be prepared the night before; refrigerate in separate airtight containers, and remove the meat from the fridge 30 minutes before cooking.)

3. Heat the olive oil in a large cast-iron pot (at least 6 quarts or 6 liters in capacity) over medium-high heat. When the oil is hot but not smoking, add the meat in a single layer, without crowding—you will have to work in batches—and cook for 10 minutes, flipping the meat every 2 minutes or so, until caramelized on all sides. Set aside and repeat with the rest of the meat. When all the meat is browned, pour out the excess fat from the pot and wipe with a paper towel.

4. Melt the butter in the pot over medium heat. Add the carrots, onions, garlic, and mushrooms, and cook for 8 minutes, stirring regularly, until the vegetables are tender and caramelized. Season lightly with fine sea salt.

5. Add the peppercorns, coriander seeds, thyme, bay leaf, and parsley, and cook for 2 minutes, stirring constantly, until fragrant. Add the tomato paste, and stir for 2 more minutes, until the vegetables are well coated.

6. Preheat the oven to 275°F (135°C). Return the meat to the pot. Add the port and stock, and pour in wine until the liquids just cover the meat; you may not need the whole bottle. Bring to a rolling boil. Remove from the heat, place a sheet of parchment paper slightly larger than the pot over the pot, and let stand for 1 minute, while the heat softens the parchment paper and makes it malleable. Using a wooden spoon or a heatproof spatula, press down on the sheet cautiously so it is in full contact with the stew; this will prevent the liquids from evaporating as the meat cooks slowly in the oven. Place the lid over the parchment paper to seal the pot.

7. Transfer to the oven and bake for 8 hours, until the meat easily separates from the bone; start checking once an hour after 6 hours. (Note: this step can also be done in a slow-cooker set on high; the parchment paper seal is unnecessary.) Remove from the oven, remove the lid and paper, and let rest for 1 hour.

8. Scoop the meat out from the pot with a slotted spoon and set it aside in a large dish. Keep the bones that hold some marrow to serve with the meat—marrow is delicious on a piece of bread, sprinkled with a little fleur de sel—and discard the others. Set the pot over high heat, bring to a rolling boil, and cook until the liquids have reduced by half, about 15 minutes, stirring every 2 minutes or so to prevent the vegetables from sticking to the bottom. The sauce is ready when it is thick enough to coat the back of a spoon.

9. Strain the sauce through a medium mesh strainer into a large bowl, pressing gently on the vegetables and herbs to release as much of the liquids as possible. (The recipe can be prepared a day ahead up to this point: let the sauce and meat cool completely, and refrigerate in separate airtight containers.)

10. Clean the pot. Return the meat and sauce to the pot and reheat over medium heat. Taste the sauce, adjust the seasoning, and serve straight from the pot.

NOTE 1: Parsley stems act as a "clarifier" in sauces and stews, making their flavors fresher and brighter. You can skip this ingredient, but it is in fact easy to keep on hand: every time you use parsley leaves in a recipe, save the stems in a food storage bag in the freezer.

NOTE 2: Veal stock helps make the sauce silky. You can either cook your own—the procedure is similar to making chicken stock—or use ready-made veal stock reduction, which can be found at some gourmet stores in packages that resemble hockey pucks. Vegetable stock can be substituted; the sauce will be a little thinner.

libraries / bookstores

If you're the kind of person who cannot resist the little voice that hides in fresh cookbooks, chanting, "Buy me! Buy me!" from every recipe and every lick-worthy photograph, I suggest you glue these pages together. If, on the other hand, you have enough willpower to browse the shelves of a cookbook-only shop without buying the stock and having to arrange for a container shipment, I think you will enjoy the following:

La Librarie Gourmande
Bookstore

Established in 1985 on rue Dante, in the Latin Quarter, this bookstore is now in the hands of Deborah Dupont, a young and charming Frenchwoman who has moved it to the lively Montorgueil area, a stone's throw from E. Dehillerin, Mora, and G. Detou (pages 273, 274, and 200).

In so doing, she has traded the old location's dusty charm for two bright and roomy floors devoted to a selection of books on food and wine—old and new, for amateurs or professionals, from France and beyond—that's comprehensive as ever. The catalog is available online, and books can be shipped everywhere in the world.

90 rue Montmartre, 2nd. CROSS STREET: Rue d'Aboukir. M° Sentier or Étienne Marcel. PHONE: 01 43 54 37 27. WEB: www.librarie-gourmande.fr. Mon–Sat 10am–7pm.

Rémi Flachard
Bookstore

In a neighborhood that's historically focused on books and antiques, it's only natural that one shop should be devoted to ancient cookbooks. This is not your average secondhand bookstore, however, as Rémi Flachard's impressive selection comprises rare books on gastronomy and oenology, the oldest of which date back to the fifteenth century.

Such collector's items are routinely sold for several thousands of euros, but there are more affordable volumes, starting around 20€. And if you're looking for one rare title in particular, Flachard can help procure it.

9 rue du Bac, 7th. CROSS STREET: Rue de Lille. M° Rue du Bac. PHONE: 01 42 86 86 87. Mon–Fri 10:30am–12:30pm and 3pm–6:30pm.

La Cocotte
Bookstore

This girly boutique is run by a young Argentinian woman, Andréa Wainer, who puts forth a quirky selection of books on food and beverages, and any book that is somehow related to either—novels, graphic novels, children's books, and art books.

Designer kitchenware and cute linen share the remaining shelf space, and the shop doubles up as a tea salon that your dolls would adore, where tea and coffee are served with homemade *dulce de leche* cookies. La Cocotte (the word means both "chick" and "stew pot") hosts author events and book signings; check the Website for details.

5 rue Paul Bert, 11th. CROSS STREET: Rue Faidherbe. M° Faidherbe-Chaligny. PHONE: 01 43 73 04 02. WEB: www.lacocotte.net. Tue–Wed 10:30am–7:30pm; Thu–Sat 10:30am–9pm.

ustensiles / cookware

The area called Les Halles gets its name from Paris's historic food market, so vividly depicted in Zola's *Le Ventre de Paris*. It was moved to the outskirts in the sixties (see page 239), and all that's left today is a handful of businesses that sell equipment to the professional chef. These stores are also open to the general public, and they're the home cook's most valuable source for tools and toys.

MORE BOOKS FOR COOKS

You will find cookbooks at all general-interest bookstores. Independently owned bookshops are likely to carry a narrower but carefully chosen selection, while the major bookselling chains (**Fnac** or **Virgin Megastore**) stock a larger and more mass-market range. **WHSmith** carries a good selection of English-language imported cookbooks.

W. H. Smith. 248 rue de Rivoli, 1st. CROSS STREET: Rue Cambon. M° Concorde. PHONE: 01 44 77 88 99. Mon–Sat 9am–7:30pm; Sun 1pm–7:30pm.

Virgin Megastore. 52 avenue des Champs-Élysées, 8th. CROSS STREET: Rue du Colisée. M° Franklin-Roosevelt. PHONE: 01 49 53 50 00. WEB: www.virginmegastore.fr. Mon–Sat 10am–midnight; Sun noon–midnight.

Fnac. 26 avenue des Ternes, 17th. CROSS STREET: Avenue Niel. M° Ternes. PHONE: 08 25 02 00 20. WEB: fnac.com. Mon–Sat 10am–7:30pm.

E. Dehillerin
Cookware

If you're looking for top-quality gear, excellent prices, and no-nonsense advice, E. Dehillerin is the place to go. The dimly lit, narrow aisles of this 1820 shop are crammed from floor to ceiling with copper pots, cast-iron cookware, silicone molds, nonstick pans, cutting boards, rolling pins, knives in all shapes and sizes, ramekins, and more utensils than you can shake a stick at.

The salesmen are knowledgeable, but they are not the coaxing type: they will tell you which type of bakeware is the sturdiest, but they won't hold your hand as you debate what size gratin dish you really want.

The prices are not labeled on the goods: you have to request them from a sales attendant, who will give you the *hors-taxe* (before tax) price point: registered professionals don't pay the VAT, but individuals are charged an extra 19.6 percent.

18 rue Coquillère, 1st. CROSS STREET: Rue Jean-Jacques Rousseau. Mᵒ Étienne Marcel or Louvre-Rivoli. PHONE: 01 42 36 53 13. WEB: www.e-dehillerin.fr. Mon 9am–12:30pm and 2pm–6pm; Tue–Sat 9am–6pm.

∼ A few steps from E. Dehillerin is **Mora**, a similar store that will pique the interest of the baker and the chocolate maker in particular: bakeware, piping bags, chocolate molds, food coloring, golden boxes and cellophane bags to wrap your confections, and even *fèves*, the tiny ceramic figures that hide in *galettes des rois*. And while you're in the area, drop by **La Bovida** (a bit pricier, but the presentation is more attractive) and **A. Simon** (restaurant-grade cook- and dinnerware).

Mora. 13 rue Montmartre, 1st. CROSS STREET: Rue du Jour. Mᵒ Étienne Marcel. PHONE: 01 45 08 19 24. WEB: www.mora.fr. Mon–Fri 9am–6:15pm; Sat 8:30am–1pm and 2pm–5pm.

La Bovida. 36 rue Montmartre, 1st. CROSS STREET: Rue Étienne Marcel. Mᵒ Étienne Marcel. PHONE: 01 42 36 09 99. Mon 10am–7pm; Tue–Fri 9am–7pm; Sat 10am–7pm.

A. Simon. 48 rue Montmartre, 2nd. CROSS STREET: Rue Étienne Marcel. Mᵒ Étienne Marcel. PHONE: 01 42 33 71 65. WEB: simon-a.com. Mon 1:30pm–6:30pm; Tue–Fri 9am–6:30pm; Sat 9:30am–6:30pm.

La Carpe

Cookware

La Carpe has been catering to the Parisian cook's needs since 1921: serious gear and cutlery cohabit with classic tableware, picnic baskets, and kitsch gadgets, and I've yet to think of some food- or wine-related accessory that they don't stock.

The prices are a bit high so I don't recommend buying large items from them (go to E. Dehillerin, Mora, or A. Simon, above, for pots, pans, and knives), but the location is convenient, and the quickest visit is sure to turn up some gizmo you never knew you needed—say, a chain mail glove to open oysters, a crumb collector like the ones they use in upscale restaurants, or a clever wheel-shaped container that prevents the cream from

oozing out of a half-eaten Camembert. The complete catalog is available for your enjoyment on their Web site.

14 rue Tronchet, 8th. CROSS STREET: Rue de Castellane. M° Madeleine or Havre-Caumartin. PHONE: 01 47 42 73 25. WEB: www.la-carpe.com. Mon 1:30pm–6:45pm; Tue–Sat 10am–6:45pm.

✑ On the opposite side of place de la Madeleine, inside the mini-mall Les Trois Quartiers, **Kitchen Bazaar** sells more modern utensils.

23 boulevard de la Madeleine, Galerie commerciale Les Trois Quartiers, 1st. CROSS STREET: Rue Duphot. M° Madeleine. PHONE: 01 42 60 50 30. WEB: www.kitchenbazaar.fr. Mon–Sat 10am–7pm.

Eurotra
Cookware

It is Fred, of L'Atelier de Fred (see page 82), who brought this no-frills cookware store to my attention: it is a notch lower than E. Dehillerin and its siblings on the quality scale, but it offers unbeatable prices on utensils, pots, and pans, with a slant toward Asian cooking (woks, bamboo steamers) and restaurant supplies (bistro-style plates and glasses, assorted signs, waiter pads, takeout boxes).

119 boulevard Richard Lenoir, 11th. CROSS STREET: Rue Jean-Pierre Timbaud. M° Oberkampf. PHONE: 01 43 38 48 48. Mon–Sat 9:30am–1pm and 2pm–7pm.

vaisselle / tableware

When it comes to dinnerware, silverware, table linen, and everything you need to prettify your table, department stores offer the widest choice by far, in a large variety of styles, brands, and price ranges.

BHV. 14 rue du Temple, 4th. CROSS STREET: Rue de Rivoli. M° Hôtel de Ville. PHONE: 01 42 74 90 00. WEB: www.bhv.fr. Mon–Tue and Thu–Sat 9:30am–7:30pm; Wed 9:30am–9pm.

Le Bon Marché. 24 rue de Sèvres. 7th. CROSS STREET: Rue du Bac. M° Sèvres-Babylone. PHONE: 01 44 39 82 80. WEB: www.lebonmarche.fr. Mon, Tue, Wed, Fri 9:30am–7pm; Thu 10am–9pm; Sat 9:30am–8pm.

Lafayette Maison. 35 boulevard Haussmann, 9th. CROSS STREET: Rue Scribe. M° Havre-Caumartin. PHONE: 01 42 82 34 56. WEB: www.galeries lafayette.com. Mon–Wed and Fri–Sat 9:30am–7:30pm; Thu 9:30am–9pm.

Printemps de la Maison. 64 boulevard Haussmann, 9th. CROSS STREET: Rue de Caumartin. M° Havre-Caumartin. PHONE: 01 42 82 57 87. WEB: printemps.com. Mon–Wed and Fri–Sat 9:35am–7pm; Thu 9:35am–10pm.

Aside from department stores, my sources of choice include the following stores and boutiques, where bargains can be found during *les soldes,* the twice-yearly sales periods that begin in early January and late June.

The Conran Shop

Owned by Englishman Terence Conran, The Conran Shop sells upscale furniture and designer objects for the home, including a beautiful range of tableware.

117 rue du Bac, 7th. CROSS STREET: Rue de Babylone. M° Sèvres-Babylone. PHONE: 01 42 84 10 01. WEB: www.conranshop.fr. Mon–Fri 10am–7pm; Sat 10am–7:30pm.

Habitat

Created in the sixties by the aforementioned Sir Terence, Habitat is now a chain of home furnishing stores that belongs to the same group as Ikea. Their lines of tableware are modern and hip, pricier than Ikea's but still affordable.

8 rue du Pont Neuf, 1st. CROSS STREET: Rue de Rivoli. M° Louvre-Rivoli. PHONE: 01 40 39 91 06. WEB: habitat.fr. Mon–Sat 10am–7:30pm.

Alternate location:

30 boulevard des Capucines, 9th. CROSS STREET: Rue de Caumartin. M° Madeleine. PHONE: 01 42 68 12 76. Mon–Sat 10am–7:30pm.

Muji

A Japanese chain store that provides everything from slippers and notebooks to dinnerware and cooking utensils, all of which demonstrate the same style: pared-down designs, natural materials, and simple lines.

47 rue des Francs Bourgeois, 4th. CROSS STREET: Rue Vieille du Temple. M° Saint-Paul. PHONE: 01 49 96 41 41. WEB: www.muji.fr. Mon–Fri 10am–7:30pm; Sat 10am–8pm.

Alternate location:

30 rue Saint-Sulpice, 6th. CROSS STREET: Rue Mabillon. M° Mabillon. PHONE: 01 44 07 37 30. Mon–Fri 10am–7:30pm; Sat 10am–8pm.

Sentou

A boutique and gallery that sells edgy designer creations, from furniture and lighting fixtures to eye-pleasing tableware.

24 rue du Pont Louis-Philippe, 4th. CROSS STREET: Rue François Miron. M° Saint-Paul. PHONE: 01 42 71 00 01. WEB: www.sentou.fr. Tue–Sat 10am–7pm.

Alternate location:

28 boulevard Raspail, 7th. CROSS STREET: Rue de Varenne. M° Sèvres-Babylone. PHONE: 01 45 49 00 05. Mon 2pm–7pm; Tue–Sat 10am–7pm.

CSAO

Artisanal products from West Africa, including linen, bowls, and plates.

9 rue Elzévir, 3rd. CROSS STREET: Rue Barbette. M° Saint-Paul.

PHONE: 01 42 71 33 17. WEB: csao.fr. Mon–Sat 11am–7pm; Sun 2pm–7pm.

Tralalart

The young designer Marie Lévêque hand-paints whimsical porcelain dishes: bowls, mugs, plates, salt shakers, eggcups . . . She can customize them for you; call or visit to inquire. She has a concession stand at Lafayette Maison (see page 276).

19 rue Milton, 9th. CROSS STREET: Rue de l'Agent Bailly. M° Notre-Dame de Lorette. PHONE: 01 48 74 68 14. WEB: tralalart.fr. Mon–Sat 11am–7pm.

Cuisinophilie and Au Petit Bonheur la Chance

Vintage tableware and cookware that seem right out of a country house.

Cuisinophilie. 28 rue du Bourg Tibourg, 4th. CROSS STREET: Rue Sainte-Croix de la Bretonnerie. M° Hôtel de Ville. PHONE: 01 40 29 07 32. Tue–Fri 2pm–7pm.

Au Petit Bonheur la Chance. 13 rue Saint-Paul, 4th. CROSS STREET: Rue des Lions Saint-Paul. M° Saint-Paul. PHONE: 01 42 74 36 38. Thu–Mon 11am–1pm and 2:30pm–7pm.

La Vaissellerie

Plain white dinnerware in every shape and form, simple and affordable.

80 boulevard Haussmann, 8th. CROSS STREET: Rue de Rome. M° Havre-Caumartin. PHONE: 01 45 22 32 47. WEB: www.lavaissellerie.fr. Mon–Sat 10am–7pm.

Alternate location:

85 rue de Rennes, 6th. CROSS STREET: Rue Coëtlogon. M° Saint-Sulpice or Rennes. PHONE: 01 42 22 61 49. Mon–Sat 10am–7pm.

SALONS AND FOOD SHOWS

Paris hosts a number of food and wine shows, referred to as *salons,* where producers present and sell their specialties. Most are held in rather unglamorous exhibition halls, but they make for fun tasting and shopping expeditions.

When faced with a large number of stalls, the wisest strategy is to make your way through all of them first, and make a note of what you're interested in buying: that way you'll be certain to buy what most appeals to you, and you won't have to lug your purchases around for quite as long. It is also a good idea to bring an empty tote bag to carry them home. Most stalls offer tasting samples; my advice is to be picky about what you taste, or you'll feel queasy within the first half hour.

These shows can get frightfully crowded: try to visit on a weekday morning, and purchase your tickets in advance if possible. Check exact dates, locations, and admission fees on the Internet.

Salon Saveurs des Plaisirs Gourmands, a.k.a. Salon Saveurs Food and wine from France and abroad.

No Web site, but if you type "Salon Saveurs" plus the year in your favorite search engine, you will find information about the next edition. Twice a year, in early May and early December, at Espace Champerret (17th).

Salon du Chocolat Chocolate makers from all around the world, exhibitions, and fashion show.

WEB: www.chocoland.com. Once a year, in late October or early November, at Porte de Versailles (15th).

Salon de l'Agriculture Agricultural show: live farm animals, and producers selling regional specialties.

WEB: www.salon-agriculture.com. Once a year, in late February or early March, at Porte de Versailles (15th).

Salon des Vignerons Indépendants Wines by independent vintners.

WEB: www.vigneron-independant.com. Twice a year, in March and November, at Espace Champerret (17th).

Salon Paris Fermier Farm-made regional specialties and wines; smaller than Salon Saveurs.

WEB: www.salonsfermiers.com. Twice a year, in late March at Parc Floral (12th) and in October at Espace Champerret (17th).

Salon Marjolaine Bio & Nature Devoted to organic and natural goods, edible or otherwise.

WEB: www.spas-expo.com. Once a year, in November, at Parc Floral (12th).

The following food-related events are also worth attending:

Fête des Vendanges de Montmartre Harvest festival for the last vineyard in Paris, the tiny Clos-Montmartre: open-air market, official ceremony, folkloric procession, and fireworks.

WEB: www.fetedesvendangesdemontmartre.com. Once a year, in late September or early October, in Montmartre (18th).

Le Fooding This movement was created in the late nineties by two food critics who wanted to break the perceived monotony of the French gastronomic scene. They organize hip yet playful events to bring good food and good wine to the man on the street—free tasting sessions, giant picnics, etc. The name is a Franglais portmanteau of "food" and "feeling."

WEB: lefooding.com

Galerie Fraîch'Attitude A gallery devoted to food art (art that uses food as its inspiration or raw material); several exhibitions each year.

60 rue du Faubourg Poissonnière, 10th. CROSS STREET: Rue de Paradis. M° Poissonnière or Bonne Nouvelle. PHONE: 01 49 49 15 15.

WEB: www.galeriefraichattitude.fr. Tue–Sat 1pm–7pm.

B=Breakfast   Br=Brunch   OS=Outdoor seating   VF=Vegetarian friendly

B=Breakfast   Br=Brunch   OS=Outdoor seating   VF=Vegetarian friendly

B=Breakfast   Br=Brunch   OS=Outdoor seating   VF=Vegetarian friendly

B=Breakfast   Br=Brunch   OS=Outdoor seating   VF=Vegetarian friendly

B=Breakfast   Br=Brunch   OS=Outdoor seating   VF=Vegetarian friendly

INDEX BY NAME

INDEX OF RECIPES

INDEX OF BOXES